Development of China in the Modern World System

30 Years of China's Reform Studies Series

Development of China in the Modern World System

LU De-ming

GALE
世纪出版

Andover • Melbourne • Mexico City • Stamford, CT • Toronto • Hong Kong • New Delhi • Seoul • Singapore • Tokyo

GALE

Development of China in the Modern World System
LU De-ming

Publishing Director: Paul K. H. Tan

Editorial Manager: Yang Liping

Development Editor (Media): Tanmayee Bhatwadekar

Senior Product Director: Janet Lim

Senior Product Manager: Vincent Cheah

Product Manager: Masaki Morisawa

Assistant Publishing Manager: Pauline Lim

Production Executive: Cindy Chai

Translator: Ding Wei

Copy Editor: Angela Dove

Cover Designer: S. T. Leng

Compositor: Integra Software Services, Pvt. Ltd.

For product information and technology assistance, contact us at
Cengage Learning Asia Customer Support, 65-6410-1200

For permission to use material from this text or product,
submit all requests online at **www.cengageasia.com/permissions**
Further permissions questions can be emailed to
asia.permissionrequest@cengage.com

ISBN-13: 978-981-4272-76-6
ISBN-10: 981-4272-76-0

This title is also available as an e-book.

ISBN-13: 978-981-4281-95-9
ISBN-10: 981-4281-95-6

Cengage Learning Asia Pte Ltd
5 Shenton Way #01-01
UIC Building
Singapore 068808

Cengage Learning is a leading provider of customized learning solutions with office locations around the globe, including Andover, Melbourne, Mexico City, Stamford (CT), Toronto, Hong Kong, New Delhi, Seoul, Singapore, and Tokyo. Locate your local office at **www.cengage.com/global**

Cengage Learning products are represented in Canada by Nelson Education, Ltd.

For product information, visit **www.cengageasia.com**

Printed in Singapore
Print Number: 07 Print Year: 2026

Table of Contents

Preface

In 1977, when the college entrance exam was first resumed, I was admitted into Fudan University, majoring in Economics. Two major subject courses were taught in the first semester (first half of 1978), which were Political Economics (on capitalism) and Economic History of Foreign Countries. Toward the end of the semester, we were given a closed-book exam on the first course and an essay assignment on the second course. At that time, my essay titled "The Latecomers Surpass the Old-timers" discussed the phenomenon of "the late developers catching up with the early developers" in the history of the world economy. Points raised included why the UK managed to overtake Holland, how the US, Germany, and Japan surpassed others, and the implications these incidents might have for the four modernizations of China. Professor Li Xiang spared no praise for this paper, marking Very Good! Wonderful! Excellent! in addition to an A score.

The phenomenon of "the late developers catching up with the early developers" was the first economic issue that occurred to me. "The Latecomers Surpass the Old-timers" was also the first economic paper I wrote. Not long ago when I moved house, I was surprised to find the dusty script. Seeing the naïve wordings, and the cliché of 30 years ago, I smiled to myself.

Influenced by the methodologies of Marxism, I chose productivity as the theme for my bachelor and Master theses, in the aim of exploring the motivation of development. I proposed a function model of "composition forces of production," yet for the uncommon character of the function, the model was shelved after it was published in the internal journal of *Reference Material for Economic Research* in 1983. Only the part concerning the "increasing-diminishing returns given the technical advancement condition" was published in the *Economic Research* in 1986.

After graduation, my sphere of research changed quite a bit, but my interest in the "relative development" between developed and developing countries (or the early development countries and the late development countries as I call them) remains strong. I focus more on China now: Why China led the world 500 years ago, and why China became so backward after 1800? How can China catch up and overtake?

I am fortunate to live in a place and time of major transition and development. Since my research focuses on the modern Chinese economy, I have been involved in the decision-making process of governments and enterprises as an advisor since long ago.

For example, I participated in the nationwide research on the economic system reform during 1988–1995 as organized by the State Reform Committee, the export group for decision-making consultation of the Shanghai municipal government during 1997–2002, the economic development consultation of Yunnan provincial government during 1999–2003, and the decision-making consultation of Suzhou, Zhenjiang, Nantong, and other developed and underdeveloped places. I have also served as an independent director for a few listed companies and as an advisor for ten private companies in different parts of China. By wearing these hats, I have availed myself of the opportunity to observe and feel the development process of China on both macro and micro levels. By and by I have gained more knowledge and understanding, which has triggered further curiosity on the driving forces behind the transition. However, to solve the puzzle of the "China Miracle," efforts must be made on the general rules and general theories of common development of the world.

In 1998, at the twentieth anniversary of the reform and opening up, Professor Wu Bailing organized the publication of a series of books in 10 volumes titled *Research on 20 Years of Economic Reform in China* with a group of young and middle-aged scholars. In the one I wrote—*Analysis of the Driving Forces of the Economic Development of China*—on top of the achievements of the previous scholars, I put forward the logical framework of the theory of development relativity, which was called the theory of development drive then and the theory of development advantage later. The theory includes seven hypotheses:(1) the early development advantage drive of early development countries (2) the late development advantage drive of late development countries (3) conditional increasing early development advantage by innovation (4) conditional diminishing late development advantage by learning (5) the primary driving force of the government of the late development countries (6) transformation of advantages and change of development track (7) relative advantages of international trade and investment. By applying the theory of development relativity on the interpretation of the fast-growing Chinese economy between 1949 and 1999, I come to the conclusion that our success lies in the learning type development path driven by the late development advantage.

Since then, there has been more research on the late development advantage. In 2004, I planned to select a few excellent doctoral dissertations I supervised for publication as a series with the title of *Series Research on Late Development Economics*, but unfortunately only one volume was completed. Last year, when I heard that Professor Shi Zhengfu was organizing a series of research on the 30 years of Chinese reform, my aspiration on the topic was once again ignited. I was granted an opportunity to undertake one of the titles in it, *Development of China in the Modern World System.*

Analysis of the Driving Force of Economic Development of China, written ten years ago, was based on the two-phase dynamic development of a nation, namely the interpretation of the fast growth of 20 years from the learning-type growth driven by late development advantage to the innovative-type growth driven by early development advantage. *Development of China in the Modern World System* views the fast growth of 30 years in the context of interaction between the innovative early development countries and learning-type late development countries. The two books are sequentially mutually complementary.

The book is based on an empirical research of the last 30 years. The main arguments grew out of years of efforts, but writing was done in merely a few months. With the book finally done, I would like to thank the Center for New Political Economy of Fudan University for its generous subsidy, and Professor Shi Zhengfu and two other anonymous peer reviewers for their precious comments.

I would also like to thank the Sanya College of Hainan University. Gao Dongfang, Sun Bin, and Gao Yilan from the college drafted some chapters with materials I provided and the framework I designed. Lu Ben from the China Center of Economic Research of Peking University and Fang Su-Juan from Shanghai Maritime University as my research assistants were also involved in the writing process. Without their participation and hard work, I would not have been able to complete the book to mark the 30th anniversary of China's reform and opening up. Thanks also go to Ms Ding Wei from Zhejiang University for translating the book into English.

Lastly, I want to extend my particular gratitude to all those who gave either material or spiritual help to me in my difficult years. I owe many thanks to these true friends.

LU De-ming
June, 2009

CHAPTER 1

The Analysis of the Modern World System

1.1 Introduction: The China Miracle in the Context of International Development

1.1.1 The Miracle of World History

In 2008, the Beijing Olympic Games impressed the whole world with a rejuvenated China. Proponents and opponents alike could not deny the great achievements made since the Reform and Opening Up process started 30 years ago.

Thirty years of fast development of the Chinese economy. Table 1.1 indicates that China's GDP grew by five times between 1978 and 2007, making China the third-largest economy in the world. The average growth rate of GDP per capita was as high as 8.7%. In the industrialization process, the weight of agriculture dropped gradually to 11.7%. By relying on its own effort, China cut the population in destitute poverty from 250 million to 15 million. While the average income per capita in 1978 was merely RMB 381, it grew by over 40 times in 30 years, to RMB 16,084 (or over US$2,000) in 2006. China has, on the whole, rid itself of poverty and backwardness, and entered the ranking of the lower middle income nations (a well-off society).

The past three decades not only witnessed the transition from an agricultural to a modern industrial society, but also the transition from a planned to a market economy. It is unprecedented for a super-large country with a population of 1.3 billion to achieve, in three decades, the progress that would have taken other countries hundreds of years to accomplish, and to do so without compromising social stability.

Table 1.1 Economic performance since the reform and opening up

	GDP		GDP Per capita			GDP Composition (%)		
Year	Annual Growth (%)	1978 = 100	RMB/Year	Growth (%)	1978 = 100	Primary industry	Secondary industry	Tertiary industry
1978	11.7	100	381	10.2	100	28.2	47.9	23.9
1979	7.6	107.6	419	6.1	106.1	31.3	47.1	21.6
1980	7.8	116.0	463	6.5	113.0	30.2	48.2	21.6
1981	5.2	122.1	492	3.9	117.5	31.9	46.1	22.0
1982	9.1	133.1	528	7.5	126.2	33.4	44.8	21.8
1983	10.9	147.6	583	9.3	137.9	33.2	44.4	22.4
1984	15.2	170.0	695	13.7	156.8	32.1	43.1	24.8
1985	13.5	192.9	858	11.9	175.5	28.4	42.9	28.7
1986	8.8	210.0	963	7.2	188.2	27.2	43.7	29.1
1987	11.6	234.3	1,112	9.8	206.6	26.8	43.6	29.6
1988	11.3	260.7	1,366	9.5	226.3	25.7	43.8	30.5
1989	4.1	271.3	1,519	2.5	231.9	25.1	42.8	32.1
1990	3.8	281.7	1,644	2.3	237.3	27.1	41.3	31.6
1991	9.2	307.6	1,893	7.7	255.6	24.5	41.8	33.7
1992	14.2	351.4	2,311	12.8	288.4	21.8	43.4	34.8
1993	14.0	400.4	2,998	12.7	324.9	19.7	43.4	34.8
1994	13.1	452.8	4,044	11.8	363.3	19.8	46.6	33.6
1995	10.9	502.3	5,046	9.7	398.6	19.9	47.2	32.9
1996	10.0	552.6	5,846	8.9	433.9	19.7	47.5	32.8
1997	9.3	603.9	6,420	8.2	469.4	18.3	47.5	34.2
1998	7.8	651.2	6,796	6.8	501.4	17.6	46.2	36.2
1999	7.6	700.9	7,159	6.7	534.9	16.5	45.8	37.7
2000	8.4	759.9	7,858	7.6	575.5	15.1	45.9	39.0
2001	8.3	823.0	8,622	7.5	618.7	14.4	45.1	40.5
2002	9.1	897.8	9,398	8.4	670.4	13.7	44.8	41.5
2003	10.0	987.8	10,542	9.3	733.1	12.8	46.0	41.2
2004	10.1	1,087.4	12,336	9.4	802.2	13.4	46.2	40.4
2005	10.4	1,200.8	14,103	9.8	880.7	12.5	47.5	40.0
2006	11.6	1,340.7	16,165	11.0	977.8	11.7	48.9	39.4
2007	11.9	1,500.7	18,934	11.4	1088.8	11.3	48.6	40.1

Source: China Statistical Yearbook, 2008.

Note: The growth indexes are calculated at comparable prices, and the structure ratio is calculated with the price of the same year.

The international comparison of the same/different period. In the history of the modern world, only the industrial revolution of Western Europe in the eighteenth and nineteenth centuries, the rising of the USA in the nineteenth century and the economic revival of Germany and Japan following WWII can be compared to the past 30 years in China. Yet, with a closer look, the China Miracle is indeed unique.

First, let us look at the information indicated in Figure 1.2. Among the Brazil, Russia, India, and China, though China has only an average national income of US$2,010 per capita, which is the equivalent of US$7,740 by purchasing power parity (PPP), it still leads in GDP growth, trade, finance, and foreign investment when compared to Brazil, Russia and India.

Table 1.3 shows the across-period comparison. We have selected the period when the average income of certain countries doubled or multiplied as a result of industrialization. According to the World Bank statistics, for the same achievement, it took the UK 58 years during the eighteenth and nineteenth centuries, the US 47 years during the nineteenth century, Germany 39 years during the nineteenth and twentieth centuries, Japan 34 years during the twentieth century, Brazil 18 years during the twentieth century, South Korea 11 years during the twentieth century, but China only nine years. Between 1978 and 1987, 1987 and 1996, and 1996 and 2005, the numbers tripled, equaling an accumulated increase of 800%. This is definitely an unparalleled and unprecedented miracle (Figure 1.1).

1.1.2 The Secret Behind the Miracle

What is the secret behind the China miracle? What are the driving forces?

Interpretations from the current research. Ten years ago, my conclusion on the high growth of the economy, which was based on the research of 20 years of reform

Table 1.2 The International benchmark of the same period

	Brazil	Russia	India	China
Population in 2006 (100 mil.)	1.89	1.42	11.1	13.12
Average national income per capita of 2006 (USD by exchange rate)	4,730	5,780	820	2,010
Average national income per capita of 2006 (USD by PPP)	8,800	11,630	3,800	7,740
Average GDP growth 2000–2006 (%)	3.0	6.4	7.4	9.8
% of manufactured goods in total export of 2005	54	19	70	92
Balance of current account of 2006 (US$100 million)	142	944.7	—	1,608.2
FDI of 2005 (US$100 million)	151.9	151.5	65.9	791.3
% of domestic credit loan in the GDP of 2006	82	21	64	138

Source: The World Bank (2008).

Table 1.3 The across-period international comparison

	Doubling time in per capita income during the industrialization period	
UK	58 years (1780–1838)	
US	47 years (1839–1886)	
Germany	39 years (1870–1909)	
Japan	34 years (1885–1919)	
Brazil	18 years (1961–1979)	
South Korea	11 years (1966–1977)	
China	9 years	1st period: 1978–1987
		2nd period: 1987–1996
		3rd period: 1996–2005

Source: The World Bank (1991,1997); *China Statistical Year Book*, 2008.

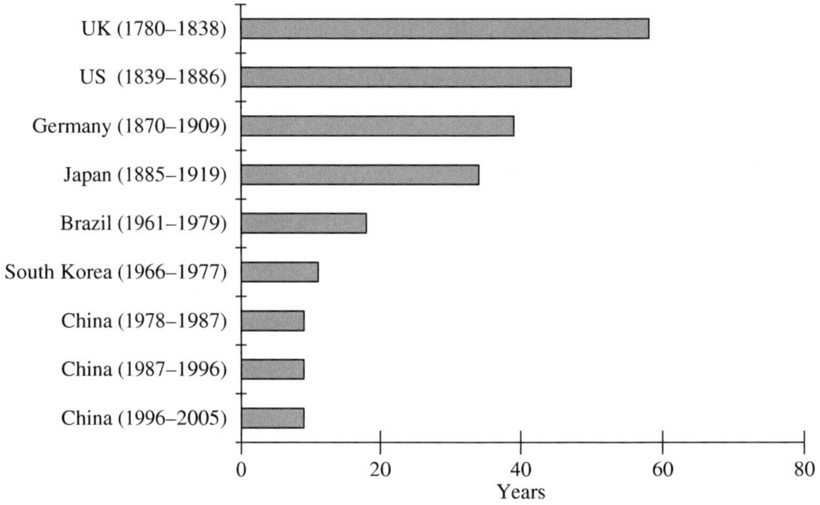

FIGURE 1.1 Doubling years in per capita income.

and opening up (1978–1998), pointed to the late development advantage of learning as the driving force (Lu De-ming 1999). The last ten years saw numerous interpretations of the fast economic growth in China, most of which are based on the growth theories, the development economics, and the new institutionalism, with some attempt at innovation.

There is a large amount of econometric analysis on the driving forces of the economic growth in China, whose conclusions are quite different due to the different models, data, and methodologies adopted. However, they all have one thing in common: The high growth is attributed to the incremental capital investment and the increase of Total Factors Productivity (TFP), the latter of which is subject to technical advancement, as well as the evolution of management systems and the change of resource allocation. For example, research adopted by the authoritative World Bank Institute (Dahlman and Aubert 2001) split the annualized growth rate of 9.7% between 1979–1998 as the follows: 39.7% from capital, 23.7% from labor and education, 37.1% from TFP. Obviously the incremented investment and technical advancement are the two main engines of the high growth.

In the Marshall Lectures of Cambridge (Lin 2007), the vice president and chief economist of the World Bank, Justin Lin, built an endogenous growth model to interpret the development and transition in China. Based on his theory of comparative advantage, Lin put forward the micro concept of "enterprise viability." Technical innovation, as he comprehends, is the fundamental driver of long-term economic development, and developing countries can only compete by selecting the industrial technologies according to their comparative advantages as determined by the endowment structure. Here the strategic selection made by the government is critically important. Before the reform, China mistakenly gave priority to capital-intensive heavy industry following the "catching up strategy," and success only came when China turned to the "comparative advantage strategy" and the labor-intensive industry since the reform. On top of this, Lin concluded that developing countries may utilize the advantage of backwardness, make technical progress through technology import, absorption, and innovation, and grow faster than the developed countries, and catch up consequently. Lin's research is now well developed, but the theoretical framework remains structuralist.

In 2008, the neo-institutionalist Steven N.S. Cheung discovered from research that the local government, represented by the county government, is the main agent of market competition in China. To seek maximum rent, they pushed for fast economic growth. Shi Zhengfu, in the same year, drew a similar conclusion from the perspective of the new political economy. According to Shi, rather than transition, the reform in China is a kind of self-dependent systematic innovation, with a different path and goal from the Western world. The governing structure of the reform is threefold, with the top leaders, the central government, and the local government all being the decision-makers. On such a basis, the market structure becomes also threefold, with the enterprises, the central government, and the local government all being the players. In this role, the local government has a dual function: In addition to the administrative function, it helps enterprises develop and join the market competition, which promotes the regional economy and the national economy.

The perspective of international development economics. The above research explains the China miracle from different perspectives. Though creative, none is an all-inclusive general theory. For example, for the importance of system as a major driver of fast development, it is not the source of development and only influences the cost of growth (like the transaction cost) and the efficiency of development. The function of the Chinese local government has Chinese characteristics, but it only reflects the operation of the market economy.

The China miracle is not an isolated event within one country, and cannot be viewed and measured with a single theory such as the conventional Growth Economics, Development Economics, or Institutional Economics. The development of China is integrated into the modern world system, and realized through interaction with other countries. For example, investment has been the prime driver of economic growth, with both domestic investment and foreign investment working together. This was particularly true in the early years when there was a shortage of domestic capital. Market consumption is another driver of growth, with the domestic market and export market functioning together. While the domestic market is huge and remains largely underdeveloped, the export market has been a major contributor to growth. As another fundamental driver, technical advancement in China is mainly based on the absorption and digestion of imported technologies, which involves interaction with the world as well.

Therefore, in order to comprehend and interpret the China miracle, we need the perspective of International Development Economics whereby the problems can be observed in the process of the development of both developing and developed countries.

1.1.3 The Structure of This Book

This book explores the driving forces of the China miracle from the perspective of international development, and is divided into the following three parts:

Chapters 1 and 2 are about the theories and strategies in general. Chapter 1 provides a theoretical or logical framework for the interpretation of the development in China. Chapter 2 aims to discuss, on a strategic level, how China grasped the opportunities over the 30 years and developed through its opening up, and how China and its foreign partners acquired the market and resources from both home and abroad through cooperation and competition.

Chapters 3 to 7 is the main part of the book, and discusses the 30 years of relative development in China in the context of international interaction from the perspective of foreign trade, foreign capital, human capital, technology import, and management systems.

Chapters 8 and 9 are the prospects and conclusion. Chapter 8 discusses the major challenges confronted by China for its long-term sustainable development. Chapter 9 concludes the whole book and echoes Chapter 1. The theory of development relativity is put forward based on the general experience of the Chinese economy in international development.

1.2 The Characteristics of the Modern World System

To view the China Miracle from an international perspective, it is important to put the development of China in the modern world system. The rest of this chapter reviews the traditional theories in the modern world system, discusses the characteristics of the modern world system and the change of market structure in the context of globalization, and analyses the opportunity window for the late developers.

1.2.1 Critique of the Traditional Theories on the World System

What is the world system like? Let's first look at the Dependency Theory.

The "Center-Periphery" structure of the dependency Theory. The Argentinean economist Raul Prebisch, also the first secretary general of the Economic Commission of Latin America of the UN, was the first one to put forward the concept of "center-periphery." According to him, the center refers to the developed Western countries, and the periphery is formed of the developing countries, and the world economic system is composed of the two parts. The system is an unequal structure, with the central countries exploiting the periphery countries with unfair game rules. According to Prebisch, the affiliated position of the periphery countries is an outcome of the historical division of labor and comparative advantage, which enslaves these countries to the ruling of the developed counties (Prebisch 1990).

The theory of world system. The theory of world system is based on the modern world system with some major arguements borrowed from the dependency theory. As a representative of the theory, the US scholar Immanuel Wallerstein considers the modern world system to be a capitalistic one led by the hegemonic countries. The economic structure can be divided into three layers as "center-semi periphery-periphery." The political structure is formed of the nation states. The "semi periphery" concept added by Immanuel acts as a buffer between the center and the periphery. Between the layers lies an unequal relationship of exchange, which contributes to the wealth accumulation of the center. According to Immanuel, the development of the central countries and the underdevelopment of the periphery countries is a historical outcome of the forming and expansion of the modern world system. It is the exploitation of the center that led to the marginalization and underdevelopment of the periphery (Wallerstein 1998).

The theoretical criticism. The traditional world system theory, based on the dependency theory, is an influential and inclusive multidisciplinary theory, of which the largest contribution is the holistic view of the modern world. Of course, the world is not solely capitalist as we see today. In fact, in the modern world system, every country depends on the international environment for development, and contributes to the transition of the world economy and politics. In writing this book, I am mostly enlightened by this holistic approach.

Yet, the conclusion and suggestion of the dependency theory seem too passive. For example, Gunder Frank (1998) and Samir Amin (2000) put forward the decoupling theory. According to Amin, the development of periphery countries will come to a stage when they have to decouple from the capitalist world system, or in other words, exclude globalization from their domestic development strategy. Cardoso and Faletto (2002) regard the development of the periphery countries as a kind of dependent development. According to them, dependency and development are not absolutely contradictory. The periphery countries may develop through the cooperation of multinational capital and domestic capital.

The world system theorists (like Wallerstein) don't accept the decoupling theory. They relate the industrialization of the emerging countries to the cyclical operation of the modern world system. Though they partially correct the defects and mistakes of the dependency theory, the unequal exchange relationship is still overemphasized, and it seems somewhat ideological to blame the developed countries for the poverty of the developing countries. In fact, the modern world system is no longer featured by the single way dependency. There is no chance for decoupling. Development in the modern world is interlinked and interactive while enjoying a degree of relative independence.

1.2.2 The Modern World System in the Globalization Context

The modern world system is a globalized system. On the economic level, with the development of cross-nation production, international trade, and international finance, the world economy is becoming increasingly integrated.

The globalized market system. As early as 1991, the Japanese scholar Ohmae Kenichi noticed that the boundaries of the world were disappearing. In 1996, two Mckinsey researchers further pointed out that there was no longer a boundary in the market (Bryan and Farrell 1997). In Marx's words, a unified world market or global market is forming. Globalized purchase, trade, and distribution came first. The globalized purchase of raw materials and components formed the globalized supply chain, and globalized trade of commodities and services led to the forming of the world trade system and the WTO.

The globalized production division system. The division of labor has been deepened with the expansion of trade volume. The international labor division system was largely vertical 20–30 years ago. With the forming and expansion of the global market, it has become more horizontal, but vertically integrated worldwide. For example, while the MNCs in the early days adopted the vertically integrated investment strategy in developing countries, they now shift to vertically integrated production in the global market, which is to split the product value chain and assign different tasks to different countries and regions for specialized production and assembling. The traditional division by industry and product has changed to the division by production stage, where MNCs of the developed countries mainly engage in capital and technology intensive tasks, like R&D or sample production, while the developing countries engage more in the labor intensive tasks, like manufacturing and assembling. The division of labor among the developed countries is horizontal (such as the globalized R&D and competition), and the division of labor among the developing countries is also horizontal (such as globalized production and labor recruitment), but the division between the developed and developing countries is vertical, which is reflected in the globalized investment and order placement.

The globalized finance system. Financial globalization refers to the opening of the financial system of one country to international capital and foreign financial institutions, or the cross-border capital flow and service provision. The last 30 years saw an increase of international capital flow by ten times in volume, amounting to US$2 trillion each year. Meanwhile global financial assets are growing 100 times faster than those of material assets. Against the backdrop of the globalization of information, a huge amount of financial assets quickly flows in the boundless market for profit. This has brought a twofold consequence: While opportunities have been created with optimized allocation of resources in the market, economic turmoil has also surfaced, bringing risk and damage to most countries and especially the late movers. Financial crises have not only happened in Mexico, Argentina, Thailand, and South Korea, but also in the US, the global financial leader. The subprime-triggered financial crisis has swept across the world, and is evolving into an international financial crisis paralleling the Great Depression. International organizations such as the IMF are put to the test.

1.2.3 The "Community of Global Interest" and the "Group of Stakeholders"

A "Community of Global Interest." The globalized allocation of resources has built a global value chain that involves financing/investment, staffing, R&D, purchasing of raw materials, production, marketing, and after sales service, making the world economy a community of common interest.

For example, there is a globalized industrial chain behind "Made in China," and a community of global interest (Figure 1.2). Typically, it is the US, Europe, and Japan that provide the capital and technologies; Asian countries that provide the raw materials, energy, and semi-finished products; and Hong Kong and Taiwan that provide finance, trade, and settlement services. All resources are later gathered in mainland China for processing, manufacturing, and assembling by its cheap labor force before being exported to the world.

Two basic "Groups of Stakeholders." The modern world system is composed of two basic groups: The developed countries (regions) and the developing countries (regions), which no longer follow the "center-periphery" or "center-semi periphery-periphery" dependent model, but are two groups of stakeholders in the community of global interest.

To start with, though the market position of the developed countries and the developing countries are unequal, the relation in between is not a unilateral type of dependency and exploitation, but interdependency.

The major cause or reflection of the "inequality" is the gap of development: Strong versus weak, advanced versus backward, early development versus late development. The developed countries are those early development economies that started early and lead the development, the developing countries are those late development economies that started late and are lagging behind.

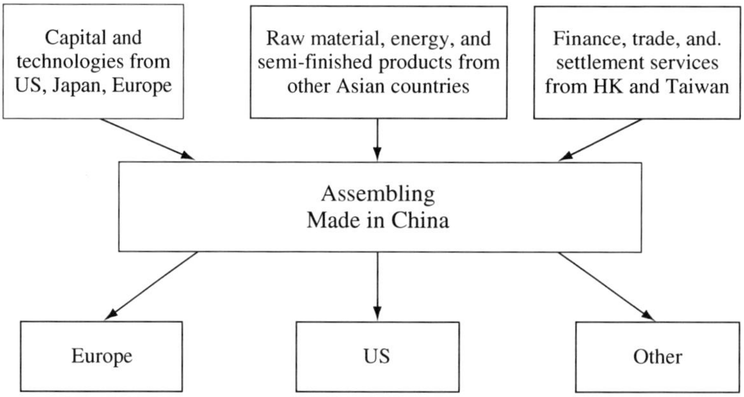

FIGURE 1.2 The "Community of Global Interest" formed by the industrial chain of "Made in China"

Thirdly, the relationship between the two groups is featured by interaction and coopetition,[1] rather than the conventional competition. While the conventional competition was exclusive and conflicting, with one winner and one loser, or is regarded as "zero sum game": $\lceil 1 + (-1) = 0 \rfloor$, the modern coopetition usually brings a win-win situation, or is regarded as "positive sum game": $1 + 1 \geq 2$

Three types of "Interlinked Economy." Developed and developing countries are two groups with interaction and coopetition, and various types of "interlinked economies" are derived on top of that.

The idea of "interlinked economies" put forward by Ohmae Kenichi (2007) refers to the iron triangle of the US, Europe, and Japan, which is similar to the EU.

The idea of "interlinked economies" raised by Du Xin (Du Xin 2007) refers to the free trade zone of China-ASEAN, which functions within the region.

If the regional trade agreement (organization) is regarded as the base of the interlinked economy, then there are nearly 300 of such economies according to the WTO report, half of which emerged after 2000. These interlinked economies (regional organizations of economic integration) can be divided into three types: The most successful "North North" type of developed countries, accounting for over 50%; the less successful "South South" type of developing countries, accounting for 15%; and the rather successful "South North" type between developed and developing countries, accounting for 35%.

As for the development trend, with information technology and the Internet, an open, equal sharing, and global Wikinomics has emerged featuring macro collaboration (Tapscott and Williams 2007).

I would argue that a "Community of Global Interest" composed of the "two groups of stakeholders" has been established. The modern world system is becoming a multipolar "interlinked economy" with common success or failure, common development or stagnancy.

1.3 The Change of the Market Structure in the Modern New World System

According to the theory of "Mutual Dependency" by Keohane and Nye (2002), the relation between developed and developing countries is a kind of unsymmetrical mutual dependency, or mutual but unequal dependency. Keohane later put forward

1. Coopetition is the concept of limited cooperation between competitors, and usually arises in rapidly changing industries where companies are compelled to work together in the face of advances by third parties.

the concept of complex interdependence, but he failed to make it clearer, as he wasn't able to find the framework of the complex interdependence—the complex market structure.

According to Neoclassic Economics, the traditional market structure is single-layered and includes four types of markets: Full competition, monopoly competition, oligopoly, and full monopoly. However, in the modern world system, the market structure has developed into a double-layered compound structure as I observe, with countries or independent economies on the upper layer, and enterprises on the lower layer.[2]

1.3.1 The International Political Economic Market

The basic structure of the international political economic market features the oligarchic coopetitive game, with the developed countries setting the game rules and the developing countries accepting the rules. Rule challengers come up occasionally.

The duo-oligarchic coopetitive game between the US and the USSR (1945–1991). The international political economic market used to be a stage for multi-oligarchic coopetition before WWII. Then, the war changed the world pattern, which led to the four-decade duo-oligarchic coopetition. With Germany, Japan, and Italy defeated, and UK and France badly hurt, competition started between the US and the USSR following the Yalta System, which was reflected in the rivalry between the US-led North Atlantic Treaty Organization and the USSR-led Warsaw Treaty Organization, resulting in the full confrontation between the East camp and the West camp; between capitalism and socialism in politics, economy and ideology.

The confrontation took the form of the Cold War with political and military competition between the two, economic cooperation within the group, and little economic exchange between the two. For example, to echo the call of Stalin to set up two parallel world markets, the internalized import and export trade within the Council for Mutual Economic Assistance (CMEA) accounted for 70% of oil trade, 95% of coal trade, 78% of mineral trade, and 61% of consumable trade in the years that followed.

The duo-oligarchic pattern remained stable for nearly half a century after WWII. Neither the "77 Nation Group" nor the "Non-alliance Movement" in the 1960s was able to challenge the pattern. In the 1970s, ex-US President Nixon pointed out that Western Europe and Japan were strong competitors for the US. They were friends and allies, but they compete hard with the US for the leadership of the world economy. With the

2. From the perspective of the new political economy (rather than traditional Neoclassic Economics), the complex market structure has become a general form of market economy for larger countries. For example, the market system in China is composed of the local government-led regional competition and the enterprise-led business competition, making it more stable and more efficient than the traditional single market structure.

collapse of the "Bretton Woods System," the US was challenged for its leadership position, but the bipolar pattern remained intact.

The coopetition led by the US alone (1992–present). The bipolar pattern started to shake in 1989 and fell apart in 1991. In November 1989, with the collapse of the Berlin wall, the two Germanys became unified, triggering a drastic change in Eastern Europe. In January 1991, the Warsaw Treaty Organization dissolved. In June the same year, the CMEA dissolved. In December the same year, the USSR disintegrated, marking the official ending of the bipolar coopetition between the US and the USSR.

The US-led coopetition started in 1992 (with one super power and multiple powers). With the disappearing of the two parallel markets, the US won back the seat for world hegemony with the edge of the "new economy." The US National Security Strategy endorsed by President Bush on September 20, 2002 officially raised the curtain for unilateralism, emphasizing that the US may take military action against others when necessary (even when not attacked).

With the long-time competitor finally gone, the US became the only super power of the world, and Europe and Japan became the second and third oligarchy, though Japan secures second place economically with efforts of over half a century. The former European Community marched one step forward to form the EU in 1993, and adopted the EU Constitution in 2004. The coopetition among the US, Japan, and the EU has dominated the world market since then.

The market position of China. China is a backward developing country. In the 1950s and 1960s, China benefited from the former USSR in terms of economic and technical assistance. However, the honeymoon ended, for China's pursuit of independent diplomacy annoyed the USSR. Around 1978, China was sandwiched between the US and the USSR. Deng Xiaoping was wise enough to notice that peace and development instead of war, would be the two main themes of the world. It was in such context that China grasped the opportunity for low profile development.

With fast growth and enhanced strength, China started to constitute a pressure on the bipolar market structure. In 1992, Deng Xiaoping called upon the nation to grasp the opportunity to deepen the reform and opening up process. Since then China has been actively involved in the process of globalization. By and by, the game rule follower has become a mild challenger. With the growing of power and improving of its international position, China has become increasingly influential and has drawn attention worldwide. There is no doubt that China will ultimately become one pole of the world market, which is conducive to the establishment of the new world economic order and the modern world system. The recent global financial crisis proves that the G7 and G8 are inadequate. The Community of Global Interest needs wider representation, especially the participation of the emerging countries like China, India, Brazil, and so on.

1.3.2 The International Business Market

The players of coopetition in the business market are enterprises, which can be divided into early development enterprises and late development enterprises. The former includes industrial leaders such as multinational corporations (MNCs) of developed countries, and the latter includes the smaller industrial leaders of developing countries. With this pattern, MNCs set the market price and industrial benchmark, and small and medium enterprises (SMEs) follow.

The MNC-led oligarchic coopetition (1945–1991). MNCs refer to enterprises with specific nationality having joint ventures or solely-owned enterprises (SIE) in two or more countries. After WWII, with the formation of the modern world system, MNCs have become the leaders of the international market. According to the statistics of the UN, there are nearly 70,000 MNCs worldwide, with over 900,000 overseas subsidiaries and branches, controlling 40% of the world economy, 60% of the world trade, and 90% of the world's foreign direct investment (FDI).

The global-company-led oligarchic coopetition (1992–present). A growing number of MNCs have adopted a global strategy in the world market, making them even more globalized. If the multinational index is above 50%, for example, over 50% of assets overseas, 50% of employees overseas, 50% of revenue from overseas, we may call the MNC a global company (Wang Zhile 2008). Global companies have larger geographic coverage and broader business scope. Since 1992, with the convergence of the two parallel world markets, and the accelerated globalization led by the US, global companies have been dominating the world market.

The international position of the Chinese enterprises. There was no enterprise, by the definition of the market economy, in China before the Reform and Opening Up policy. Since its instigation, enterprises have been growing fast, though most of them are still small and medium-sized latecomers by international standards. Today the number of Chinese MNCs is still small, and the discourse power for price setting in the international market is yet limited. Of the 22 Chinese enterprises that entered the Global 500 in 2007, most of them are state-owned, resource-type enterprises, and financial institutions.

Take the price bargain for iron ore as an example: On the supplier side, the big three (BHP Billiton, Rio Tinto, and CVRD) control supply and monopolize sea shipping. On the buyer side, China is the largest buyer with Baosteel being the chief negotiator, and Japan and Korea the competitors. In price negotiations of recent years, China has gradually had her voice heard and even obtained the right to set the initial pricing in 2007. However, negotiation remains challenging for many reasons, one of which is the extremely low concentration of iron and steel enterprises in China, putting China in a negative position. Baosteel is the largest steel company in China but it only ranks No. 307 among the Fortune 500. The market share of China's top ten iron and steel enterprises is merely 35%.

Also, being the home country for many rare metals, China lacks pricing power, for the very many small mineral enterprises act like guerrillas in the price war. When Deng visited Jiangxi in 1992, he made a famous comment, "the Middle East has oil, China has rare earth." Yet, between 1990 and 2005, although the export of rare earth increased by nearly ten times, the average price was cut by 40%. Indium is widely used for the production of LCD and military products, such as the highly sensitive missile seeker. With two-thirds of the world's total deposit of indium, China exports 80% of its indium output to South Korea and Japan at low prices, with the pricing power controlled by the importer. For domestically sold indium, the price is ironically much higher.

1.3.3 The Coordination of the International Market and Global Governance

As mentioned above, the international market of the modern world system has a double-layered compound structure, which reflects the complex interdependence between the governments of developed countries, the governments of developing countries, the enterprises of developed countries, and the enterprises of developing countries. The structure is both stable and efficient. For example, with enterprises competing in the international business market, it is the governments of concerned countries that stay behind the competition. The Long March Rocket of China Great Wall Industry Corporation is extremely competitive in the international launching market. Between 1988 and 1990, when China provided the launching service for the US Aussat, the US government stayed behind Hughes and Lockheed Martin. On the other side, since US MNCs have reaped rich profit in China, when the US congress planned to sanction China in September 2007, altogether 160 MNCs and trade associations joined together to revoke the sanction, including 122 well-known companies like Microsoft, Wal-Mart, Citigroup, GE, and 38 associations such as the China General Chamber of Commerce USA (CGCCUSA) and the National Committee on US-China Relations.

It is understandably difficult to manage and coordinate this compound market. According to the Yearbook of International Organizations, toward the end of 2005, there were altogether 58,859 international organizations (7,306 governmental, 50,658 NGOs). The political, military, trade, and financial coordination work remains far from satisfactory despite the participation of the United Nations (UN), the WTO, the International Monetary Fund (IMF), and the World Bank. The modern world system seems somewhat anarchic and is in need of a strong, supranational government in the world.

1.4 The Opportunity Window for Late Development

Michael Porter enumerated seven scenarios in which opportunities may come to change the industrial competition:

1. The invention and innovation of elementary science and technology;
2. The gap of traditional technologies (like the loss of advantage in the electronic machinery industries in the US and Germany with the emerging of the microelectronic technology);
3. The sudden increase of production cost (like the impact of the oil crisis on importers and exporters);
4. The material change in the global financial market or the exchange rates;
5. The eruption of demand in the global or regional market;
6. The important decisions of foreign governments (like the change of the European energy policy and the rising demand on solar energy, bringing opportunity to Suntech Power of Wuxi); and
7. War (like the success of Germany and Japan after WWII).

According to Porter, incidents that bring opportunities are highly important, for they reshuffle the competition, take away the edges from the original winners, and create new space for development and competition (Porter 2002).

In addition to these general and accidental opportunities, there also exists in the modern world system opportunities that can be pursued, discovered, and created.

1.4.1 The Opportunity Window Viewed from the Dilemma of Oligarchic Coopetition

The oligarchic market, on the upper layer or the lower layer, has only a small number of players (countries or enterprises) which depend on each other. The competition behavior is by nature selfish, with self interest—national interest or enterprise interest—being the first priority in the competition. Cooperation is difficult among the oligarchies because of the conflict between self interest and collaboration, just as the classic "Prisoner Dilemma" of the game theory reveals. For each oligarchy in the game, if a binding agreement can be reached, cooperation may succeed. However, since self interest is always ahead of the benefit of others, the one-off Prisoner Dilemma game won't produce any solution, for infidelity on both sides leads to the Nash equilibrium. Only through multiple rounds of the game is cooperation possible. Therefore, competition among the developed countries and MNCs comes more frequent than cooperation, which implies opportunities for developing countries and enterprises.

For example, when the US and the USSR competed for the world hegemony, developing countries had two opportunity windows: The area where the two superpowers conflict and the middle blank area with no conflict. In the US-led mono-polar game today, there are also opportunities in the coopetition between the US and Europe (France, Germany, and so on). For instance, when the US imposes sanctions for the "sake of ideology," developing countries may work with the European countries to avoid the issue, since the Europeans may not always follow the interest of the US.

When China started to develop the express train business, it aimed at the most advanced, stable, and reliable technology developed by the trade tycoons like Siemens, Alston, Kawasaki, and Bombardier. In the beginning, Siemens asked for an extremely high price and refused anything else. The Ministry of Railway came up with a "strategic buyer" plan, leaving only Qingdao Sifang Locomotive and Rolling Stock and Changchun Railway Vehicles as the negotiators for the deal, forcing the foreigners to lower their price. In 2004, Alston, Kawasaki, and Bombardier got the first opportunity for cooperation, and in 2005, Siemens could no longer afford to be left aside, and offered to slash prices by a large margin. They transferred the key technology at a reasonable price, and with that, the Chinese motor train units quickly reached world-class standards.

1.4.2 The Opportunity Window Viewed from the Rule of Technology Transfer

The general rule of technology transfer between countries is subject to the product life cycle. In the developing period of a new product, for capital and R&D reasons, production is largely done in developed countries, with the finished products exported to developing countries. Only when a product enters the standardized production stage, does the opportunity window open for developing countries. At this point, production shifts to developing countries at a lower cost (Table 1.4).

However, in a globalized context, with the change of the international division of labor, technology transfer has also extibited a new trend. In the past, when the work was divided by industry and product, different countries produced different products. Now that production is split into different phases, different countries take care of different points of the value chain. The opportunity window for developing countries and enterprises has popped up in certain points of the value chain ahead of schedule. For example, in the chain of R&D—branding—material

Table 1.4 The general rule of international technology transfer

Life cycle	R&D	Mature production	Standard production	Retiring and renewal
Country of production	Developed countries	Emerging countries	Developing countries	End of production
Trade direction	export to backward countries	export to other countries	export to developed countries	Exit market
Decisive factor in competition	Capital and technology	Human capital	Labor cost	—

supply—manufacturing—marketing—after sales service, developed countries and their enterprises are only responsible for the two ends—R&D, branding, marketing, and service—while outsourcing the middle parts to whoever offers the lowest price.

Opportunities for OEM thus arise for developing countries. For the backward and forward connection of the chain, developing countries may also have the opportunity to host the collective move of the industrial supply chain.

Take the IT industry as an example: The key technologies like CPU are still controlled by the US, with Intel, Microsoft, and IBM earning a profit of 25–35% for CPU and software. The technology- and capital-intensive manufacturing is controlled by Japan and Taiwan, with a profit rate of 15–25%. Labor-intensive manufacturing has largely been shifted to mainland China, with enterprises in Zhongguancun, Suzhou, Dongguan earning a profit of 8–12%. The computer technologies and market are still monopolized by the Wintel alliance. However, with such a huge market, China has the opportunity for late development.

1.4.3 The Advantages of Late Development

As mentioned above, some opportunities cannot be created, but others can. The key for late developers is to grasp opportunities when they come, and bring into play all the advantages to catch up, so as not to be marginalized in the modern world system.

The comparative advantage. The first advantage late countries can utilize is the comparative advantage. As a theory, it is quite complete due to the contribution of economists such as David Ricardo and Heckscher-Ohiln. The comparative advantage for the late countries is mainly reflected in resource endowment, including both natural and labor resources. This helps the primitive accumulation of capital, for one can only rely on what one has when there is nothing else. However, the statistics from 60 years ago proved "the curse of resources": The richer the resources, the poorer the economy, for the late countries lack the capital and technology to develop their natural and labor resources, so the factor endowment alone brings no development.

The competitive advantage. How did some countries gain the competitive advantage in some specific industries, like the home electronics appliance industry of Japan, the leather industry of Italy, and the media industry of the US? According to the diamond model of Michael Porter, there are four decisive factors for the competitiveness of a nation:

1. Special production factors including the primary natural resource and the artificial resource;
2. A demanding market;
3. Supporting industries; and
4. Corporate strategy, structure, and level of competition.

As a prevailing theory of competitive advantage, it is more suitable for the interpretation of the competitiveness of enterprise, while its interpretation of the competitiveness of nations is limited to only a few industries. Later, Michael Porter put forward the concept of industry cluster after the introduction of location theory, yet the source of competitive advantage of a nation remains unexplained.

The relative advantage. Judging from the perspective of dynamic development, the competitive advantage of a nation comes from the relative advantage of each nation (Lu De-ming 1999).

Developed countries enjoy the early development advantage as a result of early development of resources and advancement in science and technology, which includes: The material capital advantage accumulated through the early development of natural resources, the human capital advantage accumulated through the early development of human resources, the technical advantage accumulated through technical innovation, and the institutional advantage formulated through management innovation. All the advantages are reflected in international competitiveness of capital-intensive products and technology-intensive products.

Developing countries have the late development advantage as a result of late development of resources and the import of capital and technologies from developed countries, which includes the cost advantage of the resource-intensive products through late development of natural resources, the cost advantage of the labor intensive products through late development of labor resources, the foreign investment advantage that fills the capital gap, the technology import advantage that fills the technology gap, and the management skill learning advantage that fills the management gap.

Take China for example. Since the Reform and Opening Up process began, with low labor cost as a basis of the late development advantage, through the import of foreign capital, technologies, and management expertise, China has supplied a huge amount of cheap quality goods to the world market, creating the international competitive advantage of the labor-intensive industry.

Therefore, the late development countries have both opportunities and advantages. So long as they take initiative to integrate with the modern world system, they are able to achieve faster growth through coopetition with other nations. Should the late development advantages be fully utilized, they may even overtake the early development countries through leapfrog development.

CHAPTER 2

The Opening Strategy for the Development of China

The miracle of China can be mainly attributed to the Reform and Opening Up process. This chapter discusses the Opening Up strategy over the past three decades, in an effort to present the road map of the Opening Up from the south to the north, from the east coastal area to the inland, and from the manufacturing industry to the service industry, through which the accession to the WTO stood as a landmark in the process. Both China and its foreign participators have won markets and resources from home and abroad in common development.

2.1 Opening the Opportunity Window: Deng Xiaoping on Opening Up

On March 18, 1978, Deng Xiaoping addressed the opening ceremony of the National Conference on Science: "Only when we acknowledge the backwardness can we manage to get rid of the backwardness. Only when we learn from the developed ones are we able to surpass the developed ones. Independence does not mean shutting the door to the world, nor does self-reliance mean blind opposition to everything foreign. Science and technology is the common wealth created collectively by mankind. Every nationality or country needs to learn from the strong points of others. Not only must we learn from other nations when we are behind in science and technology, but even when we have caught up in science and technology, we still need to learn from the strength of other nations."[1]

1. Deng Xiaoping, "Speech on the Opening Ceremony of the National Conference on Science," in *Selected Works of Deng Xiaoping: Volume II* (Beijing: The People's Press, 1994), 91.

2.1.1 The Closedness and Backwardness of China in Modern Times

Dr Joseph Needham once said, it was opening up that made ancient China superior to Europe in the same period in terms of invention and discovery, especially before the fifteenth century. The same explains why the feudal economy of China prospered from the Qin and Han dynasties all the way down to the Tang, Song, and Yuan dynasties.

However, toward modern times, especially in the Qing Dynasty, the government turned to the closed-door policy for twofold reasons: On the economic level, the self-sufficient feudal economy was stable and defensive to foreign goods; on the national security level, the government wished to block the penetration of Western colonialism for safe ruling. The closed-door policy as a passive defensive means proved somewhat effective when China was under the attack of Western capitalism, at the price of leaving China gradually behind the others.

As for the downside of the policy, China lost the initiative in foreign trade, restricted the development of industry and commerce, and impeded the emergence of commodity economy and capitalism. Regardless of this, the ruling class became even more self-conceited and anti-foreign. Emperor Qianlong once sent a letter to the King of England, saying that China was abundant in resources and had no need to trade with others. The shipment of tea, ceramics, and silk to Western countries was simply a generous gesture of favor to those in bad need. This of course was detrimental to the normal exchange between China and other nations, and deprived the Chinese people of the opportunity to learn from different philosophies and cultures. It also blocked scientific exchange, leaving China behind in the development of productivity and social progress, since modern science and technology was unable to reach China. This gave rise to the weakening of the military forces, and finally made China a target of attack.

Deng once summarized: "It is probably true that when Zheng He was sent on a voyage to the western oceans by Emperor Chengzu of the Ming Dynasty, China was an open society. But with the death of Chengzu, the Ming Dynasty began to decline. Later in the Reign of Emperor Kangxi and Emperor Qianlong of the Qing Dynasty, the society was by no means open. From the middle of the Ming Dynasty to the Opium War, there was a period of over three hundred years when China closed its doors to other countries, and even if we go back only to the reign of Emperor Kangxi, that is still a period of two hundred years when China remained closed to the outside world. The lasting closed-door policy drove China into poverty and backwardness, as well as ignorance and blindness.[2]

---

2. Deng Xiaoping, "Speech at the Third Plenary Session of the Central Advisory Commission of the CPC," in *Selected Works of Deng Xiaoping: Volume III* (Beijing: The People's Press, 1993), 90.

2.1.2 Emancipating the Mind: The Case of Coca Cola in China

Thirty years ago when China opened its doors, Coca Cola, as a symbol of the Western capitalist lifestyle was the first to arrive, yet it had a tough landing (Fang Yu 2008).

In 1976, on the eve of the Opening Up, China was politically chaotic. Tong Zhiguang (the former deputy minister of the Ministry of Foreign Trade and Economic Cooperation (MOFTEC) and the chief negotiator for the second round of the World Trade Organization (WTO) accession talk) was working in the Chinese liaison office in the US. The then president of Coca Cola came to his office, expressing the wish to export Coca Cola to China and set up a bottling factory in China. In consideration of the actual domestic situation, Tong thought it was an improper idea. For the Chinese people born after 1949, Coca Cola was something they only saw in movies, and was almost always associated with the US army. After the Korean War, Coca Cola became more than just a drink; the political implication of it made it hard for China to accept such a symbol of Western lifestyle at the time.

Toward 1977, the political situation in China became more stabilized, and Deng once again came back to power. The president of Coca Cola made a visit to Beijing to discuss the possibility of setting up a factory. Tong Zhiguang, who had finished his term in the US and returned to Beijing once again, received the president on behalf of the China National Cereals, Oils, and Foodstuffs Corporation (COFCO). Talking about the possible issues concerning the export of products to China, the president expounded as follows: By setting up a bottling factory in China, it would not be the Chinese local consumers they target mainly, but the foreign travelers in China from Europe and the US. As a drink with 80 years of history, the fathers and grandfathers of this generation of Americans grew up with Coca Cola, and most Americans and Europeans were used to the taste. As for the association with the US soldiers, except for the fact that Coca Cola was the producer and the US soldiers were the consumers, there wasn't any other link. Coca Cola factories had been set up in most European countries, and since the 1960s many more have appeared in Africa and Asia. Worldwide, many young people favored the drink. Where there was a need, there was a Cola, simply because "we are business people." Also the typical comment of the "medicine taste" in the drink was actually a Chinese taste: The taste of cinnamon oil.

After multiple rounds of negotiation, on December 13, 1978, COFCO and Coca Cola agreed on the setting up of a bottling factory and the sale of Coca Cola in major Chinese cities and sightseeing places in the form of compensational trade. Between 1979 and the completion of the bottling factory, sale was to be arranged by COFCO in the form of consignment. According to the arrangement, with the assistance of Ng Fung Hong Limited, the first shipment of 3,000 cases of bottled Coca Cola was shipped from Hong Kong to Beijing at the end of 1979.

The target of sales was strictly limited to expatriates and foreign tourists, and sales were mostly conducted in friendship stores. In fact, as early as 1927, Coca Cola set up a factory in Shanghai. In 1948, it was even the largest overseas Coca Cola factory of the time, but in 1949 the company retreated from the Chinese market. Upon its return, the first preference was still Shanghai. However, when the news reached Shanghai, it immediately invited strong objection, and the municipal government was buried in such denunciations as "[an act] of treason, slave mentality, US lifestyle, undermining the national industry." Having no option, Coca Cola set up the factory in the compound of a roast duck house affiliated to the Beijing subsidiary of COFCO, with only one workshop.

At that time, business was conducted in the following way: China paid US$300,000 for concentrate each year, and Coca Cola provided all the production lines for free. Coca Cola ended up spending US$1 million for the factory. Tong later commented: "The coming of Coca Cola marked the beginning of the introduction of foreign capital to China, but the business was operated like a domestic enterprise. The introduction of foreign capital in the real sense only came several years later."

All went smooth until an old comrade voiced his opinion: "Can't Chinese cola satisfy the need of our people and the foreign people? Why Coca Cola as a must? Isn't it betrayal?" To bring things back in balance, COFCO wrote a report to respond: "The success of Coca Cola is the success of sales, since the Reform and Opening Up. More foreigners have come to China, and as a host, it is natural to satisfy the guests by providing the drink. With cinnamon oil, Coca Cola has also a Chinese ingredient, and when China is yet to have the bottling technology for soft drinks, the introduction of the equipment brings technical progress. For the US$300,000 spent each year, China earns an annual profit of 200–300%, and is in control of the factory." With this, the storm finally subsided.

In early 1982, before the global vice president and president of the international division of Coca Cola went to Guangzhou to sign the contract for the second factory, there was also an "Anti Coca Cola Movement" held there. In face of the emergency, the MOFTEC minister asked the State Council for instructions, and Vice Premier Gu Mu replied: "Everything goes as planned." The Guangzhou factory was finally put into production in 1983. With two factories set up, the third one in Shanghai opened with less trouble.

One weekend in the winter of 1982, Coca Cola conducted a store promotion campaign in Beijing: One free balloon or a free pair of chopsticks for one bottle of Coca Cola bought. This was the first ever store promotion in modern China, and was immediately challenged by different newspapers, blaming the introduction of Coca Cola as a waste of China's scarce foreign exchange. The central government then came up with the instruction: Sell only to foreigners, and not a single bottle to the Chinese. In the spirit of the instruction, the Ministry of Commerce officially stopped the sale of Coca Cola in Beijing. In such a context, Chen Guang, director of the sugar and wine division of COFCO wrote a letter to the central government. In the letter, he mentioned the fact that 96% of the raw materials used for production were from China, with the concentrate from Coca Cola accounting for only 4% of the total cost. Through the sales in the tourist hotels, a great amount of foreign exchange had been earned, and with the rest of the products distributed to the domestic market, it enriched the market and brought huge profit to the factories. Finally, Coca Cola won back the right for domestic sales.

2.1.3 Let Some Areas Open First, Develop First, and Get Rich First

It was in May 1979 that Deng Xiaoping explicitly expounded the concept of "Opening up." Opening up, as he thought, was to attract foreign capital and technology to push forward the construction of the four modernizations. He added later in 1984: "Today the world is an open world. One important cause for the backwardness of China after the industrialization of Western countries was the closed-door policy. After the founding of new China, while the sanction from other countries remains, to some extent we are also blocking ourselves from others, making things more difficult. The experiences over the past 30 years reveal the truth that construction and development with our doors closed is not feasible."[3]

According to Deng, to develop and construct a nation, we must open up. But in what way? Can we open the whole nation in one shot? As early as 1978, Deng raised the theory of unbalanced development, deciding that some areas would develop ahead of others, and some people would get rich ahead of other people. Therefore, the coastal areas, especially the Special Economic Zones (SEZs) became the first beneficiary of the policy.

Deng pointed out that "one of the important steps of the Reform and Opening Up process is to speed up the opening of the coastal areas, so that the vast areas with a population of 200 million can develop first, and drive the development of the inland. This is the master plan. The inland areas are to show consideration to this arrangement, and in turn, when the coastal areas are developed to a certain degree, they are to give more support to the inland areas, which is also what the master plan is about. When that time comes, the coastal areas are to subject to this part of the master plan as well."[4]

The opening up trial started with the southeast coastal area. Neighboring Hong Kong and Taiwan, Guangdong and Fujian were first chosen as the base for the SEZs.

3. "Constructing Socialism with Chinese Characteristics," in *Selected Works of Deng Xiaoping: Volume 3*, 64.
4. "Central Authoritativeness," in *Selected Works of Deng Xiaoping: Volume 3*, 277–78.

After that, with the experience learnt, 14 coastal cities were opened up and development zones were set up in the three deltas (the Yangtze River Delta, the Pearl River Delta, and the Southeast Fujian Delta). Later, Pudong and some cities along the Yangtze River were opened up, together with the inland provincial capitals. With this, a nationwide network of opened up cities gradually came into being.

The "south to north and east to west" opening up strategy was an important part of the development strategy of "the first mover cities driving the late mover cities." According to Deng, the socialist road leads to common wealth but in a gradual manner. The concept of common wealth was to develop some eligible areas first, and let these areas give help to the backward areas toward the goal of common wealth.

2.2 Special Economic Zones (SEZs), Opening of Coastal Cities, and the Case of Shenzhen

2.2.1 The First Gunfire Shot in the Shekou Industrial Park

The slogan "Time is money, efficiency is life," was a spring thunder in the early 1980s, making a huge impact on the mindset of the Chinese people. Starting from the birthplace of the slogan—the Shekou Industrial Park of Shenzhen, the whole nation shifted toward the market economy (Liu Jianqiang 2008; Chen and Chen 2008).

Shekou Industrial Park is the industrial park established by the China Merchants Hong Kong, which is a Hong Kong-based state-owned Enterprise (SOE) under the Ministry of Communications.

On December 23, 1872, Viceroy Li Hongzhang proposed to set up China Merchants Steam Navigation Co. Ltd (China Merchants) to compete against the foreign shipping companies, and won the approval from Emperor Tongzhi of the Qing Dynasty. In addition to "attracting merchants worldwide and opening shipping lines to the five continents," China Merchants injected a large amount of capital to found the first group of industrial and commercial enterprises in China, such as Kai Ping Mine Bureau, China's first machine-operated coal mine; Han Ye Ping Corporation, China's first large iron & steel and coal conglomerate; Shanghai Machine Spinning Bureau, China's first cotton spinning enterprise; the Commercial Bank of China, China's first bank; and Bureau of China Merchants Insurance, China's first insurance company. In January 1950, as a branch of China Merchants, China Merchants Hong Kong was taken over by the Ministry of Communications, with the name remaining unchanged.

On October 12, 1978, the State Council approved the *Proposal on the Full Utilization of China Merchants Hong Kong* as drafted by Yuan Geng and submitted by the Ministry of Communications. On January 6, 1979, the Revolutionary Committee of Guangdong Province and the Ministry of Communications submitted the *Report on the Setting Up of Bao'an Industrial Park by China Merchants Hong Kong*. Approval came on January 31. In the spirit of the central government, Yuan Geng, the then standing vice chairman of China Merchants Hong Kong, selected the 2.14-square km Shekou to set up the foreign-oriented industrial park.

When Deng visited Shekou in January 1984, the place was already well known for its achievement within five years since its establishment. It was also the place with the youngest and highest-paid officials and employees. The success of Shekou can be attributed to a series of reform experiments such as the following:

1. Honoring the economic rules in the construction of the industrial park;
2. Reforming the management system and institutions;
3. Adopting open and democratic election of officials; and
4. Reforming the salary and housing system.

As the outcome of this reform, a market economy system and a number of excellent enterprises (CIMC, CMB, Ping'an, Huawei, Vanke) surfaced. Just as Yuan Geng recalled after retirement: "In 1878, when Edison invented the light bulb, it only brought brightness for eight minutes, yet the eight minutes marked a new era because the world was brightened all over shortly afterwards. It is not important when the filament of the first bulb got burnt out. What is important is the thinking on demand and the hope for the future." (Chen and Chen 2008).

2.2.2 The SEZ: The Case of Shenzhen

The SEZ refers to a designated area within the PRC that allows for the investment activities of foreign companies and individuals as well as the overseas Chinese and compatriots from Hong Kong and Macau, with special economic policies and special economic management systems offered. In April 1979, during the working session of the central government, the then Guangdong provincial leaders Xi Zhongxun and Yang Shangkun proposed to Deng Xiaoping the idea of setting up export processing zones in Shenzhen, Zhuhai, and Shantou, so as to attract foreign investment. This was how Deng came up with the concept of the SEZ.

On August, 26, 1980, during the 15th session of the Fifth NPC, it was officially announced that Shenzhen, Zhuhai, and Shantou had been chosen for the SEZs. On December 10 the same year, Xiamen was added to the list by the State Council. This was the first step toward opening up. On April 13, 1988, the proposal on founding Hainan province and Hainan economic zone was approved at the first session of the seventh NPC. By then, altogether there were five SEZs.

During the 1970s and 1980s, the bottleneck of economic construction was the shortage of capital, technologies, and experiences. With the SEZs, foreign capital and technologies could be brought into these zones to carry out policy experiments and accumulate experience.

Then why the five places? As Deng said in Shanghai in 1991, in choosing Shenzhen, Zhuhai, Shantou, and Xiamen, geographic condition was the first consideration. Shenzhen is close to Hong Kong, as Zhuhai is to Macau. Shantou is the hometown for the Teo Chew people in Southeast Asia, as Xiamen is the hometown for the Southern Fujian people overseas.[5]

The Opening Up strategy was firstly offered to businesses from Hong Kong, Macau, and Taiwan, especially Hong Kong, which links the mainland to the world as an international financial, trade, and shipping center. As the major hometown for the overseas Chinese, Guangdong and Fujian enjoy an advantage in attracting overseas Chinese. Also, being a part of China, Hong Kong and Macau would come back to China sooner or later. By strengthening economic ties, the heightened mutual understanding would pave the way for future political solutions. Hainan has abundant resources such as iron ore, natural gas, oil, rubber, and tropical plants. It would be great if Hainan is developed.[6]

Now let us look at the development case of the Shenzhen SEZ. In July 1979, the central government issued Circular No.50, unveiling the curtain for the establishment of the Shenzhen SEZ. In August 1980, the Shenzhen SEZ was officially founded through legislation. The central government issued Circular No. 41 in 1980, Circular No. 27 in 1981, Circular No. 50 in 1982, Circular No. 13 in 1984, and Circular No. 46 in 1985 to endorse Shenzhen with a series of favorable policies and flexible measures, including the fiscal responsibility system, the foreign exchange reserve system, the deduction and exemption of import and export tariff, the deduction of corporate income tax, favorable border entry and exit, and so on.

By 1984, with support of the central government and the whole nation, Shenzhen had become a mid-level and quite prosperous city. In the beginning of 1984, when Deng first visited Shenzhen, he commented: "The development and experience of Shenzhen proves our policy on the SEZs to be correct."[7] Deng pointed out: "The SEZs are windows of technology, windows of management, and windows of knowledge, as well as windows of foreign policy."[8] "There is a guiding thinking to be confirmed—the Opening Up policy for the SEZs is to be further liberated rather tightened."[9]

5. "Talks on Visiting Shanghai," in *Selected Works of Deng Xiaoping: Volume 3*, 366.
6. "The Pace of Reform is to Be Accelerated," in *Selected Works of Deng Xiaoping: Volume 3*, 239.
7. "Build Special Economic Zones and Open up More Cities," in *Selected Works of Deng Xiaoping, Volume 3*, 51.
8. Ibid.
9. Ibid.

Shortly before the spring festival of 1986, the Second National Working Meeting on the SEZs was held in Shenzhen. During this meeting, it was decided that the focus of development would shift from infrastructure to more efficient production, with more advanced technologies and more foreign investment. In the latter half of 1986, when the Shenzhen government changed the officials upon completion of term, the first stage of development came to an end.

In October 1986, the State Council issued the *Provisions on the Encouragement of Foreign Investment* (22 clauses), and the attraction and utilization of foreign capital embarked on a new journey. The then vice premier, Gu Mu, ordered the Shenzhen government to implement the 22 clauses for the creation of a microclimate for the attraction of foreign capital, so as to pave the way for the building of a macroclimate nationwide.

In the autumn of 1988, Shenzhen took advantage of the Japanese Yen appreciation and the reshuffle of the international economic order, and engaged in many large projects that helped build the microclimate. In November 1988, Shenzhen was approved by the State Council as a city with independent planning jurisdiction, enjoying provincial level status in the management of economic affairs.

Since Shenzhen was chosen as a pilot base, the trial effort has not been limited to the economic field only. After the 13th Congress of the CPC, the municipal government shifted the focus of the reform to finance, taxation, price, salary, SOE, land system, housing, and social security, among which the most influential innovation was the compensated transfer of the land use rights as authorized by the central government. With the deepening of the reform and the increasing demand for capital investment, by referring to the experience of Hong Kong, the Shenzhen municipal government submitted to the central government *The Proposal on the Trial of Compensated Transfer of Land Use Rights in Some Areas.* In 1987, the State Council approved the proposal, and Shenzhen, Shanghai, Tianjin, and Guangzhou became the first group of pilot cities. In September 1987, Shenzhen started the reform. In April 1988, the NPC adopted the *Revision of the Constitution of the PRC*, and amended the provisions which had prohibited the transfer of land use rights according to the 1982 Constitution.

In September 1988, to address the problems in the development of the national economy, a rectification plan was announced during the third session of the 13th Central Committee of the CPC. Compared to 1988, the actual investment in joint ventures dropped by 28.7% in 1989, the actual investment in solely foreign-invested enterprises (FIEs) dropped by 41.9%, and exports also showed signs of declining. In the face of the challenges, Shenzhen once again grasped opportunity with its geographic edge and development momentum. With the help of Shenzhen SEZ, the inland areas were connected to Hong Kong. Besides, the stable growth of Shenzhen also contributed to the prosperity of Hong Kong. The strategic position of Shenzhen was not impaired in the nationwide rectification. Rather it was once again solidified and enhanced.

During the Fourth National Working Meeting on the SEZs in February 1990, the central government decided that the focus of the SEZs was to be shifted from labor-intensive industries to technology-intensive ones, as well as the foreign-oriented economy. In June and November the same year, Jiang Zemin visited Shenzhen twice. On November 26, 1990, Jiang addressed the Reception of the 10th Anniversary of Shenzhen SEZ, saying that the achievement of Shenzhen had proven the correctness of the Reform and Opening Up strategy. By combining theory and practice, it enriched our understanding on the building of socialism with Chinese characteristics. In December the same year, the first congress of party representatives was held in Shenzhen, during which the mission and goal for the new period was set: "Develop Shenzhen into a multifunctional industrial metropolitan with a relatively mature tertiary industry and relatively advanced high technologies." It was decided that on top of "Shenzhen Speed," "Shenzhen Efficiency" would be targeted.

In January and February 1992, Deng visited Wuchang, Shenzhen, Zhuhai, and Shanghai, and delivered a series of important talks. Upon arriving in Shenzhen, he said: "Once the target is located, attempts and efforts should be made with courage. The precious experience of Shenzhen lies in the courage to try."[10]

The talk delivered during Deng Xiaoping's southern tour, and the convening of the 14th Congress marked the new historical period of the reform, and greatly pushed forward the development of all undertakings in Shenzhen. In 1992 and 1993, the GNP and the total industrial output of Shenzhen grew by over 30% annually. The actual utilization of foreign capital in 1993 doubled the amount of 1992, and the export volume ranked the top in China. The landmark of the reform of the new period was the establishment of the socialist market economy system. In 1993, based on the practical experiences of the past decade, five systematic indexes of the socialist market economy were set, which were expanded to eight in the following year. In 1997, Shenzhen announced that after years of efforts, the framework of the socialist market economy was established, and ten socialist economic systems were formed, that is, the ownership system that allows for fair competition of multiple types of economy with public ownership being the main body; the capital-tied supervision and operation system for state-owned assets; the market-based price system; the commodity market-based and factor market-supported market system; the market economy-oriented national budgeting and corporate accounting system; the social-individual-combined security system; the work-based

10. "Talking Points for the Talks in Wuchang, Shenzhen, Zhuhai, Shanghai and Other Places," in *Selected Works of Deng Xiaoping: Volume 3*, 372. (Here the achievement of Shenzhen was fully acknowledged).

and performance-related compensation system; the all-inclusive economic regulation system with mostly indirect means; and the socialist market economy-oriented legal system. The summary of the ten systems became an important reference and basis for the construction of the socialist market economy system.

On December 11, 2001 China entered the WTO, and the specialness of the SEZ was challenged. The principle of national treatment and nondiscrimination of the WTO aims at the protection of the fair interest of the foreign investors in the host country. No member country is allowed to treat the foreign investors differently from home investors by giving either favor or punishment. In the spirit of this principle, the favorable policies offered to the foreign investors in the SEZs contradicted the WTO commitment and were to be nullified sooner or later.

Against this new backdrop, the connotation of the SEZs was in need of update and enrichment. The future focus of the SEZs was not to attract foreign capital or earn foreign exchange. Rather, it was to shift from policy favors to a comprehensive business environment. In recent years, Shenzhen has managed to keep its momentum in opening up, innovation, and development.

2.2.3 The Coastal Opened Cities—The Coastal Economic and Technical Development Zones—The Coastal Economic Opening Areas

The opening up and economic stimulus guidelines set during the third session of the 11th CPC was a significant strategic decision in the new historical period. In the following years, by utilizing foreign capital and importing technologies, many joint ventures, Sino-foreign cooperative enterprises, and FIEs were established, and great achievements were made in foreign economic affairs. Noticing the progress made, the central government decided to deepen the reform.

In May 1984, 14 coastal cities were officially opened up. They were Dalian, Qinhuangdao, Tianjin, Yantai, Qingdao, Lianyungang, Nantong, Shanghai, Ningbo, Wenzhou, Fuzhou, Guangzhou, Zhanjiang, and Beihai. Such was the second step of opening up.

In September that year, the State Council approved Dalian to set up an economic and technical development zone. Between then and January 1985, Qinhuangdao, Yantai, Qingdao, Ningbo, Zhanjiang, Tianjin, Lianyungang, Nantong, Fuzhou, and Guangzhou were approved in succession to set up economic and technical development zones. In August 1986, the State Council approved the Minhang Economic and Technical Development Zone, and the Hongqiao Economic and Technical Development Zone of Shanghai, and in 1988, the Caohejing High-tech Zone of Shanghai was also approved, increasing the total number of economic and technical development zones to 14.

Each of these coastal cities enjoys the heritage of economic and cultural ties with the outside world since ancient times, as well as a long history of commodity economy, a solid industrial foundation, advanced technologies, culture, and management expertise. At the same time, most are located in the traffic hubs for water carriage, land transportation, and airway. Having experiences with both foreign trade and inland collaboration, they were the more developed areas in China. By easing some policies and reforming some administration systems, they could become more vital. Should the utilization of foreign resources (such as capital, material, technologies, knowledge, and talents), the development of international market, the restructuring of industries, the technical advancement of enterprises, and the reform on administration systems be integrated, these places could surely move faster in economic development, and bring higher profitability to enterprises, and better living for the people.

The opening up of the 14 cities was to deepen the Opening Up strategy. The favorable policies included independent rights in the handling of foreign affairs and tax reduction.

The independent rights are as follows: Supporting the utilization of foreign capital and advanced technologies in the reengineering of old enterprises and the opening of new factories; loosening the examination and approval of foreign capital setting up economic and technical development zones; importing the advanced technologies in urgent demand, especially the knowledge- and technology-intensive projects; further loosening the examination and approval of foreign capital projects by referring to the standard of the SEZs; and increasing the quota for foreign exchange and FX loan to ensure the import of key facilities and instruments in need.

Each of these coastal cities has a designated area for the construction of the economic and technical development zone, and the import of advanced technologies in urgent demand. Joint ventures, joint cooperative enterprises, or joint R&D institutes were invited to develop and manufacture new products in the zones. Foreigners are also welcome to set up FIEs. Some zones also later developed into transshipment hubs.

To activate the economy and expand the scope of opening up, on February 18, 1985, the central government and the State Council approved *The Minutes of the Meeting on Yangtze River Delta, Pearl River Delta, and South Fujian Delta,* and issued a notice on the setting up of economic zones in these places. Later, the Bohai Bay area, and many more coastal cities and counties were opened up. These areas enjoy favorable state policies, including independent rights, the preferential taxation on foreign investors, and simplified entry/exit. It was recorded in the minutes that the processing industry was to be developed to support the export trade, and agriculture and production of other raw materials were to be developed to support the processing industry, in the aim of expanding export and earning foreign exchange. Meanwhile, these places would also serve as windows for the foreign-oriented economic affairs.

In this way, with the opening up of coastal cities, the coastal economic and technical development zones, and the coastal economic zones, a long and narrow opening frontline of 18,000 kilometers from south to north was established. Over the past 20 years, great achievements have been made along this frontline. The experience accumulated (like the economic development model, the market economy philosophy, and management concept) and the lessons learnt have been used for reference by the rest of the country.

2.2.4 The Foreign-oriented Development Strategy of the Coastal Region

In the early 1980s, the Rung Shift Theory was put forward by some Chinese economists, the gist of which was to divide China into three rungs from the east to the middle, and then to the west, which are low, middle, and high in altitude, but high, middle and low in terms of economic development. Based on this theory, the strategic focus of economic development should be put on the east coastal region and gradually move to the central and west, to coincide with the thinking of unbalanced development. Though proven effective in the beginning stage of the reform, it also invited criticism from the inland.

By the late 1980s, with progress made in the reform, the coastal areas were given a precious opportunity: With the change of labor costs, developed countries and regions were moving the labor-intensive industries to cheaper regions, and the coastal areas in China were highly competitive with low labor costs, convenient transportation, and manageable infrastructure. This gave rise to the emergence of the "Theory of International Economic Circulation," the gist of which was to grasp opportunities to expand the opening up of the coastal regions and the development of the labor-intensive export processing trade, to better utilize the foreign capital and technologies, and to employ redundant rural laborers. The circulation requires both the export market and the raw materials from overseas, so as not to compete with the inland for domestic market and resources. After discussion, a consensus was reached as follows.

The first priority was to develop labor-intensive industry. With abundant human resources and low labor costs, the price ratio was competitive, it is therefore reasonable to develop labor-intensive processing industries, and industries that combine both labor and knowledge. "Processing with imported materials," as a product-based labor export, should also be supported.

Next was to maintain international input and output for the processing industry, with both ends (raw materials and sales market) extending to the overseas market. With the increasing demand for raw materials in the coastal areas, and the development of the inland, should the coastal areas rely upon the domestic materials, they would have to compete hard with the inland for resources. The coastal areas were, therefore, encouraged to purchase raw materials from overseas and sell the finished products to the international market. When conditions were met, manufacturing of components and spare parts as well as raw materials should be encouraged to substitute the import and raise the product value and grade.

As a representative of this theory, Wang Jian, a researcher of the State Planning Committee, published an article titled "The Possibility and Requirement for Adopting the Macro International Economic Circulation Development Strategy," in an internal journal of the Xinhua Agency on November 1, 1987. The article was later published in the *Economic Daily*, with the title of "Adopting the Correct Long-term Strategy—the Concept of Macro International Economic Circulation Development Strategy" on January 5, 1988. The theory caught focused attention from the central leaders, and served as a basis for the forming of the "Economic Development Strategy of the Coastal Region" in 1988.

In the plenary session of the Politburo on February 6, 1988, it was confirmed that the economic development strategy of the coastal region should not only push the coastal areas to the international market for competition and exchange, but also drive the economic development of the central and western regions. This significant overall strategy should be carried out in a consistent manner. The following 20 years have proven the strategy to be most correct and successful.

2.3 Pudong New District, Opening of Yangtze River and Border Cities, and the Development of the Central and Western Areas

2.3.1 The Case of Shanghai—Pudong

In the 1980s, in developing the foreign-oriented economy, China established the SEZs in Guangdong and Fujian by offering favorable policies and flexible measures. The SEZs contributed a lot toward the national economy and impressed the world, yet the achievements were still limited to a small region. In May 1984, China further opened up 14 coastal cities; and in February 1985, China set up the economic zones in the Yangtze River Delta, the Pearl River Delta, and the South Fujian Delta. Started in Fujian and Guangdong, the opening up strategy gradually moved northward, yet the important city of Shanghai was missed in the process.

With unique resources and economic legacy, Shanghai only played the rearguard role in the opening up of the 1980s. Although Shanghai achieved some moderate economic progress, for various reasons, it lagged behind the southern region. During his southern China tour in 1992, Deng commented: "Take Shanghai for an example. It has all the possible conditions for faster development. Shanghai enjoys evident advantages in human resources, technology, and management. Looking back, my big mistake was to neglect Shanghai in building the SEZs. Otherwise, the situation now in the Yangtze

River Delta, the whole Yangtze River area, and even the whole country would be different."[11]

As early as 1984, when formulating the *Outline of Economic Development Strategy of Shanghai* and *The General Urban Plan of Shanghai*, the municipal government decided on the idea of developing Pudong. Lying on the Yangtze River Delta, Pudong is on the estuary of the "golden coastline" and the "golden waterway" of China, and enjoys advantageous location for international trade and domestic transportation. For the lack of bridge or tunnel on the river in the past, the development of Pudong remained long untapped.

As for Shanghai, developing Pudong presented an opportunity for the upgrading of the urban infrastructure, industrial structure, and economic strength. The development of Pudong could also release the population pressure on the west town and make room for urban reconstruction. In February 1990, the municipal government officially submitted the application for the development of Pudong to the Central CPC and the State Council. Deng attached great importance to the development of Pudong and actively supported the initiative.

In the 1980s, the SEZs functioned as role models, yet since all the SEZs are southern cities with a lower starting point and weaker technical and educational base, it was still hard for them to drive the whole nation and pose a stronger impact. Therefore, Deng said: "It's true that Shanghai is included in the 14 coastal opened cities, yet that was the general opening up. Should Pudong have been developed years earlier as with Shenzhen, that would have been fantastic. The development of Pudong has significant impact, since it does not concern Pudong only, but the whole city of Shanghai, and the Yangtze River Delta and the Yangtze River area with Shanghai as a base. Waste no time in developing Pudong until it is done."[12]

On April 18, 1990, the then premier Li Peng, on behalf of the Central CPC and the State Council, announced the decision on the development of Pudong, describing it as a significant step toward the deepening of the Reform and Opening Up process. In this way, the development of Pudong was upgraded from a local strategy to a national one.

The policy innovation and system innovation of Pudong includes:

1. Levying 15% income tax for the manufacturing joint ventures, FIEs and Sino-foreign cooperative enterprises; two years' tax exemption and three years' tax deduction by half since the first profitable year for enterprises with over ten years' operation.

11. "Talking Points of Talks in Wuchang, Shenzhen, Zhuhai, Shanghai and Other Places," in *Selected Works of Deng Xiaoping, Volume 3* (People's Press, 1993), 376.
12. "Talks in Visiting Shanghai," in *Selected Works of Deng Xiaoping: Volume 3*, 366.

2. Exemption of customs tariffs and industrial and commercial tax for imported equipment, vehicles, and building materials for construction purposes; exemption of customs tariffs and industrial and commercial tax for imported equipment, materials, vehicles, office facilities, household necessities, and transportation vehicles for expatriates with joint ventures, FIEs and Sino-foreign cooperative enterprises; exemption of customs tariffs and industrial and commercial tax for exported goods complying with the state provisions.
3. The products of the foreign manufacturers in Pudong should be export oriented, and can only be sold in the domestic market upon approval from the competent departments and with tariff/industrial and commercial tax paid.
4. Foreigners are allowed to make investment in airports, harbors, railroads, motorways, and power plants with five years' tax exemption followed by five years' tax deduction by half since the first profitable year.
5. Foreigners are encouraged to engage in the tertiary industry including the otherwise denied financial and commodity retail business upon approval.
6. Foreigners are allowed to set up foreign banks in Pudong starting with financial firms. Based on the actual business development, a certain number of banks may set up branches. The income tax rate for the foreign banks would be lowered moderately and different tax rates would be offered to different businesses. Related provisions would be promulgated to guarantee the normal operation of the foreign banks.
7. Foreign trading firms are allowed to conduct transshipment business in the bonded zone of Pudong, and provide agency services for raw materials dealing, spare parts import, and products export. The corporate executives in the bonded zone may apply for multiple entry/exit visa to facilitate business travel.
8. Differentiated treatment would be given to the Chinese enterprises in Pudong including the enterprises with investment from other Chinese cities. Tax exemption and reduction may be given to those contributing to the development and opening up of Pudong.
9. Foreign investors may develop land in Pudong based on the policy on the compensated transfer of land use rights for a term of 50 to 70 years.
10. The fiscal revenue of Pudong would be used for further development to accelerate the opening up.

With support of Shanghai and the whole nation, after 18 years, Pudong underwent a facelift, and now presents to the world a modern international image. The GDP jumped from RMB 6 billion in 1990 to RMB 275.1 billion in 2007, with an annual growth of over 15%. The achievement cannot be separated from the continuous efforts in overcoming the system and mechanism barriers, as well as the firm adoption of the development strategy.

From being questioned by the speculative international investors in the beginning of the opening up to the first round of reform on the administration system between 1992 and 1993, from the land price hike in 1995 to the Asian financial crisis in 1997, from the hard shift from the project-based development to the function-based development at the beginning of the twenty-first century to the building of the first comprehensive reform trial base in 2005, Pudong managed to grasp every opportunity when challenged.

In June 2005, Pudong was approved by the State Council as a trial base for the comprehensive reform, marking a new stage of development. The role model effect and system surplus effect surfaced soon after. The bonded zone model, the export processing zone model, and the high-tech park model were duplicated nationwide, and proven policies like the "nine clauses of foreign exchange" and the "fourteen clauses of quality inspection" were rolled out. The 500 financial institutions in the Lujiazui area of Pudong have become the propellers of economic development in the Yangtze River Delta and the rest of the country. Over half of the goods imported and exported through the Waigaoqiao bonded zone covered the Yangtze River Delta; many domestic enterprises have set up headquarters in Pudong to pave the way for nationwide and worldwide business development; and 96 MNCs set up their regional headquarters in Pudong to reach out to the whole Chinese market.

Mind emancipation and innovative development is the driving force for Pudong. Now, Lujiazui is building itself as an international financial center, the Zhangjiang high-tech park a pilot base of innovation, the Waigaoqiao bonded zone a world trade base, and the Jinqiao export processing zone a manufacturing service industry center. With innovation and globalization, Pudong will surely have a brighter tomorrow.

2.3.2 The Opening Up of the Yangtze River Area

After the southern tour of Deng Xiaoping, China further developed, expanded, and deepened the Opening Up policy in practice. Following Shanghai and Nanjing, in June 1992, five more cities along the Yangtze River were opened up, namely Wuhu, Jiujiang, Yueyang, Wuhan, and Chongqing. This represented the third step China took toward opening up. Meanwhile Shanghai port, Nantong port, Zhangjiagang port, Zhenjiang port, Nanjing port, Wuhu port, Jiujiang port, and Wuhan port were also opened up, making the 1,200-km riverside along the Yangtze River open to the world. The opening up of these cities was not only significant for these cities themselves, but also for the whole Yangtze River belt and even the whole country.

The Yangtze River is the axis of productivity and the hub of the national economy. With a favorable geographic location and abundant resources, it is ideal for industrialization and urbanization. By taking the opportunity in the development of Pudong and the Three Gorges project, and with Shanghai, Nanjing, Wuhan, and Chongqing as backbones of the river, an economic belt gradually formed to drive the development of the massive inland.

2.3.3 The Opening of the Inland and Border Cities

From March to July of 1992, the State Council decided to open 13 border cities including Heihe, Suifenhe, Huichun, Manchuria, Yining, Tacheng, Pinxiang, Dongxing, Wanting, Ruili, Hekou, and Erlianhot. This was China's foruth step of opening up.

The policy and system innovation for the 13 cities was as follows: The provinces (or autonomous regions) to which the cities belonged may authorize the cities to approve and manage trade, economic cooperation, and investment within the jurisdiction; a special state loan would be set aside for the construction of the economic zones and a preferential tax policy would be offered to the FIEs as follows: Upon approval of the local tax department, the FIEs would be entitled to a favorable 24% income tax; the goods exchanged from the neighboring countries may be sold at will, with 50% deduction of tariff and turnover tax upon import.

Compared with the east coastal areas, the border cities are very different in geographic condition, economic development level, historical background, cultural habit, and lifestyle. While the coastal cities are already quite developed, most border cities are backward with low technologies, weak infrastructure, and an uneducated population; while the coastal cities have received huge foreign capital, the money flow of the border cities follows a double way model, since the neighboring countries were more or less on the same economic level. However, the border cities are rich in natural resources, and have huge potential in developing tourism. Also, with similar habit and culture, labor export to the neighboring countries is feasible.

Shortly after the opening of the border cities, China opened the fifth door. In June and July of 1992, the State Council and the Central Committee of the CPC decided to open 18 inland provincial capitals and autonomous region capitals including Urumqi, Nanning, Kunming, Harbin, Changchun, Huhehot, Shijiazhuang, Taiyuan, Hefei, Nanchang, Zhengzhou, Changsha, Chengdu, Guiyang, Xian, Lanzhou, Xining, and Yinchuan, offering the same preferential policies as with the coastal areas. Thus, a multilayered and dimensional pattern of opening up came into existence.

2.3.4 The Opening and Development of Western China

On June 17, 1999, in a seminar on the enterprise reform and development of the five northwest provinces and regions, the then president, Jiang Zemin, pointed out that it was time for the development of western China and it would be a major strategy of the party and the nation from then onward. The development of western China echoed the "two master plans" strategy of Deng Xiaoping.

Before the Reform and Opening Up process began, the conflict between cities and rural areas was tense, and there was no labor flow in between or market allocation of capital. The dual economy is characterized by urban-rural separation and economic underdevelopment. After the opening up of the east coastal region, western China, with less than desirable development, was left further behind, worsening the shortcoming of the dualistic economy: Industries in the east and agriculture in the west.

Technically speaking, the eastern region enjoys the first mover advantage and the western region the late mover advantage. But in reality, the western region was so slow in development that it started to handicap the sustainable development of the eastern region and even the healthy and coordinated development of the whole nation. Therefore, the "Western Campaign" strategy was adopted to accelerate the development of the west toward the goal of common wealth.

The market mechanism alone does not provide the solution. For the natural condition, historical baggage, and geographical reasons, the market in western China is far less developed than that in the east. To narrow the gap, many favorable policies were offered to the western region, including: Easing the requirements for the setting up and foreign share ratio of the FIEs of the restricted category, encouraging the FIEs in eastern China to reinvest in western China, offering FIE treatment to projects with over 25% foreign investment, applying the 15% income tax rate to the FIEs of the encouraged category within three years after the expiry of the tax holiday period; support from the credit loan department of the National Development Bank, and a total investment of up to RMB 200 billion in the forestry and ecological construction.

Unlike the coastal region and the border cities, western China is open to both foreign and domestic capital, especially the private investors from eastern China.

2.3.5 The Return of Hong Kong and Macau

Since the reform, Hong Kong and Macau have served as the window and bridge between the mainland and the world. After Hong Kong and Macau returned to China in 1997 and 1999, respectively, with their favorable geographic location and developed economy, they continue to push forward the opening up of the mainland within the Closer Economic Partnership Arrangement (CEPA) framework.

As an international financial center, trade center, tourism center, and shipping center, Hong Kong is the most liberalized economy in the world. Situated on the southern tip of China, Hong Kong is a major entry port for people and goods coming from the

US, Europe, Japan, and Southeast Asia to south China. Hong Kong is also the most free harbor among all, with free flow of duty free commodities, people, and capital, making the place a distributing center of import and export.

The initial period of economic cooperation between the mainland and Hong Kong extends from 1978 to 1992. Amid the gradual opening up and the reform of the economic system, Hong Kong fully utilized the free harbor advantage, and made the Pearl River Delta region a major production base and distribution center for transshipment. The development strategy and favorable policies attracted a huge amount of Hong Kong capital to the mainland. As a result, the mainland gained a great amount of capital, overseas market, and management expertise, and the move of the Hong Kong manufacturing business to the mainland also accelerated the construction of the Pearl River Delta as a manufacturing center. From 1992 to 1997 the economic cooperation of both sides expanded from trade and processing to a wider scope covering transportation, urban infrastructure, high-tech industry, finance, tourism, and so on. The return of Hong Kong to the mainland in 1997 signaled the beginning of the enhancement period, with the two sides becoming more closely tied in common development. With support from the mainland, Hong Kong survived the financial crisis, and through Hong Kong, the mainland has obtained all kinds of international finance and trade services.

Before the return of Hong Kong and Macau, the east coastal region was the frontier of opening up, and after the return, the frontier was further extended to Hong Kong and Macau. Now the mainland, Hong Kong, Macau and Taiwan have formed a close "interlinked economy," or in other words, the Greater China Region.

In June and October 2003, the Chinese government signed with Hong Kong and Macau the CEPA. Since then, the free trade relationship was established between the mainland and Hong Kong/Macau, giving rise to expanded capital investment and trade. Hong Kong/Macau now functions better as the international finance, trade, and shipping center, and investment platform, which is conducive to the upgrade of the manufacturing business and construction of the service industries in the mainland.

2.4 The Overall Opening since the Accession to the WTO

On December 11, 2001, China accepted the rigid accession conditions and officially joined the WTO, committing a five-year transition period for market opening. This marked the overall opening up of China. Fifteen years had been spent on hard negotiation before that day: Starting from July 10, 1986, China first submitted the application to resume the position as a signatory member of the General Agreement on Tariffs and Trade (GATT). However, for various reasons, China failed. In 1995, the GATT was replaced by the WTO. On November 15, 1999, the bilateral WTO agreement between China and the US was signed, putting an end to the substantial negotiation of the WTO accession. The untiring effort was finally rewarded.

2.4.1 From Policy Opening to Institutional Opening

Since 1978, China has opened its door in a gradual way through a series of policies, which may be called "policy opening" (Liang Xiaomeng 2001). In the early years, as tied by the legacy of the planned economy and the closed-door thinking, there was no legal base for the establishment of the market economy, and policy innovation came up as the major means. As a set of conduct codes for the government bodies and party organizations serving the mission and goal of certain historical periods, policy has the function of controlling, managing, and coordinating.

In practice, the policy opening includes: policies for the SEZs, the coastal opened up cities, the coastal economic zones, the attraction of foreign capital, and so on. While being effective, these policies had defects also:

1. As the opening up policy was an innovation which was not included in the system, there was conflict between the opening up policies and the existing systems, including the unfair competition between the SOEs and FIEs/JVs, between the SEZs and other areas.
2. As opening up was a dynamic process and required continuous efforts, the policy opening lacked stability and predictability.
3. While the reform within the system encountered multiple barriers, policy opening met less trouble. Yet, outdated systems, such as the administration system, still inhibited the market opening, and watered down the due effect.
4. For the differentiated taxation benefits, foreign capital and domestic resources would naturally move to more favorable regions, widening the existing gap between the coastal areas and the inland.

After accession to the WTO, with the deepening of opening up in all dimensions, policy opening could no longer handle the new situation. System opening in the legal framework was in need to address the new issues, so that all types of entities could be given national treatment for fair competition, and all practices could be in line with the WTO rules.

The "institutional opening" refers to the alignment with international practice, and the adoption of an overall and stable legal framework as conduct code and incentive mechanism. The WTO promoted the legalization and standardization of the international trade system, and symbolized economic globalization. By joining the organization, which is a whole set of multilateral rules based on the market economy, China would have to acknowledge and accept the set of rules in the first place. To that end, in the five-year transition period, China cleaned up all the administrative and legal systems, and hundreds of administrative and legal documents were nullified, revised, and drafted.

2.4.2 Opening from the Manufacturing Industry to the Service Industry

For the first 20 years of the reform, efforts were focused on the manufacturing industry, from auto, home electronic appliances, and food to steel, chemical, machinery, textile, electronics, and medicine. At that time, manufacturing was the economic sector exposed to competition while the service industry was hidden and protected, as a result of the low income level in China in the 1980s and 1990s.

In the early years, many foreign manufacturers shifted their operations to China to benefit from the higher skills and lower cost of the Chinese workforce. Through the opening up of the manufacturing business, China accumulated a large amount of capital, advanced technologies, and management expertise.

After China joined the WTO in 2001, focus then shifted to the service industry as a result of the improved personal income and the deepened industrialization. The foreign investors arriving in China after 2000 are mostly interested in this sector as well. In recent years, finance, trade, and IT have become exposed to competition.

On the evening of May 24, 2007, when the ex-Vice Premier Madam Wu Yi addressed the US-China Trade Commission, she said:

> When China joined the WTO, we made extensive commitment on the market access to trade in service. Over the past five years, China has honored its commitment in an all-round manner, and opened the 100-plus service trade sectors to foreign capital in accordance with the WTO classification, to the same extent of the developed countries. Since accession to the WTO, the amount of foreign capital absorbed in trade, distribution, logistics, finance, courier, communication, tourism, transportation, law, construction services grew fast. In the finance sector, China has opened the RMB business in an all-round manner and lifted the bans on regions and customers. In 2005 and 2006 alone, the banking industry attracted over US$18.2 billion of FDI, which was much higher than the amount of most developed countries. Up to the end of 2006, 74 overseas banks had set up 312 offices in China; 28 overseas strategic investors had invested in 21 Chinese banks; 31 overseas financial institutions had set up 31 joint securities firms and fund companies; and 44 overseas insurance companies had set up 115 offices in China.

2.4.3 From "Bringing in" to "Going Global"

Since the reform, China has given full play to the late development advantage by importing capital, technologies, and management expertise, which resulted in fast economic growth and strengthened international competitiveness. After accession to the WTO, China enhanced the effort on attracting business and raised new programs such as the

"Northeast Rejuvenation Program" and the development of the Tianjin Binhai new district. In November 2002, during the 16th Congress of the CPC, it was pointed out in the report that the "bringing in" strategy should be combined with a "going global" strategy so as to engage in the international economic and technical coopetition "in a wider range and on a higher level," and fully utilize the overseas and domestic market to optimize resource allocation and make room for further development. Since then, the "bringing in" strategies has been replaced by a combination of "bringing in" and "going global" strategies, marking a new period of opening up. Before the accession to the WTO, the "going global" strategy was mostly applied in the commodity trade. Since the accession, China has taken off in areas of overseas investment and economic cooperation with other countries.

2.5 The Relative Advantages of the Sino-Foreign Coopetition in the Opening Up Process

Multiple participants have benefited from the opening up of China, for the process of opening up is featured by interaction among different parties, with each party obtaining a new market and a new type of resource.

2.5.1 The Late Development Benefit of China

As a developing (late development) country, the purpose of opening up is to have both the domestic market and the overseas market, and gain access to both domestic and overseas resources. The past three decades have proven the strategy to be successful as China has given full play to the late development advantage and obtained huge late development benefit.

The acquisition of external resources. While China is rich in labor resource, it lacks capital, technologies, and management. Over the past 30 years, the import of the above resources boosted the economic growth.

Over these years, China altogether brought in (actual utilization) nearly US$1 trillion and set up 300,000 FIEs. Should the coordinated investment from the Chinese partners be factored in, foreign capital is certainly a major driving force of high economic growth.

The technical import is also considerable. In addition to the assembly lines and equipment which are "hard technologies," there are also "soft technologies" including technical licensing, consulting, and joint production, which amounted to US$259.3 billion in value up to the end of 2007. Upon arriving, the imported technologies are digested, absorbed, and innovated, so as to raise the TFP. Apart from that, management expertise and experience learning are also acquired as hidden gains.

The development of the external market. With a population of 1.3 billion, China has a huge domestic market. Yet with lower average income, the domestic market still remained underdeveloped. Since the reform, China has attached great importance to the overseas market, including Europe, North America, Japan and Asia, Africa, and Latin America, covering almost the whole world.

With the foreign trade volume jumping from US$9.96 billion 30 years ago to US$1.34463 trillion today, or an increase of 135 times, it is one of the major contributors to the economic growth. The competitive power of "Made in China" lies in the late development advantage of labor-intensive products. Though low in added value and thin in profit, they are considerable in volume.

Growth driven by the late development advantage. By utilizing the market and resources both domestically and abroad, China achieved fast growth driven by the late development advantage, with FDI, technology transfer, and export being the main contributors to the high growth.

2.5.2 The Early Development Benefit of the Foreign Participants

Most of the foreign participants involved in the opening up of China are developed countries and emerging industrialized economies. With the early development advantage against China, they have harvested huge benefit in China.

Occupying the market in China. As the third-largest importer in the world after 30 years of opening up, imports received by China amounted to US$955.8 billion in 2007. The imports of China are the exports of the foreign parties, which cover luxury goods, resources, raw materials, semi-finished products, and so on. Since the goods exported to China are mostly capital-intensive or technology-intensive products, they have brought rich profits to the exporters, which reflects the accumulated capital/technology advantage.

The huge commodity market China offers to the world has created many job opportunities for other countries, especially in Asia, who have achieved growth by exporting to China. For example, the increasing demand for motor vehicles and tires in China boosted the price of rubber in a small Thai town where rubber was the largest cash crop, bringing prosperity to the local farmers. The economic boom in China has created continuous demand for raw materials.

On the other hand, inexpensive quality products made in China benefit global consumers. By purchasing from China, many foreign companies have lowered costs and enhanced their competitive edge, which was most true for the auto industry. By purchasing spare parts and components in China, MNCs have greatly reduced their average cost. One example is Ford, which has reduced its average cost of spare parts and components by 30–40%. Another example is the Barbie dolls made in Dongguan and Wenzhou. With a cost price of US$1 and a retail price of US$9.99 in the US, thick profit has been transferred from China to the foreign party.

Obtaining the resources in China. China is not only a large commodity market, but also a large investment market. As mentioned before, over 300,000 FIEs have been established in China since the reform, and they come for two things: Big market and cheap resources, especially the abundant labor resources. With the early development of the human resources sector, the labor cost in developed countries is getting increasingly higher, making the competitiveness of commodities weaker. Yet, in China, with the late development of labor resources, the cost is still relatively low. Plus, the labor quality is not bad, at least better than most developing countries. Therefore, foreign companies, especially MNCs, swarmed to China to set up factories or outsource business to Chinese enterprises. As proof of the competence of Chinese technicians and scholars, many MNCs have set up R&D centers in China and recruited local researchers.

The interaction between wealth and growth. Over the past 30 years, the philosophy of the Chinese people toward wealth and profit has changed dramatically. Instead of detesting and opposing, Chinese people now welcome foreign investors to China to make money. Actually, by coming to China, the foreign companies gain not only profit, but also growth and closer ties with their trading partners.

2.6 Case Study of the Accession to the WTO: The Dynamic Win-Win Game of 15 Years

2.6.1 The Mission and Essence of the Accession to the GATT/WTO

The application for the resumption of the GATT membership made in July, 1986 was based on four considerations:

1. After the founding of the SEZs, China started to benefit from the Reform and Opening Up process, and wished to carry it further. With the GATT membership resumption, China may better integrate itself into the world economic system and prosper with both markets and resources domestically and abroad.
2. The trade volume of the GATT member countries accounted for 85% of the world total, and the trade volume between China and GATT members accounted for 85% of the national total. China could not afford to be left outside the GATT.
3. The capital, technologies, and management expertise brought into China since the reform require a more favorable international market in order to accommodate its productivity.

4. After China joined the World Bank and International Monetary Fund in 1980, it was natural to apply for the membership of the multilateral trade organization.

The resumption of the GATT membership or the accession to the WTO (in 1995 the WTO was founded and the task of GATT resumption changed to the accession to the WTO) took many rounds of talks and the target of negotiations were twofold:

1. Make China an eligible GATT/WTO member within the market economy. For conditions yet to be met, special clauses were to be signed for the transition period.
2. Define the obligations and rights of China as a member. All the issues were to be negotiated in bilateral or multilateral talks. The key of GATT/WTO was the list of tariff reductions based on the principle of the balance of obligations and rights, which involved the interest of various parties and required many rounds of talks.

According to the GATT/WTO rules, technically each member could be the negotiation counterpart for China, but in reality, not all members requested bilateral negotiation for market access. Based on the level of difficulty, there were four groups of countries: The first group was the small developing member countries or regions, most of whom were given special care in the multilateral trade system. Since they were all quite backward and had few ties with the outside world, the impact of China's accession was only limited to a certain aspect, making the talks easier. The second group was the major developing countries or regions, like Brazil, Argentina, Mexico, India, and so on. Since they were more concerned with their domestic affairs, the change of the international society had little impact on them. Generally speaking, those with more interest intertwined with China asked for higher prices. The third group was Japan, Australia, New Zealand, Norway, and so on. As beneficiaries of the multilateral trade system, they were highly concerned with their own interests and cared less about the general and systematic issues. The fourth group was the US and the EU, the hardest negotiation counterparts of all. As the dominating powers of the system, they cared not only for their own interests but also systematic and strategic issues.

2.6.2 The Arduous Journey to the GATT/WTO

The GATT/WTO talks could be divided into four stages according to the procedure and agenda (Liu Guangxi 2007).

1. **Filing application and making preparation.** On July 10, 1986, China filed the application. In March 1987, the GATT China working team was set up.
2. **Defining the systematic conditions for the GATT resumption.** According to the list compiled at the 15th working meeting of the China team in October 1993, there were two major tasks: 1) Taking questions from the GATT members and passing them

to the State Planning Committee, the Commission for Economic Restructuring, the General Customs Office, and the Ministry of Foreign Affairs for answer. 2) Solving the market economy issue. China defined the goal of reform as constructing the socialist market economy, establishing the systematic base for China's accession to the multilateral trade system.

3. **Preparing for the bilateral talks on market access.** This was the most essential part of the negotiation, and covered the two most complicated and important talks with the US and the EU concerning tariff reduction, cancellation of non tariff measures, opening of service industry, and IPR. In December 1994, with the objection from the US-led developed countries, China failed in the effort. In January 1995, the GATT gave its place to the WTO; in November the same year, China decided to apply for WTO membership. According to the WTO rules, China needed to have bilateral talks with 37 members, among which the Sino-US talks alone took 25 rounds, and the Sino-EU talks took 15 rounds. The mission at this stage was to address the development, construction, and improvement of the market economy, which involved the condition, speed, scope, and endurance of the opening up, and related to the opening of agriculture, manufacturing, and IPR, the key of which was the timetable for market opening. These bilateral talks served as a base for the multilateral talks on the protocol on the WTO accession and the list of tariff reductions.
4. **Conducting multilateral procedure talks.** In March, June, and July 2000, the Chinese delegation visited Geneva three times for multilateral talks on procedure. On September 17, 2001, the fundamental document on China's accession was adopted in Geneva. On November 10, 2001, the Fourth Ministerial Meeting of the WTO examined and passed the decision. On November 11, 2001, the Chinese government signed the agreement and on December 11, 2001, China became an official member of the WTO.

The journey toward the GATT/WTO was hard. How come it took 15 years? The answer lies in the conflicting and intertwining interests of different parties. The bilateral and multilateral talks on market access mainly addressed three issues: Gradual reduction of tariffs, gradual removal of import restrictions, and gradual opening of service trade. The multilateral talks addressed the specific obligations and rights in the legal documents.

The Sino-US talk was the most difficult, extensive, and complicated of all the bilateral talks. Before 1989, there were four rounds of Sino-US talks, and conflict mainly focused on the following issues: 1. Whether the US was to give China the Most Favored Nation (MFN) treatment unconditionally. 2. Whether China allows the US and others to use the selective safeguard clauses to protect domestic industries after the resumption. In May

1989, during the fifth talk in Beijing, both parties reached a series of understandings and agreements, making substantial progress. It was expected that the talks might wrap up within the year. However, the political turmoil in 1989 disrupted the pace and the US-led Western countries started to take economic sanctions on China, criticizing the rectification of the economy as retrogressive. Such was the first setback.

In January 1991, during the working meeting of the GATT China team, it was decided that the protocol on resumption would be drafted in July the same year. Due to strong objection to the domestic pricing system, annual import/export plan, and import license system, the US and the EC recommended a cautious attitude toward the resumption. Both the US and the EC strongly requested China to accept the selective safeguard clauses and gradually remove the limit on the export to China. By linking the progress of the market access talks with the MFN treatment and GATT resumption, the US imposed pressure on China and demanded more concessions. Between December 1992 and July 1994, the GATT China team held six working meetings altogether. Based on its own condition and the GATT rules, the Chinese government adopted a flexible and pragmatic strategy, and made a series of promises on tariff reductions, NTB, trade policy, transparency, and so on. However, in the sixth round of the Sino-US talks in Beijing in March 1993, the US delegation responded by saying that China was not a standard market economy by itself and the resumption would bring technical issues. The US would not recognize China's position as a developing country. In the seventh Sino-US talks in Washington in July the same year, the US went to extremes on the RMB exchange rate, customs valuation and declaration, and the implementation of market access. The US insisted that the "selective safeguard clauses" be written into the protocol, and the GATT should be allowed to check the implementation of the GATT obligations and conduct biannual consultations to monitor the pace of the economic reform in China, which was to be included in the "transitional review mechanism" in the protocol, providing the theoretical base for intervening in the economic and trade decisions of China. For fear that after the resumption of the GATT membership, China may request the US to move issues concerning trade imbalance, market access, and IPR from the bilateral context to the multilateral system by referring to the GATT rules, so as to check the unilateralism against China and reduce the excessive interest obtained through the bilateral talks, the US tried all means to delay the course. In 1994, due to the unreasonable opposition from the US-led developed countries, China lost the chance to be the founding member of the WTO. Such was the second setback.

In face of these setbacks from Western countries, the Chinese government adopted a measured and patient approach, making it hard for outsiders to assess the true attitude of

China toward the newborn WTO. In due course, the US government came to realize that the Sino-US trade relations involved extensive domestic issues, such as industry policy, investment, and market access that required solutions in the multilateral framework of the WTO, which better served the long-term interests of the US.

In October 1996, during the bilateral consultations between China and the US in Geneva, the US delegates expressed the wish to wind up the talks. The bilateral talks focused on the opening of some key sectors including telecommunication, finance, auto, agriculture, and so on, for which the US asked for the following: For the telecommunication sector, within four years after the accession to the WTO, China was to allow foreign capital to invest in all telecommunications entities with up to 49% share, and 51% share in value-added services. All restrictions on imported mobile handsets should be removed, and the fixed-line business should be opened within six years. For the financial sector (banks, securities, insurance), foreign banks should be allowed to conduct RMB business within two years of the accession, and retail business within five years. Foreign capital should be allowed to invest in Chinese securities and the bond market, hold up to 51% of shares of insurance companies, and establish solely funded branches within two years. For the auto sector, the import duty would be reduced from the then 80% to 25% before 2005, and the average duty for imported spares and components would be reduced to 10%, with removal of quota from that year.

With that, China replied as follows: For the telecommunication sector, up to 25% foreign share for major operation and 30% foreign share for the value-added operation. No foreign-owned Internet company. The RMB business had already started with foreign banks in Shanghai and Shenzhen and may be extended to other cities. No foreign-owned retail business. China had never promised to open the securities and bond market to foreign capital. China had agreed to remove the import quota on auto and spare/components.

For the agricultural sector, China promised to cancel the non-tariff measures, and adopt bound tariff for import, and tariff quotas for major produce. The bilateral talks covered two topics:

1. Tariff reductions year by year within the five-year transition period, to an average of 17% by 2004.
2. Quota management for wheat, rice, corn, cotton, bean oil, and sugar.

On March 15, 1999, the then Premier Zhu Rongji addressed the press conference: "The GATT and WTO talk has been going on for 13 years. The once young negotiators have gray hair now. It's time to bring an end to the talk ... China has made the largest possible concession and effort to join the WTO." In the following four months, Zhu visited the US, and both sides planned to reach an agreement. However, for reasons involving the US congress, China suffered a third setback.

On September 6, 1999, the Sino-US talks resumed. On September 11, 1999, the then President Jiang Zemin reiterated the principles of the WTO accession when meeting the then US President Clinton. On November 15, 1999, after intensive talks of six days and nights, China and the US reached an agreement, marking the completion of the substantial negotiations. On May 19, 2000, China and the EC reached an agreement. On December 11, 2001 China accepted the conditions and became an official member of the WTO.

2.6.3 The Win-Win Result of the WTO Talk

The GATT/WTO talk was hard and lasting, but finally rights and obligations were balanced in a win-win scenario (Liu Guangxi 2007).

The major obligations of China. In the WTO context, the major obligations included: Observing the WTO rules and treating all members equally. By being a WTO member, all the international trade activities of China, especially those concerning commodity trade, would be subject to the WTO rules and the legitimate supervision of all WTO institutions. Within China, all foreign individuals and institutions (including those with no investment or registration in China) enjoy equal treatment with the Chinese enterprises in commodity trade rights. China would cancel the dual pricing system and the differentiated treatment to products for domestic sales and export sales to reflect the WTO principle of non-discrimination. Price control cannot be used to protect the domestic producers and the service sector. The Chinese legislation would be revised according to the WTO agreement to honor the commitment.

The basic rights of China. In the WTO context, China is entitled to the following rights: Unconditional, permanent, multilateral, and stable MFN treatment and national treatment from 135 members for commodity, service, and IPR; Generalized System of Preferences (GSP) treatment for the export of industrial products or semi-finished products to most developed countries; most of the favorable or transitional arrangement for the developing members; the benefit of enlarged market access of commodities and services to other WTO members; access to the dispute-solving mechanism for fair, objective, and reasonable handling of trade conflicts with other members; multilateral trade activities and access to the decision/rule making power for the international trade rules; exception or safeguard measures to protect domestic trade and economic development.

The win-win result. With the compromises and concessions made during the GATT/WTO talks, all parties also benefited from China's accession. The then US President Clinton indicated upon learning the signing of the Sino-US agreement that this was a win-win agreement for China and US, and win-win-win with the rest of world.

As for China, years ago, people feared that with the "wolf coming," the once protected sectors like agriculture, telecommunication, and finance would be exposed to competition and may even be out of control. However, years have passed since the wolf came. Nobody has been eaten up, and, on the contrary, Chinese products are now more competitive in the world market.

CHAPTER 3

Relative Development in International Trade

Market demand is the driving force for economic growth and development of a nation. China has a large population with huge potential demand yet low average income, which explains the insufficiency of effective demand in the early days of the Reform and Opening Up process. Since China opened its door, the top agenda has been to access the foreign market. Over the 30 years, foreign trade has become a major contributor to its fast economic growth. Based on the theory of relative development of countries in international trade, this chapter reviews the evolution of the system and policies of foreign trade in China over the 30 years, analyses the growth of import and export, and discusses the relative benefits of both sides in international trade.

3.1 The Reform and Opening of the Foreign Trade System and Policies in China

3.1.1 The Traditional System, Policies, and Foreign Trade

From 1949 to 1978 (from the founding of the PRC to the starting of the reform), foreign trade business in China could be generalized as follows: High concentration and rigid control by the government with no division of responsibilities between the government and enterprises. Profits and losses were solely borne by the state fiscal budget with the government as both the operator and the administrator. In practice, business was operated by specialized foreign trade companies in a unified manner, with administrative orders from the government as the major means of management. Both the gains and losses were assumed by the Ministry of Finance, and both the receiving and using of foreign exchange were controlled by the government.

In a particular historical context, the centralization of the trade system promoted the construction of an independent and complete industrial system and national economic system, and was conducive to the convergence of resources and the expansion of exports, the planning of the import of key commodities, the administration of import and export for a balanced structure, the protection of infant domestic industries, and the development of friendly relations with other countries.

However, there were also serious defects in the highly centralized foreign trade system:

1. With the state-owned specialized foreign trade companies solely conducting business, the monopolized operation dampened the enthusiasm of other production sectors and enterprises. With the production enterprises paying no attention to the market situation, they were not able to produce what the international market needed, which impaired the competitive power and trade quality.
2. With the government intervening too much in the operation of enterprises, ignoring the economic rules, and for the lack of division of responsibilities between the government and enterprises, enterprises were cornered and deprived of the power to join international competition.
3. With the state fiscal budget assuming profits and losses, there was no incentive mechanism and no balance of interest between the state, the enterprise, and the individuals, which was detrimental to the operation, management and development of foreign trade. Therefore, a reform on the foreign trade system was required to accommodate economic development.

3.1.2 The Reform of the Foreign Trade System

Stage one (1979–86): Delegating power and sharing profit. This stage was featured by the replacement of the state monopoly by power delegation for a multilayered structure, with details as follows:

1. The monopoly of the specialized foreign trade companies was terminated, and each functional ministry set up its own foreign trade firms. By the end of 1981, altogether 32 foreign trade firms affiliated to the ministries were set up. In July 1979, the State Council gave the green light to Guangdong and Fujian to adopt special foreign trade policies for foreign trade affairs within the province. A decision was also made to turn Shenzhen, Zhuhai, Shantou, and Xiamen into SEZs, followed by the opening of 14 coastal cities. In 1987, the central government decided to establish Hainan as a province and build it into the largest SEZ of China. By doing so, the enthusiasm of various parties was activated and a multilayered structure came into being.

2. Guidance planning and market regulations were combined to limit the power of mandatory plans.
3. The macro control system was strengthened by adopting the import/export license system, quota system, tariff system, export subsidy, and export tax rebate to give incentives to trade.

Stage two (1987–93): Rolling out and improving the contract responsibility system for foreign trade. Since 1987, all foreign trade entities started to adopt the contract responsibility system and assume sole responsibility for profits and losses. This stage was featured by the government subsidized trade contracts and the enhanced support on the policy level, with details as follows:

1. The foreign trade contract responsibility system was rolled out nationwide with the government of all provinces, autonomous regions, municipal cities, and foreign trade firms establishing contracts with the state on three items (the FX revenue from export, cost of currency exchange, and profit/loss).
2. The light industry, handicraft industry, and garment industry were chosen as the three trial bases for the cancellation of export subsidy and the establishment of self-responsibility for profits and losses.
3. The reform of the administration system of foreign trade was deepened, with the competent departments shifting their roles from direct control to indirect control. The government started to adopt the legal, economic, and administrative means to regulate the market and guide the enterprises.

In December 1990, the State Council promulgated *The Decision on Several Issues Concerning the Further Reform and Improvement on the Foreign Trade System*, mapping out the following measures:

1. Canceling the state fiscal subsidy on export and adopting the self responsibility system for profits and losses;
2. Changing the retaining of foreign exchange (FX) from region-based to commodity-based;
3. Adopting economic means such as exchange rates and tariffs to regulate import and export;
4. Conducting market regulation and increasing the margin for FX swap;
5. Adding the supply of FX to enterprises. The reform led foreign trade firms to a healthy trajectory with consistent policy, equal competition, self-ruled operation, self-responsibility for profits and losses, a combination of industry and trade, and the agency system (Tang and Ma 2008).

Stage three (1994–2001): Reforming the exchange rate. In January 1994, the State Council issued the *Decision on the Further Deepening of Foreign Trade System Reform.* The reform at this stage was symbolized by the convergence of exchange rates with details as follows:

1. Building the macro control system for the foreign trade business including: 1) canceling the contract responsibility system and converging the RMB exchange rates to a unitary, regulated, and supply-based floating exchange rate; 2) cutting the import tariff and canceling the import tariff reduction/exemption on some commodities; 3) promulgating *The Foreign Trade Law for the People's Republic of China* (Foreign Trade Law) on July 1, 1994. Foreign Trade Law is the fundamental law for foreign trade business in China.
2. Deepening the reform on the operation system through: 1) promoting the corporate recapitalization for the industrialization and globalization of large foreign trade enterprises; 2) reforming the administrative measures, shifting from the license system to the registration system; and 3) conducting trial experiments on the foreign trade business with joint ventures.
3. Deepening reform of the coordination system. Strengthening the leadership of the chambers and enhancing the macro control function of competent departments.

Stage four (2002–present): The accession to the wto and the integration of the Chinese foreign trade system into the world system. Ever since the accession to the WTO in 2001, China has been honoring its commitment and obligations in market access, national treatment to foreign capital, service trade, and so on, and has been acknowledged by the WTO and the World Bank for the work done. This stage is featured by the integration of the foreign trade policy system in China into the world trade system, which accords with the interests of China as well as the norms of the world, with details as follows:

1. Change of the government functions. To honor the commitment made when joining the WTO, the Chinese governments at different levels have been reforming the public service, improving administration efficiency, and updating the service philosophy to create the conditions and opportunities for enterprises to join the international competition.
2. Improving and complying with various laws and regulations on foreign trade, so as to fill the gap left as a legacy of the planned economy.
3. Deepening the reform of the state-owned foreign trade enterprises.

3.1.3 The Tariff Policy and the System Reform

Stage one (1979–92): When the tariff system accommodated the commodity economy on the whole. The tariff system at this stage accommodated the planned commodity economy, and the tariffs of different commodities could be varied according to the market demand. In 1982 and 1983, there were two major changes of the import/export tariff to encourage the export and import of necessities, and to protect and promote the national economy. In March 1985, the *Regulations of the People's Republic of China on Import and Export Duties* and the *Customs Tariff of Import and Export of the People's Republic of China* were published for the first time, and in July 1986 the Chinese government officially applied for the resumption of GATT membership, and adopted multiple measures such as market liberation, tariff reduction, and tariff standardization to facilitate the resumption. On July 1, 1987 the *Customs Law of the People's Republic of China* was adopted, marking the use of legal means in the administration of foreign trade. The Reform and Opening Up process from 1979 to 1992 provided a favorable background for the reform on tariff policy, yet for the lack of a market economy system, the tariff system was far from complete, and the nominal tariff rate was as high as 40%. License and quota were still the dominant practice for the import and export business.

Stage two (1992–2001): Reforming the tariff system. Since 1992, China started the wide use of tariffs and exchange rates as the major means to regulate import/export and construct a foreign trade system with mostly legal and economic means, and some administrative means, in preparation for the GATT negotiations. In the spirit of the decision on the establishment of the socialist market economy as was made during the third session of the 14th CPC, the State Council put forward a new request for tariff policy reform, which was "to build a unified, equal and open import/export tax policy that accommodates the socialist market economy, and clean up the tax reduction/exemption rules for an equal and fair market competition environment with lowered tariffs." From 1992 to 1999, the government updated the provisions on the exemption and reduction of import tax, moving gradually from the exemption/reduction of tariffs to the varied tariff rates in regulation. From January 1, 1992, China started to use the *International Convention for Harmonized Commodity Description and Coding System* and lowered the import tax rate for 225 tax items. From January 1, 2001, China again lowered the general tariff from 16.4% to 15.3%, with an average cut of 6.6%. A total of 3,462 tax items were involved, accounting for 49%. Changes were also made to the provisional tax rate and tax items, with 49 newly added tax items, increasing the total number to 7,111. This voluntary reduction of general tax in the beginning of the twenty-first century displayed the resolution of China to develop foreign trade.

Stage three (2001–present): Updating the tariff system after the accession to the WTO. On December 11, 2001, China joined the WTO. To observe the WTO rules, China has been gradually reducing tariffs. From January 1, 2002, China started to comply with the Bangkok Agreement and the tariff exemption/reduction obligations of 2002, by updating import tax rates, and dividing the tariffs into the MFN tariff, conventional tariff, preferential tariff, and general tariff. Changes were also made to the import tax items of 2002, lowering the average tariff to 12%, which was further lowered to 11% on January 1, 2003. On January 1, 2004, 30 import tax items were added, increasing the total number to 7,475. While the general tax rate remained unchanged, the MFN rate for 2,414 tax items were cut, lowering the general tariff to 10.4%. On January 1, 2005, China lowered the tax rate for 900 tax items, after which the general tariff was 9.9%. With the successive tax cuts, by 2005 China has fulfilled the tariff reduction obligations it committed to when joining the WTO. By lowering the tariff, the tariff structure was streamlined, the national fiscal revenue was increased, and the regulation function of tariffs on import/export was strengthened, which promoted the fast growth of trade, and the stable development of the national economy.

3.1.4 The Export Tax Refund Reform

From April 1, 1985, China started to levy tax on imported items and refund tax on exported items by refunding the equal amount levied upon export, which covers VAT, commodity tax, operation tax, and special consumption tax. From 1985 to 1993, exports grew fast and the tax refund also grew fast at an annual rate of 46.99%, higher than the average export growth rate. In 1994, China adopted a new tax system limiting the tax refund policy to the VAT and consumption tax paid for exported goods in the domestic production and sales process. On February 19, 1994, the State Tax Bureau formulated the *Methods on Management of Tax Refund of Exported Goods*. In 1995, The Ministry of Finance and the State Tax Bureau promulgated the *Provisions on Several Issues Concerning Tax Refund of Exported Goods*, updating the scope and methods for tax refund. With these changes, the work on taxation became more standardized and the actual tax rate became higher.

In the face of the 1997 Asian financial crisis and its impact on Chinese exports, the State Council, in order to support certain industries and expand exports, approved the increase of the tax refund rate for: Textile machinery from January 1, 1998, the shipping industry from June 1 1998, and farming machinery and another nine types of machinery products from July 1, 1998. To alleviate the impact on Chinese exports and enhance their competitive power in the market, from January 1999, the average tax refund rate was increased to 15%. While the higher refund rate promoted the growth of exports, it also brought on problems as follows:

1. The total amount of tax refund was too large to be borne solely by the central fiscal budget.
2. The attractive refund rate led to some rampant expansion of exports and even cheating just for the sake of refunds.
3. The high refund rate impaired the optimization of the export product mix and invited trade conflict (Tang and Ma 2008).

To address these issues, China continued to fine-tune the tax refund system by lowering the refund rate from 13% to 8% in 2004, and splitting the refund between the central government and local government at 75:25. In 2005, the rate was further lowered from 8% to 5%, with the ratio changed to 92.5:7.5, relieving the pressure on local fiscal expenditure. To optimize the export product mix, from September 15, 2006, China lowered the refund rate for 1,130 tax items, canceled the refund for 255 tax items and increased the refund rate for 191 tax items.

To moderate the excessive trade surplus, in July 1, 2007, China revised the export refund policy for 2,831 items, accounting for 37% of the total commodity. The revision covered three main aspects:

1. Canceling the export refund for 553 "high energy consuming, high polluting, and high resource consuming" products (including endangered animals and plants, salt, cement, fertilizer, dye, metal carbide, leather, certain wood board and disposable wood products, general carbon weld pipes, other simple nonferrous products, and so on.)
2. Lowering the export refund rate for 2,268 sensitive commodities including garments, footwear, bags and cases, toys, paper products, vegetable oil, plastic and rubber products, certain stone and ceramic products, certain iron and steel products, low value-added machinery products like motorcycles, furniture, and so on.
3. Replacing the tax refund policy with a tax free policy for ten commodities, including peanuts, oil paintings, stamps, carved board and fiscal stamps (Tang and Ma 2008).

3.2 The Growth of Export Trade

3.2.1 The Total Volume and Growth Speed

Following the start of the Reform and Opening Up process in 1978, export trade grew fast with both the total volume and the growth rate increasing year after year. Total export grew from US$9.955 billion in 1978 to US$1.344627 trillion in 2007, a 35-time increase within 30 years. The weight of Chinese exports in the world total also increased from 0.76% in 1978 to 7.84% in 2007.

Yet, before 1992, total Chinese exports were still lower than US$100 billion in value. In 1992, it only accounted for 2.01% of the world total. From 1993 to 1999, exports grew faster and reached US$100 billion in 1993 and US$221.096 billion in 1999. In 1999, Chinese exports accounted for 3.11% of the world total. From 2000 on, exports grew even faster, from US$279.349 billion in 2000 to US$1.344627 trillion in 2007, an increase of 4.8 times in value and 4% in proportion (Figure 3.1 and Table 3.1).

3.2.2 The Characteristics of the Trade Structure

The product structure-*Commodity Trade and Service Trade.* With the fast development of the Reform and Opening Up process, both commodity trade and service trade have been growing steadily in China. As indicated in Figure 3.2 and Table 3.1, the commodity trade is 10 times larger than the service trade in value and has been dominating Chinese exports since 1978. From 1978 to 2007, Chinese exports grew by 122 times, from US$9.95 billion to US$1.217939 trillion. Its proportion of the world total also grew from 0.76% in 1978 to 7.10% in 2007.

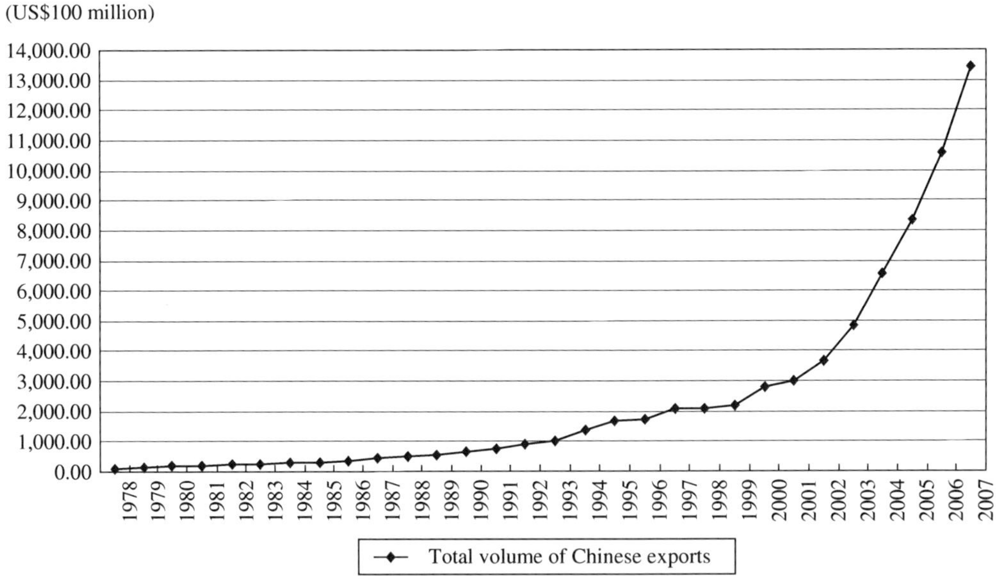

FIGURE 3.1 The trend of Chinese export development from 1978 to 2007

Source: WTO data.

Table 3.1 The Chinese exports in value and the percentage in the world total between 1978 to 2007

	Volume of Chinese exports (US$100 million)		Volume of Chinese exports (US$100 million)	Total volume of World exports (US$100 million)	Percentage of Chinese exports (%)		
Year	Commodity trade	Service trade	Commodity + service	Commodity + service	Commodity trade	Service trade	Commodity + service
1978	99.55	—	99.55	13,070	0.76	—	0.76
1979	136.14	—	136.14	16,590	0.82	—	0.82
1980	180.99	—	180.99	23,990	0.75	—	0.75
1981	220.07	—	220.07	23,840	0.92	—	0.92
1982	223.21	24.76	247.97	22,476	0.99	0.11	1.10
1983	222.26	24.66	246.92	22,003	1.01	0.11	1.12
1984	261.39	27.83	289.22	23,216	1.13	0.12	1.25
1985	273.50	29.25	302.75	23,356	1.17	0.13	1.30
1986	309.42	36.12	345.54	25,858	1.20	0.14	1.34
1987	394.37	42.33	436.70	30,474	1.29	0.14	1.43
1988	475.16	47.21	522.37	34,693	1.37	0.14	1.51
1989	525.38	44.52	569.90	37,546	1.40	0.12	1.52
1990	620.91	57.48	678.39	42,295	1.47	0.14	1.60
1991	719.10	68.64	787.74	43,397	1.66	0.16	1.82
1992	849.40	91.08	940.48	46,893	1.81	0.19	2.01
1993	917.44	109.92	1,027.36	47,230	1.94	0.23	2.18
1994	1,210.06	163.54	1,373.60	53,599	2.26	0.31	2.56
1995	1,487.80	184.30	1,672.10	63,401	2.35	0.29	2.64
1996	1,510.48	205.67	1,716.15	66,633	2.27	0.31	2.58
1997	1,827.92	245.04	2,072.96	69,022	2.65	0.36	3.00
1998	1,837.12	238.79	2,075.91	68,448	2.68	0.35	3.03
1999	1,949.31	261.65	2,210.96	71,079	2.74	0.37	3.11
2000	2,492.03	301.46	2,793.49	79,373	3.14	0.38	3.52
2001	2,660.98	329.01	2,989.99	76,756	3.47	0.43	3.90
2002	3,255.96	393.81	3,649.77	80,885	4.03	0.49	4.51
2003	4,382.28	463.75	4,846.03	94,150	4.65	0.49	5.15
2004	5,933.26	620.56	6,553.82	114,279	5.19	0.54	5.73
2005	7,619.53	739.09	8,358.62	129,514	5.88	0.57	6.45
2006	9,689.36	914.21	10,603.57	148,737	6.51	0.61	7.13
2007	12,179.39	1,266.88	13,446.27	171,553	7.10	0.74	7.84

Source: www.wto.org.

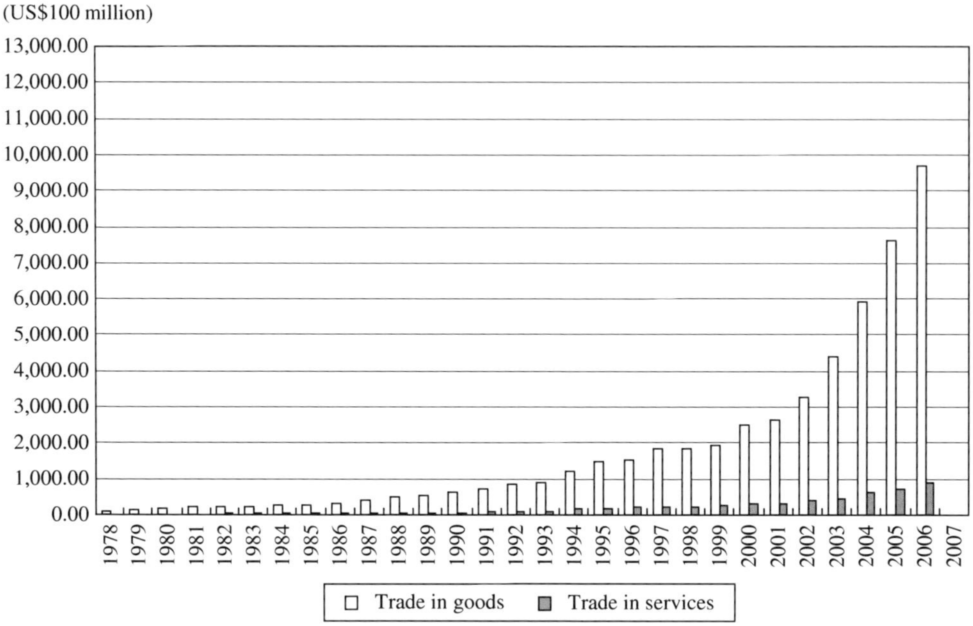

FIGURE 3.2 The development of the Chinese commodity and service exports from 1978 to 2007

Source: WTO data.

Meanwhile the service trade grew by 51 times from US$2.476 billion in 1982 to US$126.688 billion in 2007. It hit US$10 billion in 1993 and US$100 billion in 2007, with the percentage rising from 0.11% in 1982 to 0.74% in 2007. According to the report of the WTO, in 2007 Chinese service trade export accounted for 3.9% of the world total, ranking seventh place (the first six being the USA, the UK, Germany, Japan, France, and Spain). The top four service trade partners of China are Hong Kong, the USA, Japan, and South Korea.

The Resource type primary products—the labor intensive industrial products—the capital- or technology-intensive industrial products. *The Standard International Trade Classification* (SITC) divides the trade data into nine categories, with categories 0 to 4 being the traditional products and primary products, categories 5 to 9 being the industrial products, including iron and steel, textile, clothes, chemical products, machinery and transportation equipment, office and communication equipment, auto, and so on, among which category 5 and category 7 are capital- or technology-intensive industrial products, and category 6 and category 8 are labor-intensive, industrial products. According to the SITC, the commodity exports from China are classified as three types: The resource type primary products (SITC category 0 to 4), the labor-intensive industrial products (SITC category 6+8), and the capital- or technology-intensive industrial products (SITC category 5 + 7). The small percentage of category 9 is not included here.

As indicated in Figure 3.3 and Table 3.2, from 1980 to 2007, exports grew steadily in value, with the later two categories of products growing fast since 2001, and the first category shrinking in percentage from 50.36% in 1980 to 4.58% in 2007. The export of capital- or technology-intensive industrial products grew from US$1.963 billion in 1980 to US$637.55 billion in 2007. Between 1980 and 2002, the labor-intensive industrial products were ahead of the capital- or technology-intensive products in export value, whereas between 2003 and 2007, the situation was reversed. The percentage of labor-intensive products dropped from 40.26% in 2003 to 38.43% in 2007, and the percentage of capital- or technology-intensive products grew from 42.79% in 2003 to 47.41% in 2007.

This is a sign of the optimization of the export structure with the deepening of the economic reform. In the early stage of the reform, the primary products accounted for over half of the US$18.099 billion in 1980 and 45.67% of the US$30.275 billion in 1985.

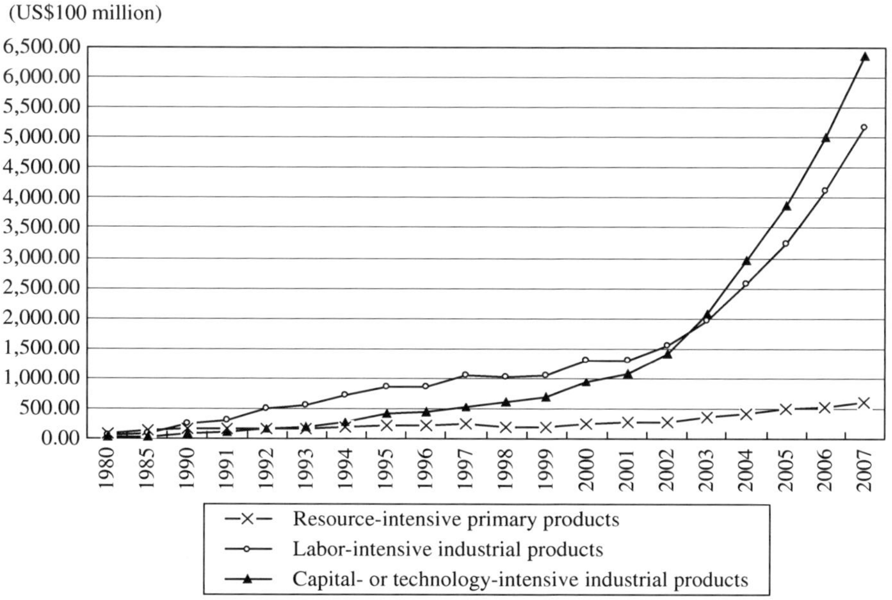

FIGURE 3.3 The change of the Chinese export structure from 1980 to 2007

Source: China Statistical Year Book, 2007 and www.mofcom.gov.cn

Table 3.2 The change of the Chinese export structure from 1980 to 2007

(Unit: US$100 million)

Year	Export in value (Commodity trade + Service trade)	Resource-intensive primary products		Labor-intensive industrial products		Capital- or technology-intensive industrial products	
		Value	Percentage	Value	Percentage	Value	Percentage
1980	180.99	91.14	50.36	68.35	37.76	19.63	10.85
1985	302.75	138.28	45.67	79.79	26.36	21.30	7.04
1990	678.39	158.86	23.42	252.62	37.24	93.18	13.74
1991	787.74	161.45	20.50	310.76	39.45	109.67	13.92
1992	940.48	170.04	18.08	503.69	53.56	175.67	18.68
1993	1,027.36	166.66	16.22	551.73	53.70	199.05	19.37
1994	1,373.60	197.08	14.35	731.55	53.26	281.31	20.48
1995	1,672.10	214.85	12.85	867.88	51.90	405.01	24.22
1996	1,716.15	219.25	12.78	849.22	49.48	441.89	25.75
1997	2,072.96	239.53	11.55	1,048.99	50.60	539.36	26.02
1998	2,075.91	204.89	9.87	1,026.77	49.46	605.38	29.16
1999	2,210.96	199.41	9.02	1,057.72	47.84	692.09	31.30
2000	2,793.49	254.60	9.11	1,288.24	46.12	946.98	33.90
2001	2,989.99	263.38	8.81	1,309.23	43.79	1,082.53	36.21
2002	3,649.77	285.40	7.82	1,541.08	42.22	1,423.01	38.99
2003	4,846.03	348.12	7.18	1,951.06	40.26	2,073.54	42.79
2004	6,553.82	405.49	6.19	2,570.44	39.22	2,946.20	44.95
2005	8,358.62	490.37	5.87	3,233.04	38.68	3,880.06	46.42
2006	10,603.57	529.19	4.99	4,128.30	38.93	5,008.73	47.24
2007	13,446.27	615.50	4.58	5,167.40	38.43	6,375.50	47.41

Source: China Statistical Year Book, 2007 and www.mofcom.gov.cn.

With the development of the export trade, from 1990 onward, the percentage of industrial products of the total trade climbed steadily. While between 1990 and 2002 the industrial products were mainly the labor-intensive types, between 2003 and 2007 the majority were the capital- or technology-intensive types. As for the primary products, though they grew in value from US$9.114 billion in 1980 to US$61.55 billion in 2007, the percentage dropped each year to only 4.58% in 2007.

The market structure. While the commodity structure is being continuously optimized, the destination of the exports has also changed dramatically. In 1995, the largest export market was Asia, with US$92 billion or 61.8%; the second was North America, with US$26.24 billion or 17.6%; and the third was Europe with US$22.98 billion or 15.4%. Between 1995 and 2006, the ranking remained the same, yet in 2007, while Asia stilled ranked the top with 46.64%, Europe overtook North America with 23.64% against 20.71%. From 1995 to 2007, exports to Latin America, Africa, and Australia grew steadily from US$3.15 billion in 1995 to US$51.54 billion in 2007. While exports to Africa in 1995 were US$2.5 billion, or 1.7%, they amounted to US$37.29 billion in 2007, or 3.06%. While exports to Australia totaled US$1.9 billion in 1995, or 1.3%, they amounted to US$21.11 billion in 2007, or 1.73%. A multidimensional export structure has gradually formed (Table 3.3).

From 2000 to 2007, the ranking of the top ten export destination countries (regions) further changed. Between 2000 and 2006, the USA was the number one export trading partner for China, but in 2007 it was replaced by the EU. Between 2000 and 2006, the ASEAN, South Korea, and Taiwan ranked the fifth, sixth and seventh places, but Taiwan was lowered to ninth place with Russia climbing to the seventh position in the rankings in 2007. Also worth noting is the lowered ranking of Australia between 2000 and 2005, from eighth to the tenth position. In 2007 the top ten destination countries (regions) were the EU, the USA, Hong Kong, Japan, ASEAN, South Korea, Russia, India, Taiwan, and Canada (Table 3.4).

The structure and category. With the total export trade volume growing and the export product structure being optimized, processing trade as a new fashion of trade has been expanding dramatically in scale. (See Figure 3.4 and Table 3.5).

Between 1981 and 1994, common trade dominated export trade, between 1995 and 2007, both common trade and processing trade grew fast, with the latter growing faster (Figure 3.4 and Table 3.5). In 1978, Dongguan Taiping Handbag Factory started the first case of processing trade with supplied materials, and after that the development of processing trade experienced three stages:

1. Between 1978 and 1987, the primary stage with mostly processing with supplied materials and little processing with imported materials.
2. Between 1988 and 1991, the middle stage with more processing with imported materials than supplied materials.
3. Between 1992 and 2007, the high growth stage with increasing weight in the trade structure.

Table 3.3 The major destinations of the Chinese export by continent between 2000 to 2007

(Unit: US$100 million, %)

Year		2000		2002		2004		2006		2007	
Ranking	Commodity export in value	2492.03	Percentage	3255.96	Percentage	5933.26	Percentage	9,689.36	Percentage	12,179.39	Percentage
1	Asia	1,323.10	53.09	1703.20	52.31	2,955.00	49.80	4,558.40	47.05	5,680.10	46.64
2	North America	552.80	22.18	742.80	22.81	1,332.40	22.46	2,191.40	22.62	2,521.80	20.71
3	Europe	454.80	18.25	592.30	18.19	1,224.00	20.63	2,153.70	22.23	2,878.80	23.64
4	Latin America	71.90	2.89	94.90	2.91	182.40	3.07	360.30	3.72	515.40	4.23
5	Africa	50.40	2.02	69.60	2.14	138.20	2.33	266.90	2.75	372.90	3.06
6	Oceania	39.10	1.57	52.90	1.62	101.70	1.71	160.10	1.65	211.10	1.73

Source: www.mofcom.gov.cn.

Table 3.4 The top ten export destinations (Regions) between 2000 to 2007

(Unit: US$100 million)

Commodity export in value	2000	2001	2002		2003		2004		2005		2006		2007	
	2,492.03	2,660.98	3,255.96	Ranking	4,382.28	Ranking	5,933.26	Ranking	7,619.53	Ranking	9,689.36	Ranking	1,2179.39	Ranking
US	520.80	542.80	699.50	1	924.70	1	1,249.50	1	1,629.00	1	2,034.70	1	2,327.00	2
Hong Kong	446.10	465.50	584.70	2	762.90	2	1,008.80	3	1,244.80	3	1,553.90	3	1,844.30	3
Japan	416.20	449.60	484.40	3	594.20	4	735.10	4	839.90	4	916.40	4	1,020.70	4
EU	381.30	409.00	482.10	4	721.50	3	1,071.60	2	1,437.10	2	1,819.80	2	2,451.90	1
ASEAN	174.40	183.90	235.70	5	309.30	5	429.00	5	553.70	5	713.10	5	941.80	5
South Korea	112.10	125.20	155.00	6	201.00	6	278.20	6	351.10	6	445.30	6	561.40	6
Taiwan	49.80	50.00	65.90	7	90.00	7	135.50	7	165.50	7	207.40	7	234.60	9
Australia	34.90	35.70	45.90	8	62.60	8	88.40	9	110.60	10	—	—	—	—
Canada	32.40	33.50	43.00	9	56.30	10	81.60	10	116.50	9	155.20	9	194.00	10
Russia	22.40	27.10	35.20	10	60.30	9	91.00	8	132.10	8	158.30	8	284.90	7
India	—	—	—	—	—	—	—	—	—	—	145.80	10	240.20	8

Source: www.mofcom.gov.cn.

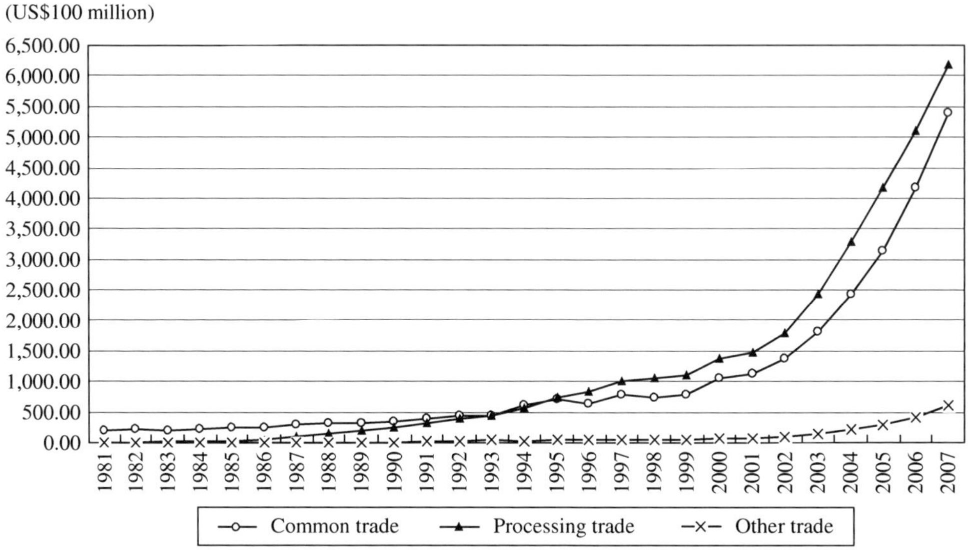

FIGURE 3.4 The modes of commodity export between 1981 to 2007.

Source: China Statistical Year Book, 2007 and www.mofcom.gov.cn.

Table 3.5 The trend of commodity export between 1981 to 2007

(Unit: US$100 million)

Year	Commodity exports in value	Common trade	Processing trade	Other trade
1981	220.07	208.00	11.31	0.76
1982	223.21	222.45	0.53	0.23
1983	222.26	201.60	19.44	1.22
1984	261.39	231.62	29.29	0.48
1985	273.50	237.30	33.16	3.04
1986	309.42	250.95	56.20	2.27
1987	394.37	296.43	89.94	8.00
1988	475.16	326.22	140.60	8.34
1989	525.38	315.52	197.85	12.01
1990	620.91	354.60	254.20	12.11
1991	719.10	381.20	324.30	13.60
1992	849.40	436.80	396.20	16.40
1993	917.44	432.00	442.50	42.94
1994	1,210.06	615.60	569.80	24.66

Table 3.5 (continued)

Year	Commodity exports in value	Common trade	Processing trade	Other trade
1995	1,487.80	713.70	737.00	37.10
1996	1,510.48	628.40	843.30	38.78
1997	1,827.92	779.74	996.02	52.16
1998	1,837.12	742.35	1,044.54	50.23
1999	1,949.31	791.35	1,108.82	49.14
2000	2,492.03	1,051.81	1,376.52	63.70
2001	2,660.98	1,118.81	1,474.33	67.84
2002	3,255.96	1,361.87	1,799.28	94.81
2003	4,382.28	1,820.34	2,418.51	143.43
2004	5,933.26	2,436.06	3,279.70	217.49
2005	7,619.53	3,150.63	4,164.67	304.23
2006	9,689.36	4,162.00	5,103.55	423.81
2007	1,2179.39	5,385.80	6,176.50	617.09

Source: China Statistical Year Book, 2007 and www.mofcom.gov.cn.

The structure of export base. The export business has always been unbalanced in China, with the coastal regions exporting a lot more than the inland. From 2000 to 2007, six of the top ten export bases were in the coastal regions, with Guangdong ranking first place, accounting for 30% of the national total. Jiangsu ranked second place in 2000 with 10.58% of the national total, which grew to 16.72% in 2007. Shanghai ranked third with 10% of the national total between 2000 and 2007. Guangdong, Jiangsu, and Shanghai alone took up over half of the national total, manifesting the great success of the Reform and Opening Up process in the coastal regions (Table 3.6).

The structure of enterprises. With the deepening of the reform on managerial authority, the structure of foreign trade has also changed with the SOEs, private enterprises, and FIEs working together.

In terms of the export growth rates, though all enterprises registered double digit growth, private enterprises led the growth, followed by the FIEs and then the SOEs. As for the weight of exports, the FIEs ranked the top with 57.11% in 2007, followed by private enterprises with 24.44% in 2007, replacing the SOEs in second place starting from 2006. The weight of SOEs dropped from 46.70% in 2000 to 18.46% in 2007 (Table 3.7 and Figure 3.5).

Table 3.6 The top ten regions in export value between 2000 and 2007

(Unit: US$100 million)

	2000		2001	2002	2003		2004		2005	2006	2007	
	Export value	Ranking	Export value	Export value	Export value	Ranking	Export value	Ranking	Export value	Export value	Export value	Ranking
Guangdong	934.28	1	954.26	1,184.70	1,529.40	1	1,915.60	1	2,381.60	3,019.50	3,692.60	1
Jiangsu	263.77	2	288.74	384.70	591.20	2	875.00	2	1,229.80	1,604.20	2,037.00	2
Shanghai	246.40	3	276.24	320.50	484.60	3	735.10	3	907.20	1,135.90	1,438.90	3
Zhejiang	204.82	4	229.76	294.20	416.00	4	581.60	4	768.00	1,009.00	1,282.90	4
Shandong	160.93	5	181.21	211.10	265.60	5	358.50	5	461.30	586.00	751.30	5
Fujian	136.23	6	139.26	173.30	211.40	6	294.00	6	348.40	412.60	499.40	6
Beijing	76.67	7	117.87	126.10	168.50	7	205.70	8	308.70	379.80	489.20	7
Liaoning	105.89	8	110.08	123.70	146.30	8	189.20	9	234.40	283.20	353.30	8
Tianjin	76.74	9	94.92	115.70	143.70	9	208.60	7	273.80	335.00	381.50	9
Hebei	32.78	10	39.56	45.90	59.30	10	93.40	10	109.30	128.40	170.10	10

Source: China Statistical Year Book, 2007 and www.mofcom.gov.cn.

Table 3.7 The structure of export enterprises between 2000 to 2007

(Unit: US$100 million)

		SOE		Private enterprise		FIE	
Year	Commodity export in value	Export value	Percentage	Export value	Percentage	Export value	Percentage
2000	2,492.03	1,163.78	46.70	134.57	5.40	1,193.68	47.90
2001	2,660.98	1,132.30	42.55	196.28	7.38	1,332.40	50.07
2002	3,255.96	1,228.60	37.73	327.96	10.07	1,699.40	52.19
2003	4,382.28	1,380.30	31.50	598.58	13.66	2,403.40	54.84
2004	5,933.26	1,535.90	25.89	1,011.26	17.04	3,386.10	57.07
2005	7,619.53	1,688.10	22.15	1,489.33	19.55	4,442.10	58.30
2006	9,689.36	1,913.40	19.75	2,137.66	22.06	5,638.30	58.19
2007	12,179.39	2,248.10	18.46	2,976.09	24.44	6,955.20	57.11

Source: www.mofcom.gov.cn.

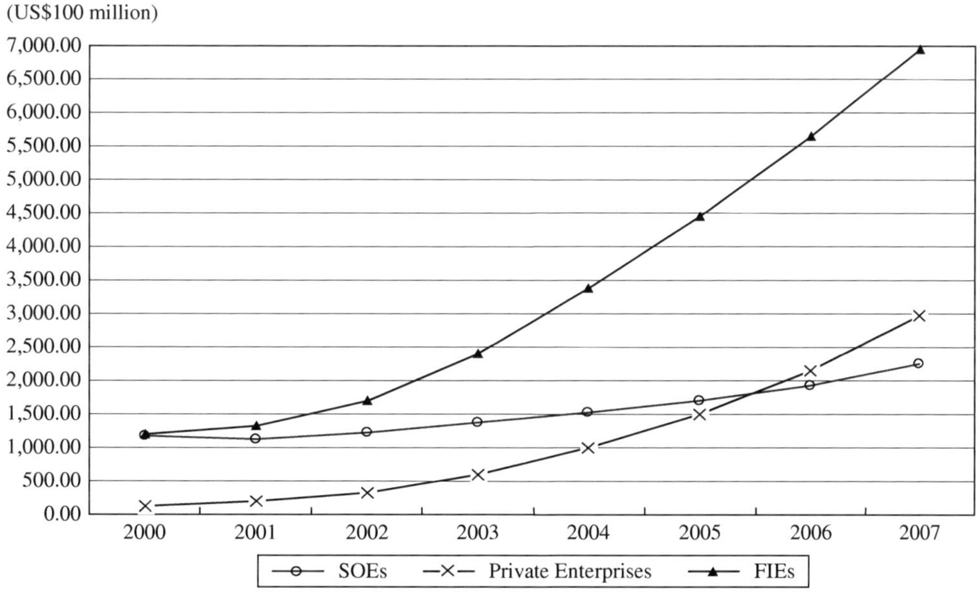

FIGURE 3.5 The structure of export enterprises between 2000 to 2007

Source: www.mofcom.gov.cn.

3.3 The Growth of Import Trade

3.3.1 The Total Volume and Growth Speed

From 1978 to 2007, the import trade developed as fast as the export trade, with the total value growing from US$11.131 billion to US$1.084759 trillion, a 97-time increase within 30 years. Its weight of the world total also jumped from 0.82% to 6.28%.

Between 1978 and 1992, import trade grew slowly to US$89.792 billion, only accounting for 2.01% of the world total. Between 1993 and 1999, import trade grew faster, hitting US$100 billion in 1993, and US$196.666 billion in 1999, accounting for 2.70% of the world total. From 2000 onward, import trade grew rapidly from US$260.952 billion to US$1.084759 trillion in 2007, and the weight also jumped by 3% from the 3.19% in 2000 (Figure 3.6 and Table 3.8).

As indicated in Figure 3.7 and Table 3.8, commodity imports dominated import trade. Between 1978 and 2007, commodity imports grew from US$11.131 billion to US$955.845 billion. Commodity imports hit US$100 billion in 1993 and were estimated to hit US$1 trillion in 2008. Its weight of the world trade total also jumped from 0.82% in 1978 to 5.53% in 2007.

Meanwhile service imports also grew year after year. From 1982 to 2007, service imports grew by 69 times, from US$1.865 billion in 1982 to US$128.914 billion in 2007. The weight jumped from 0.08% in 1982 to 0.75% in 2007. According to a report by the

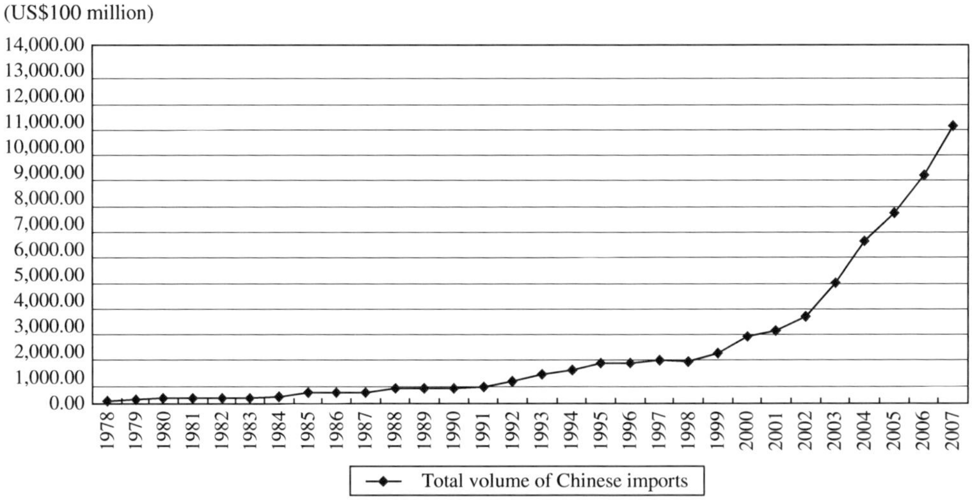

FIGURE 3.6 The trend of import trade in China between 1978 and 2007

Source: WTO data.

Table 3.8 The import value and the percentage in the world total between 1978 and 2007

(Unit:US$100 million)

	Imports of China		Imports of China	Imports of the world	% of Chinese imports in the world total		
Year	Commodity trade	Service trade	Commodity + service	Commodity + service	Commodity trade	Service trade	Commodity + service
1978	111.31	—	111.31	13,580	0.82	—	0.82
1979	156.21	—	156.21	16,940	0.92	—	0.92
1980	199.41	—	199.41	24,774	0.80	—	0.80
1981	220.14	—	220.14	24,838	0.89	—	0.89
1982	192.85	18.65	211.50	23,438	0.82	0.08	0.90
1983	213.90	18.40	232.30	22,729	0.94	0.08	1.02
1984	274.10	26.34	300.44	24,103	1.14	0.11	1.25
1985	422.52	22.61	445.13	24,161	1.75	0.09	1.84
1986	429.04	20.25	449.29	26,640	1.61	0.08	1.69
1987	432.16	23.35	455.51	31,259	1.38	0.07	1.46
1988	552.68	33.26	585.94	35,897	1.54	0.09	1.63
1989	591.42	35.73	627.15	38,865	1.52	0.09	1.61
1990	533.45	41.13	574.58	43,713	1.22	0.09	1.31
1991	637.91	39.37	677.28	44,843	1.42	0.09	1.51
1992	805.85	92.07	897.92	48,283	1.67	0.19	1.86
1993	1,039.59	115.63	1,155.22	48,356	2.15	0.24	2.39
1994	1,156.15	157.81	1,313.96	54,718	2.11	0.29	2.40
1995	1,320.84	246.35	1,567.19	64,767	2.04	0.38	2.42
1996	1,388.33	223.69	1,612.02	68,037	2.04	0.33	2.37
1997	1,423.70	277.24	1,700.94	70,309	2.02	0.39	2.42
1998	1,402.37	264.67	1,667.04	70,045	2.00	0.38	2.38
1999	1,656.99	309.67	1,966.66	72,942	2.27	0.42	2.70
2000	2,250.94	358.58	2,609.52	81,893	2.75	0.44	3.19
2001	2,435.53	390.32	2,825.85	79,644	3.06	0.49	3.55
2002	2,951.70	460.80	3,412.50	83,080	3.55	0.55	4.11
2003	4,127.60	548.52	4,676.12	96,439	4.28	0.57	4.85
2004	5,612.29	716.02	6,328.31	116,883	4.80	0.61	5.41
2005	6,599.53	831.73	7,431.26	132,143	4.99	0.63	5.62
2006	7,914.61	1,003.27	8,917.88	150,540	5.26	0.67	5.92

Source: www.wto.org.

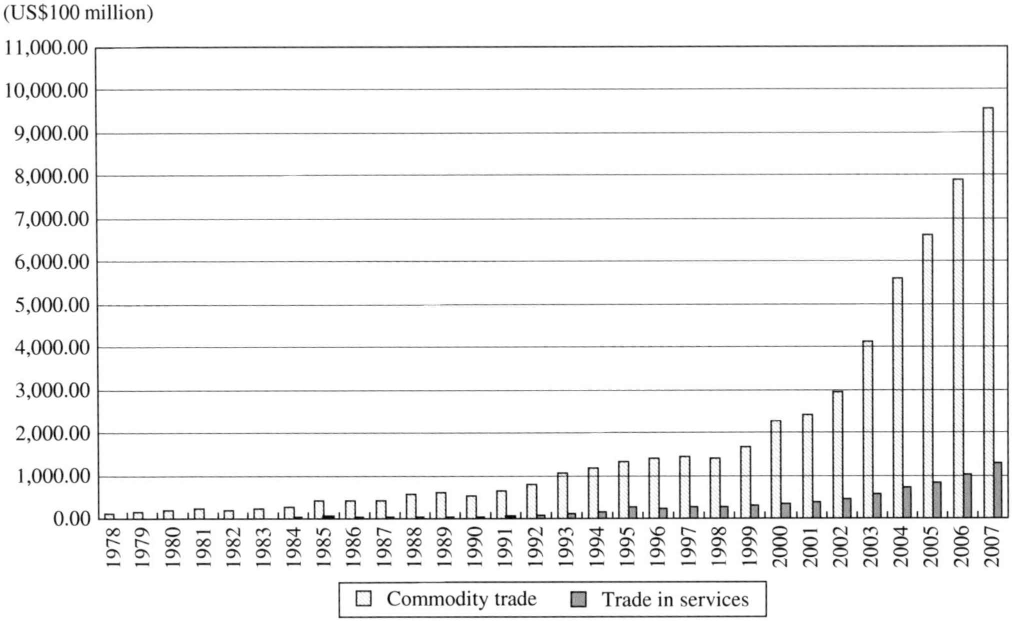

FIGURE 3.7 The trend of commodity and service import between 1978 and 2007

Source: WTO data.

WTO in 2007, in 2007, service imports of China accounted for 4.2% of the world total, and the ranking jumped from seventh place in 2006 to fifth place. (The first four were the USA, Germany, the UK, and Japan).

3.3.2 The Structural characteristics

The inter-industrial trade dependent on processing trade. Between 1981 and 2007, the import trade in China was mainly composed of common trade and processing trade, with other types of trade slowly growing. Between 1981 and 1993, common trade was larger than processing trade in import value. While the gap between the two fluctuated between US$16.5–US$30 billion before 1987, it was reduced to US$1.6 billion after 1987. Especially between 1994 and 1999, processing trade overtook common trade in import value. From 2000 on, common trade won back its position as a major fashion of import, and processing trade tightly followed (Figure 3.8 and Table 3.9).

The fast development of processing trade in China is a reflection of the new technology revolution in the global division of labor and inter-industrial trade. With the quick development of science and technology, rather than participating in the entire

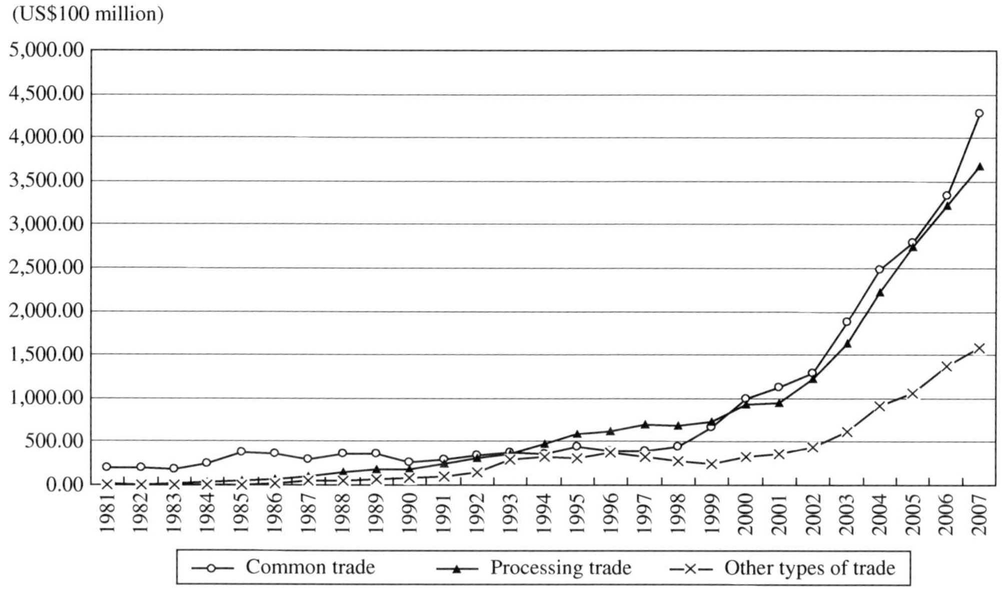

FIGURE 3.8 The modes of commodity import in China between 1981 and 2007

Source: China Statistical Year Book, 2007 and www.mofcom.gov.cn.

Table 3.9 The trend of commodity import in China between 1981 and 2007

(Unit: US$100 million)

Year	Commodity imports in value	Common trade	Processing trade	Other types of trade
1981	220.14	203.66	15.04	1.44
1982	192.85	188.85	2.76	1.24
1983	213.90	187.68	22.72	3.50
1984	274.10	238.49	31.47	4.14
1985	422.52	372.72	42.74	7.06
1986	429.04	352.07	67.03	9.94
1987	432.16	287.72	101.91	42.53
1988	552.68	352.04	151.05	49.59
1989	591.42	356.14	171.64	63.64
1990	533.45	262.00	187.60	83.85
1991	637.91	295.40	250.30	92.21
1992	805.85	336.20	315.40	154.25
1993	1,039.59	380.50	363.70	295.39

Table 3.9 (continued)

Year	Commodity imports in value	Common trade	Processing trade	Other types of trade
1994	1,156.15	355.20	475.70	325.25
1995	1,320.84	433.70	583.70	303.44
1996	1,388.33	393.60	622.70	372.03
1997	1,423.70	390.30	702.06	331.34
1998	1,402.37	436.80	685.99	279.58
1999	1,656.99	670.40	735.78	250.81
2000	2,250.94	1,000.79	925.58	324.57
2001	2,435.53	1,134.56	939.74	361.24
2002	2,951.70	1,291.11	1,222.01	438.58
2003	4,127.60	1,876.51	1,629.04	622.05
2004	5,612.29	2,481.45	2,216.94	913.90
2005	6,599.53	2,796.33	2,740.12	1,063.08
2006	7,914.61	3,330.74	3,214.72	1,369.15
2007	9,558.45	4,286.50	3,684.00	1,587.95

Source: China Statistical Year Book, 2007 and www.mofcom.gov.cn.

process of production, one country only engages in one or a few parts of the process, where it can best utilize its comparative advantage so as to optimize the resource allocation. Processing trade refers to importing raw material, supplementary material, spare parts, components, supporting parts from abroad, processing and assembling in the home country, and exporting the finished products to the foreign market. By utilizing its abundant labor resource, China entered the labor-intensive part of production in the international division of labor and gradually occupied the global market in textiles, clothes, light industry, and home electronic appliances industry, and accumulated a huge amount of capital. The industrial structure has also been upgraded and optimized, creating the economic miracle. With the continuous development of MNCs, imported materials have changed from the common raw materials to semi-finished products, integrating the Chinese enterprises into the upper part of the value chain of the MNCs, and moving the processing in China from the labor-intensive production to the capital- and technology-intensive production.

The asymmetric distribution of the import/export market. Between 2000 and 2007, over 60% of Chinese imports came from Asia, followed by Europe and North America (Table 3.10).

Table 3.10 The major continents (region) from which China imported between 2000 and 2007

(Unit: US$100 million)

Year	2000		2001	2002	2003		2004	2005	2006	2007	
Commodity import in value	2,250.94	Ranking	2,435.53	2,951.70	4,127.60	Ranking	5,612.29	6,599.53	7,914.61	9,558.45	Ranking
Asia	1,413.40	1	1,471.80	1,903.10	2,729.30	1	3,695.30	4,415.40	5,255.00	6,199.00	1
Europe	407.80	2	484.00	534.30	697.40	2	890.40	964.50	1,148.60	1,396.80	2
North America	261.20	3	302.40	308.70	382.60	3	520.50	562.70	669.20	804.00	3
Latin America	54.10	6	67.00	83.40	149.30	4	217.80	267.70	341.90	510.70	4
Oceania	58.80	4	62.90	68.30	86.00	5	133.30	180.10	213.20	284.20	6
Africa	55.60	5	47.90	54.30	83.60	6	156.50	210.60	287.70	362.80	5

Source: www.mofcom.gov.cn.

Between 2000 and 2007, China (the mainland) imported the most from Japan, followed by the EU (except for 2005), Taiwan, ASEAN, and South Korea. Since 2002, the US has been in the sixth place. Between 2000 and 2002, Canada registered the tenth place, but was replaced by Brazil in 2003 and 2004, and by Saudi Arabia in 2005. From 2006 on, Canada and Hong Kong have been replaced by Brazil and Saudi Arabia. In 2007, the top 10 countries (region) were Japan, the EU, ASEAN, South Korea, Taiwan, the US, Australia, Russia, Brazil, and Saudi Arabia (Table 3.11).

However, comparison between the import market and the export market of China reveals a huge contrast: While the export market was in the US, the EU, Hong Kong, and Japan, the import market was in Japan, the EU, Taiwan, ASEAN, and South Korea. The asymmetry of the import and export markets gave rise to the trade conflicts between China and the US/EU.

The trade imbalance and trade friction. The above analysis reveals the root of the trade imbalance and trade friction between China and the USA/EU. The restriction on the exports of high-tech products to China by the US and the EU slowed down China's imports, and the pricey US/EU industrial products impeded large imports, resulting in a huge trade surplus as time went by. From 2002 onward, China has become the largest source of trade deficit for the US and the EU, which put China in a passive position in the trade talks.

Table 3.11 The top ten countries (regions) from which China imported between 2000 and 2007

(Unit: US$100 million)

Year	2000		2001		2002		2003		2004		2005		2006		2007	
Commodity import in value	2,250.94	Ranking	2,435.53	Ranking	2,951.70	Ranking	4,127.60	Ranking	5,612.29	Ranking	6,599.53	Ranking	7,914.61	Ranking	9,558.45	Ranking
Japan	415.10	1	428.00	1	534.70	1	741.50	1	943.70	1	1,004.50	1	1,157.20	1	1,339.50	1
EU	308.00	2	357.20	2	385.40	2	530.60	2	701.20	2	736.00	5	903.20	2	1,109.60	2
Taiwan	254.90	3	273.40	3	380.60	3	493.60	3	647.80	3	746.80	4	871.10	5	1,010.20	5
ASEAN	221.80	6	232.30	6	312.00	4	473.30	4	629.80	4	750.00	3	895.30	4	1,083.70	3
South Korea	232.10	4	233.90	5	285.70	5	431.30	5	622.50	5	768.20	2	897.80	3	1,037.60	4
US	223.60	5	262.00	4	272.30	6	338.60	6	446.80	6	487.30	6	592.10	6	693.80	6
Hong Kong	94.30	7	94.20	7	107.40	7	111.20	7	118.00	8	122.30	10	—	—	—	—
Russia	57.70	8	79.60	8	84.10	8	97.30	8	121.30	7	158.90	8	175.50	8	196.80	8
Australia	50.20	9	54.30	9	58.50	9	73.00	9	115.50	9	161.90	7	193.20	7	258.50	7
Canada	37.50	10	40.30	10	36.30	10	—	—	—	—	—	—	—	—	—	—
Brazil	—	—	—	—	—	—	58.40	10	86.80	10	—	—	129.20	10	183.30	9
Saudi Arabia	—	—	—	—	—	—	—	—	—	—	122.50	9	150.80	9	175.60	10

Source: Data based on the website of the Ministry of Commerce of China.

Taking the Sino-US trade friction as an example, according to the statistics of the US Department of Commerce, in the early 1980s, the main targets of the anti-dumping lawsuits from the US were the textile and chemical products. In the mid- to late 1980s, the targets changed to the iron and steel products. In the 1990s, the targets further changed to the chemical products, iron and steel products and all kinds of finished products, and the situation has remained so since 2000.

3.4 The Relative Advantages of the Sino-Foreign Trade Coopetition

3.4.1 The Late Development Benefit of China

The huge trade surplus of labor intensive products. Since the Reform and Opening Up process began, with the fast growth of foreign trade, China has become a trade power in the international market. The huge trade surplus between China and the US/EU is a consequence of the late development advantage of China in the international competition brought by the export of labor-intensive products.

Labor-intensive products take up a considerable proportion of the Chinese export market. Among the top ten exported products, seven are labor-intensive ones. Abundant labor resources and the low cost of late development make China highly competitive in the international labor market and commodity market. To create jobs and develop the economy, the Chinese governments at different levels have been supportive to the development of the labor-intensive industries. Although labor cost in China is also rising and the late mover advantage is diminishing, for the time being labor-intensive products remains competitive.

According to the traditional comparative advantage theory and the resource endowment theory, developed countries import the resource-intensive and labor-intensive products, export the capital- or technology-intensive products, while the developing countries import the capital- or technology-intensive products and export the labor-intensive products. These theories can be applied to China, which mainly imports technology-intensive machinery equipment and exports labor/resource-intensive textiles and garments. However, since 2003, the export structure has changed somewhat, with the capital- or technology-intensive products (mostly machinery and transportation equipment) becoming the major export, indicating the upgrade of the export structure. Yet for the low technology contained in these products, as compared to the high value-added products of the same products produced abroad, they still belong to the labor-intensive category by nature. Therefore, China should encourage the export of manufactured products with more high-tech content.

Though by exporting labor-intensive products, China may utilize the late development advantage of low cost. It is after all not sustainable, for in the labor-intensive market, developed countries can always replace the labor factor with the capital or technology factors, taking away the competitive advantage of labor-intensive products from the developing countries. In the long run, with the deepening of human resource development and the increase of salary, the low cost advantage is to diminish. Apart from that, in face of the domestic employment pressure, developed countries would set up all barriers to block the cheap labor-intensive products from China and weaken the international competitive power of Chinese products, such as is now happening with Chinese textile products.

The economic growth effect. In theory, trade growth and economic growth are interdependent. On one hand, the expansion of foreign trade drives economic growth, in particular, the export growth may produce the Keynesian Multiple Effect, and drive the economic growth through the demand pull in the short run. In the long run, import growth may promote technical progress and improve the allocation of resources and the expansion of economic scale. On the other hand, economic growth may also push the expansion of foreign trade, for the enlargement of economic volume brings the scale economy, making export enterprises more competitive in the market, which brings back more revenue to support the further demand on imports.

The net export growth in China made great contribution to the upgrade of the industrial structure. Since the 1980s, the export structure has changed dramatically. Before 1985, China exported mostly primary products, but after 1986, the proportion of industrial manufactured products increased year on year, and overtook the primary products finally. By 2007, industrial products accounted for over 80% of the total export. Between 1980 and 2007, the category 7 "machinery and transportation equipment" registered the fastest growth, with its proportion growing from 4.7% in 1980 to 47.1% in 2007. The competitive advantage of the Chinese manufacturing business has been gradually established, along with the optimization of the industrial structure towards the higher end of the value chain.

Over the years, people have tended to focus more on the contribution of exports to economic growth rather than that of imports. Yet more research in the recent years indicates that import contributes more than estimated. In China, many of the imported products compensate the domestic products, like the combination of the imported materials with the domestic supplementary materials for the processing of products for export. So some imports actually increase the demand for domestic products. In summary, there are three kinds of positive relations between imports and economic growth in China:

1. With the imports also came the advanced science and technologies, saving time for R&D and narrowing the technical gap between China and development countries, which promotes the transition of the economic growth model.

2. With the imports also came the scarce natural resources, filling the blank for raw materials, which facilitates the upgrade of the industrial structure.
3. Imports push the establishment of the market economy system and bring the domestic enterprises to competition, which encourages the reform on corporate management, and the optimization of product structure.

The employment effect (the transfer of rural laborers) and the income effect. Since foreign trade drives economic growth and economic growth promotes employment, the increase of import and export volumes always creates more jobs. While the jobs brought by export growth are visible, they also invisibly created by import as a result of technical advancement. Therefore, the expansion of foreign trade may well improve employment and increase the national income.

Since 1978, with the growing size of the working population, the elasticity coefficient has been declining constantly. The 1980s was the heyday for employment, with a high elasticity coefficient for employment in the second industry. For the competitive advantage of the labor-intensive products, textile, clothes, footwear, and toy industries absorbed the largest proportion of the working population. Since the 1990s, though China maintained high growth, both the growing speed and elasticity coefficient followed a down trend, mainly because the contribution of labor input to the economic growth declined in weight, with the growing input of capital and technology. After China joined the WTO in the twenty-first century, lowered tariffs stimulated imports, promoted the adoption of advanced technical equipment by local enterprises, heightened both the capacity and production efficiency, and created jobs through technical upgrade. However, the expansion of imports brought a huge impact on the employment of the first industry, for the competition between the imported produce against the domestic produce threatened the income of farmers. Meanwhile the quality competition forced Chinese farmers to raise the technical content of rural production, creating the dual pressure of fewer jobs and rising demand in the first industry, which further widened the gap between rural and urban income, and forced the redundant rural laborers to seek jobs in cities.

Since the Reform and Opening Up process began, with the rural redundant laborers moving to the coastal cities, the employment structure has been improved and personal income has been increased. With the processing trade as a major trend of foreign trade, China has become the world manufacturing base with many MNCs transferring more production to China and even outsourcing some spare/component production to Chinese enterprises. For example, the export manufacturing enterprises in the coastal region (in particular the processing trade enterprises) absorbed a large number of rural laborers and trained them to become skilled workers for mass production.

3.4.2 The Early Development Benefit of Foreign Parties

The trade gains with the capital-technology-intensive products. The structure of the unbalanced commodity demand in China led to the fact that China exports mostly low value-added primary products and labor-intensive products (like raw materials for textiles and manufactured textiles, mineral products, and agricultural products), and imports mostly capital- or technology-intensive products (like machinery products, auto and chemical products). Major trading partners like the US, the EU, Japan, and South Korea have obtained huge early development benefits from trading with China.

The benefits of the foreign parties come from three means:

1. By doing processing trade with China, many Chinese enterprises import equipment, spare parts and components, and raw materials from abroad, process, and export the finished products to the raw materials provider or other countries.
2. By setting up factories in China, MNCs swarm to China to take advantage of the low labor cost and bypass trade barriers. Since China only assembles high value-added spare/component imports, the larger part of the profit still remains in the hand of the developed countries. For instance, in the international division of labor for electronic products, the US gains 50%–60% of the profit by producing the high value-added chips and software, Japan and South Korea share 20%–30% by producing the key components, and developing countries like China only share 10% by producing the less important spare/component parts and doing the assembling.
3. While restricting the Chinese labor-intensive products by setting up all trade barriers, many developed countries (region) export high value-added capital- or technology-intensive products to China, obtaining greater trade benefit from the unbalanced exchange.

Take the US as an example. China as a developing country enjoys lower labor cost but is in shortage of capital and advanced technologies. The US as a developed country leads the world in capital and technology but is high in labor cost. As a result, China exports labor-intensive products with low added value and thin profit, such as textiles, clothes, footwear, toys, and electronic appliances, and the US exports airplanes, power equipment, machinery equipment, electronic component, telecommunications equipment, and chemical products with high added value and heavy profit. The product structures of the two countries mutually compensate each other and bring huge benefit to the US in the following ways:

1. The cheap, quality commodities from China satisfy the need of the American consumer, so that the local resources can be invested in the high-tech industries to optimize the US' industrial structure and maintain its leading position.

2. The labor-intensive products from China stabilize the price in the US, so that the US government may adopt a low tax rate, low interest rate, and high fiscal deficit to stimulate the economy and maintain a huge military budget without worrying about inflation.
3. As for the trade itself, though both sides benefit, it is still the US enterprises that benefit more. Through transitional pricing, profit sharing, and dividend allocation, the foreign investors have reaped profits higher than what was booked on the balance sheet, not to mention the contribution of the Chinese commodities to the employment of the tertiary industries in the developed countries, such as logistics, transportation, wholesale, retail, insurance, and finance.

The consumer surplus: The one year adventure of a US family in the absence of Chinese commodities. On August 23, 2007, Wang Chao, the assistant minister of the Ministry of Commerce (MOC) spoke at a press conference of the State Council: "With many countries involved in the manufacturing business in China, "Made in China" is also "Made in the World," and if "Made in China" is harmed, the harm is done to the world. Chinese commodities are popular for both quality and price. Over 50% of the export trade belongs to the processing trade, which is based on the international standard. 58% of the products are exported from the foreign invested enterprises. It is the SOEs, private enterprises and FIEs that build together the name "Made in China," so "Made in China" is also "Made in the World" (Zhang and Huang 2007).

The cheap quality products from China save the world's consumers money and produce consumer surplus. For example, according to the research report of the German Institute of Economy, "Made in China" saves each German family 350 Euros annually, as most Chinese products are two-thirds cheaper than the same products made in Germany.

In order to better understand the trade relation between the US and China, Sara Bongiorni, an American author, decided to boycott Chinese commodities for one year following the discovery, in the Christmas of 2005, that among 39 Christmas gifts, 25 were made in China. In addition, she realized that her DVDs, shoes, socks, toys, and lamps were all also made in China. Acting in panic, she decided to experience one year of family life without "Made in China" to see if Americans could survive. In the absence of "Made in China," shopping became a huge inconvenience. Without plastic wheels from China, her husband could not make a wooden toy car for their son. Without hardware from China, Sara could not fix the drawers in the kitchen. Without mouse traps from China, the rats ran free, and in order to buy a pair of shoes for the kids, Sara needed to search the whole town before she paid US$68 for a pair of Italian shoes. Buying birthday gifts also became a headache, not to mention candles, ink cartridges, sunglasses, coffee machines, and so on. With all the trouble, Sara drew the conclusion:

> "We finally agree that we had better live together with the Chinese products. It is just not practical to swear not to use Chinese products. While the cheaper price benefits China and helps the rise of the Chinese economy, it has also made it difficult for American consumers to live without Chinese products. My experience forces me to rethink the distance between China and myself, with all the efforts to push China away from our lives, I draw the conclusion that China is already deeply rooted in our lives." (Sara Bongiorni, 2008)

Yet Sara had considered only the labels marked "Made in China," neglecting the fact that even the products made in the USA may also have components from China, and vice versa. The pattern of international trade is shifting from the inter-industrial trade to the intra-industrial trade. Today as the second-largest trading partner for each other, the Sino-US trade coopetition is featured by mutual benefit and win-win, which brings benefit to the two peoples and the world economy.

The growth of the Asian economies. ***South Korea.*** Since the establishment of diplomatic relations between the two countries in 1992, cross-border trade has been growing steadily. Between 1990 and 1995, the annual growth rate of bilateral trade was as high as 42.13%, and the total volume amounted to US$16.545 billion in 1995. Between 1995 and 1999, bilateral trade grew at a rate of 8.05% annually, and between 1999 and 2002, at a rate of 18.17% annually. The trade volume hit US$44.07 billion in 2002, and US$159.9 billion in 2007. Today China has become the largest trading partner for South Korea, yet with a huge deficit of US$47.62 billion in 2007. The deficit came from the import of machinery products, auto, electronic equipment, spare parts/components and other capital- or technology-intensive products, driving economic growth in South Korea.

Japan. China is the largest source of import and the second-largest trading partner for Japan. Since the twenty-first century, the Sino-Japanese trade relations has played an increasingly important role for the development of the two economies. Since 2000, over 90% of the exports to Japan have been industrial products, and the export of agricultural products and mineral products has declined to 2%. Most of the imports from Japan are also industrial products, indicating the fast growth of intra-industrial trade. Yet Japan is also a source of trade deficit for China. In 2007, the deficit amounted to US$31.88 billion, indicating the imbalance of intra-industrial trade: While Japan imports mostly labor-intensive industrial products from China, it exports mostly capital- or technology intensive industrial products to China. Japan has obtained huge first mover benefits from China through trade, amid which the industrial transfer from Japan to China has also promoted the upgrade of the industrial structure in China. The huge trade surplus from China pulled Japan out of the economic downturn in the 1990s.

ASEAN. The trade volume between ASEAN and China grew by over 70% between 1996 and 2007, and the growth rate exceeded that between the ASEAN and Japan, the US and the EU over the past 10 years. Since 2000, bilateral trade between China and Thailand, Malaysia, and the Philippines has warmed up, making China the most important export market for the Southeast Asian countries, proving the role of China in the region as an engine or locomotive. Take Singapore as an example. Since 1997, according to the statistics from Singapore, trade relations between Singapore and China have survived the Asian financial crisis, and the total amount jumped from US$10.2 billion in 1997 to US$40.858 billion in 2007, and with surplus on the Singapore side amounting to US$12.12 billion in 2007. China is now the largest export market for Singapore and a major engine for its economic growth.

3.5 Case Analysis: The Pearl River Delta and the Yangtze River Delta

3.5.1 Foreign Trade and Economic Growth in the Pearl River Delta

In 1979, there were altogether 13 places in the Pearl River Delta conducting processing trade: Guangzhou, Shenzhen, Zhuhai, Foshan, Jiangmen, Dongguan, Zhongshan, Huizhou, Huidong, Boluo, Zhaoqing, Gaoyao, and Sihui. The development of processing trade made Guangdong the most vigorous and robust place in China. In 1980, exports from the Pearl River Delta accounted for 28.4% of the provincial total and 2.4% of the national total, and by 2006, 78.2% and 23.7%, respectively. In 2006, the total export volume also grew from US$616 million in 1980 to US$288.745 billion, an increase of 469 times. The foreign trade dependency ratio of the region was as high as 186.89% in 2006, higher than the national average of 120.65%. The export dependency also jumped from 100.61% in 2005 to 106.45%. Seven of the nine cities in the Pearl River Delta surpassed US$10 billion in export value, among which Shenzhen was the first in China to hit US$100 billion. The growth of foreign trade has also driven the economy of the whole region, with the GDP accounting for 10.21% of the national total and 82.50% of the provincial total in 2006, 7.4% and 47.08% higher than 1990.

Shenzhen and Dongguan are the two typical examples of the export-oriented economy in the Pearl River Delta. With an export volume of US$135.919 billion in 2006, Shenzhen ranked top in China, followed by Shanghai, and then Dongguan with US$47.376 billion. Between the two cities, Dongguan is even more export oriented. Take the statistics in 1998 as an example. Of the total industrial output of US$73.222 billion, SOEs accounted for 15.91%, shareholding ownership accounted for 6.16%, private ownership accounted for 3.38%, Hong Kong, Macau, and Taiwan ownership accounted for 56.59%, and foreign capital (all except for Hong Kong, Macau, and Taiwan) accounted for 17.95%. In 1998, exports from Dongguan accounted for 7.11% of the national total and 17.25% of the provincial total, 6.71% and 14.44% higher as compared to 1978. But the GNP was only 0.45% of the national total and 4.48% of the provincial total, 0.28% and 1.17% higher than 1978.

As for the trading partners of the Pearl River Delta, the Hong Kong enterprises are the most important ones. The trade between Hong Kong and the Pearl River Delta (including the transit trade via Hong Kong) accounted for over 80% of the total business. Since the 1980s, processing trade has become the major economic tie between Hong Kong and the region. According to the statistics from the Hong Kong Administration, in 1996 the total export and outsourced processing amounted to US$55.7 billion, accounting for 76.2% of the total export from the mainland to Hong Kong, and 84% of the total export from Guangdong to Hong Kong. After the return of Hong Kong in 1997, the total amount of exports and outsourced processing amounted to US$59.9 billion in value upon arriving in Hong Kong for transit, and US$73 billion upon leaving Hong Kong. According to the statistics from the Statistics Bureau of Guangdong Province, in 1980, the export and processing trade of the region only accounted for 3.75% of the national total. In 1990, it increased to 72.04%, in 2000 to 78.09%, and in 2001 to the historical high of 80.17%.

Among the products exported from the Pearl River Delta to Hong Kong, about 90% were further delivered via Hong Kong to the world market. With the trading firms in Hong Kong, more market channels were established for the export of the region. Since the 1990s, trade ties have been established with Hong Kong, the US, the EU, and Japan. In the late 1990s, the regional economic cooperation was further strengthened by expanding the "Small Pearl River Delta" to the "Greater Pearl River Delta" covering the small delta, Hong Kong, and Macau. In 2003, the "Pan Pearl River Delta" (including Fujian, Jiangxi, Guangxi, Hainan, Hunan, Sichuan, Yunnan, Guizhou, and Guangdong, plus Hong Kong and Macau, or "9 + 2") was established. By utilizing the location advantage, the economy has been full-fledged over the years, and moved towards the mature industrialization stage. It is estimated that the foreign trade dependency ratio of the region is twice as high as that of the national average. During the 10th Five-year Period, the annual GDP growth rate of the region reached 15.58%, higher than the provincial rate of 2.28% and the national rate of 6.08%.

However, attention should also be given to the problems that go along with trade development, which handicapped further development of the economy. First, since the processing trade still dominates the foreign trade of the region, most products were labor-intensive in the light industry. Second, the excessive high dependency on foreign trade and export enslaves the region to the international trade market, trade barriers and friction, as well as the reform of the RMB exchange rate. In addition, with the land resource in the region becoming increasingly scarce, the cost of urbanization and industrialization has also become higher, and with the rising of the international oil price, production cost would also rise for the heavy dependency on imported energy. Therefore, it is critically necessary for the Pearl River Delta to optimize and upgrade the product structure, and transfer from labor-intensive manufacturing to technology-intensive manufacturing so as to enhance its competitive power in the international market.

3.5.2 Foreign Trade and Economic Growth in the Yangtze River Delta

The Yangtze River Delta, which has always enjoyed strong economy is compared to the land of Milk and Honey. Just like the Pearl River Delta, from the beginning of the reform to the late 1980s, the economic development in this region followed a reform-oriented path. Typical examples are the "South Jiangsu Model" and the "Wenzhou Model," which were the role models for the township enterprises and the private enterprises, respectively. The early 1990s was a watershed, for the decision to open Shanghai Pudong in 1990 and the southern tour in 1992 pushed the export-oriented economy of the region.

The development of Pudong promoted the revival of Shanghai. Since 1992, with the opening up of Pudong, and Shanghai as a whole, the Jinqiao processing zone, the Waigaoqiao free trade zone, and the Lujiazui finance and trade zone were established one after another, making Shanghai a window of foreign trade. A "Pudong Model' with finance and trade as the dual core came into being by combining development and opening up to attract the advanced manufacturing MNCs and the high-tech industries. Meanwhile the Wenzhou Model and southern Jiangsu Model also shifted toward the export-oriented model. During the 1990s, the foreign trade volume of the region grew by nearly nine times, accounting for 28.5% of the national total in 2001, a 14.1% increase compared to 1991. The foreign trade dependency ratio also jumped from 25.0% in 1990 to 56.7% in 2001. The regional GDP has taken up a larger proportion of the national total. While in 1978, the GDP of Zhejiang, Jiangsu and Shanghai amounted to RMB 64.577 billion, or 17.82% of the national total, in 2000, it reached RMB 1.917022 trillion, or 21.44% of the national total.

After the accession to the WTO, export from the region further expanded and maintained a high growth rate. After 2003, with imports to the region slowing down, the total import/export remained high (Figure 3.9). In 2006, the total import/export reached US$650.644 billion in value, among which exports amounted to US$374.889

billion. Compare with the national average, though the import rate of 19.29% was lower than the national rate of 19.93%, since the export growth rate was 1.9% higher than the national average, the total import/export value still surpassed the national average by 1.02%. Meanwhile the GDP of the region further increased. Compared to 2001, the GDP of the region grew from RMB 2.12109 trillion to RMB 4.775396 trillion in 2006. The foreign trade and export dependency ratio grew from 6.84% and 3.75% in 2001 to 13.62% and 7.85% in 2006.

Since the opening up of Pudong, Shanghai has become the locomotive of the region, and maintained fast growth in foreign trade. Between 1998 and 2001, the total foreign trade volume of Shanghai reached US$185.55 billion, an annual growth of 25.2%, among which the export reached US$87.72 billion, an annual growth of 17%. The port import/export trade reached US$369.59 billion, an annual growth of 19.7%. Meanwhile the overseas business also grew rapidly, with project contracting and overseas investment achieving great success. The convening of the Fortune Forum and the APEC Summit displayed the new image of Shanghai as a metropolitan city. Since the accession to the WTO, the added value of the import/export of Shanghai has been rising, with fast growth of the low energy consuming, low material consuming, low-polluting and high value-added exports, among which the high-tech products contributed 40% to the total export of the city.

The opening up of Pudong presented Jiangsu a great opportunity to utilize the international market for foreign trade. Since 1992, Jiangsu has established a successful model to attract foreign capital. In 2001, among the 1,600 newly established enterprises with

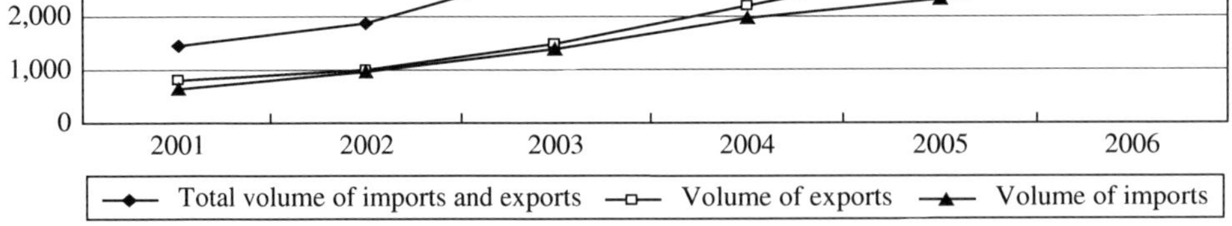

FIGURE 3.9 The import and export of the Yangtze River Delta

Source: China Statistical Year Book, 2003, 2005, 2007.

export business, most were FIEs, which led the optimization of the export structure. In 2001, the export of machinery products accounted for half of the provincial total, with the high-tech products sharing a bigger proportion. Currently 300 Jiangsu enterprises have been included in the list of the national high-tech enterprises. The export of some well-known ones such as the Little Swan, Wuxi; Epson, Suzhou; and Seagate Technology, Wuxi exceeds US$600 million in value every year.

Since the 1990s, foreign trade has also grown rapidly in Zhejiang. Different from the model of Jiangsu, most of the trading entities in Zhejiang are local enterprises rather than FIEs, and the destinations are not limited to the developed market, due to the efforts made by the overseas Zhejiang merchants and Zhejiang emigrants worldwide. It is estimated that by the end of 2002, the Zhejiang merchants had opened 1,033 enterprises overseas, doing business in both developed and developing countries/regions including Russia, Italy, France, South Africa, Brazil, Argentina, Mexico, and so on. In the first half of 2002, exports to developing countries grew by 31.8%, and in the following years, Zhejiang topped all provinces in common trade and trade surplus. From 2001 to 2006, the export of Zhejiang grew from US$22.974 billion to US$100.891 billion, an annual growth of 67.83%, 15% higher than the national average. Meanwhile the GDP grew from US$674.815 billion in 2001 to US$1.574251 trillion in 2006, an increase of 133.29%, 37.3% higher than the national rate of the same period. In 2006, the foreign trade and export dependency ratios were 88.39% and 64.09%, far higher than the national ratios of 8.31% and 4.57%.

CHAPTER

4

Relative Development in International Investment

Investment is the primary driver of the rapid economic growth in China, and the huge investment in China is fueled by high domestic savings as well as foreign capital and coordinated investment. Based on the theory of relative development in international investment, this chapter is starts with a review of the capital gap, the attitude toward foreign capital, and the change of policy, and then discusses the foreign direct investment (FDI), China's overseas investment by China, and the relative benefits of both participants in the international investment.

4.1 Capital Accumulation and Economic Growth in China

4.1.1 The Shortage of Savings and Foreign Exchange in the Early Days of the Reform and Opening Up Process

Before the Reform and Opening Up process began, China was short of capital. Between 1950 and 1979, the total savings were small, and the foreign exchange reserve amounted to only US$58.47 billion, far from what was needed for economic development. Therefore, in the early days of the reform, China focused on the attraction of foreign capital, which was reflected in the variance of foreign exchange (FX) reserves. In 1980, the FX reserve was negative, but became positive from 1981 onward. Between 1981 and 1983, the FX reserve grew fast, but starting from 1984, it dropped from US$8.22 billion to US$2.072 billion by 1986. Between 1987 and 1989 the numbers picked up again, though with a moderate increase. In 1990, the FX reserve reached US$10 billion for the first time, and in 1995, US$73.597 billion. With the increase in domestic capital reserve, the contribution of foreign capital to the Chinese economy slowed down. In 1996, the FX reserve reached US$100 billion for the first time. In the following decade, it grew still faster, and China started to engage in international investment activities, and mergers and acquisitions (M&A) (Table 4.1).

In the early days of the reform, with low FX reserves and RMB savings, it was hard to accommodate the economic development. In 1978 and 1980, the RMB savings were merely RMB 21.06 billion and RMB 39.95 billion, respectively, but in the following years, the amount grew to RMB 100 billion by 1985 and RMB 1 trillion by 1992. In the following 10 years, the RMB savings continued to grow, and China managed to build up a large capital stock (Table 4.2).

Table 4.1 **The FX reserve in China between 1950 and 2006**

Year	FX reserve (US$100 million)	Year	FX reserve (US$100 million)	Year	FX reserve (US$100 million)
1950–1954	4.88	1986	20.72	1998	1,449.59
1955–1959	5.95	1987	29.23	1999	1,546.75
1960–1964	5.01	1988	33.72	2000	1,655.74
1965–1969	12.60	1989	55.50	2001	2,121.65
1970–1974	2.80	1990	110.93	2002	2,864.07
1975–1979	27.23	1991	217.12	2003	4,032.51
1980	−12.96	1992	194.43	2004	6,099.32
1981	27.08	1993	211.99	2005	8,188.72
1982	69.86	1994	516.20	2006	10,663.00
1983	89.01	1995	735.97	2007	15,282.6
1984	82.20	1996	1,050.49	—	—
1985	26.44	1997	1,398.90	—	—

Source: http://www.sina.com.cn.

Table 4.2 **RMB savings in the urban and rural areas in China between 1978 and 2006**

Year	Savings (RMB 100 million)	Year	Savings (RMB 100 million)	Year	Savings (RMB 100 million)
1978	210.60	1994	21,518.80	2001	73,762.40
1980	399.50	1995	29,662.30	2002	86,910.60
1985	1,622.60	1996	38,520.84	2003	103,617.30
1990	7,119.80	1997	46,279.80	2004	119,555.40
1991	9,241.60	1998	53,407.47	2005	141,051.00
1992	11,759.40	1999	59,621.80	2006	161,587.30
1993	15,203.50	2000	64,332.40	—	—

Source: China Statistical Year Book, 2007.

4.1.2 Introduction of Foreign Capital as a Major Driver of Fast Economic Growth in China

Despite rich natural resources and labor resources, the Chinese economy has been relatively backward for the lack of capital, technology, and management expertise. Since the Reform and Opening Up process began, China has established the market economy system, participated in the international division of labor, and imported a great amount of foreign capital and technologies to develop the economy. Driven by the FDI, the trade volume in China continued to grow, leading to more diversified products and larger international market share, and a huge amount of foreign exchange. Meanwhile the injection of foreign capital also paved the way for the transfer of foreign industries to China, which was conducive for the learning of advanced technologies and management expertise, for the optimization and upgrade of the industrial structure, and for the best allocation of two types of resources in the domestic and overseas markets.

The injection of foreign capital has had a profound impact on the Chinese economy, which is reflected in the following aspects:

More jobs. Foreign capital has played an important role in absorbing the redundant urban and rural labors. At the end of 2006, over 14 million people worked in the FIEs, accounting for 8% of the total working population. Foreign investment in the labor-intensive industries helped create more jobs, which balanced economic development.
More exports. In recent years, over half of Chinese exports were manufactured by the FIEs as measured by value, which enhanced the competitive power of Chinese exports.
Technology spillover effect. Foreign investment not only brought in capital, advanced technologies and management expertise, but also accelerated the transfer of foreign enterprises to China, which brought the technology spillover effect, and promoted technical advancement and industrial upgrade in China.

4.1.3 Attitude toward Foreign Capital: The Case of CITIC

On July, 1, 1979, the second session of the fifth NPC adopted *The Law of the PRC on Chinese-Foreign Equity JV*, displaying to the world the resolution of China to open up. On April 10, 1980, the first ever Sino-Foreign JV: Beijing Aviation Food Co., Ltd was founded upon the approval of the Administrative Commission for Foreign Investment. This marked the beginning of foreign investment and the establishment of three types of foreign-funded enterprises in China. Yet the attitude towards foreign capital has not always been positive. An example here is CITIC, which was established on October 4, 1979 (Zhao Haijun 2008).

On January 17, 1979, Deng Xiaoping invited five industrial and commercial leaders including Rong Yiren to a discussion in the People's Hall. On that occasion Rong proposed to attract foreign capital for business, and Deng echoed with great interest, replying that compensation trade might be one option for the attraction of foreign capital, and joint operation in industries with quick capital turnover might be another option. In early February, Rong submitted a report on the primary opinions on the establishment of CITIC, and on October 4, a CITIC which was directly under the State Council, was officially founded with Rong being the founding president.

During the preparation stage of CITIC, the central government was drafting *The Law of the PRC on Chinese—Foreign Equity JV*, the most controversial part of which was whether the percentage of foreign shares should be limited. According to article four of the draft law, "The foreign investment in the Sino-foreign equity joint ventures should not exceed 49%," and "A two-thirds majority approval is required for the resolution of major issues." Rong raised objection to the limit of foreign capital, saying that "it is for the shortage of capital that China plans to import foreign technical equipment. If the limit is set as 49%, that is simply to pay more for the capital received, which contradicts the original intention. These two clauses would dampen the enthusiasm of the foreign investors, and China would fail to attract enough capital for construction. I suggest the attraction of more foreign capital and technologies in the principle of mutual benefit and equality under the precondition of not losing sovereignty." Deng thought highly of Rong's opinion, and the percentage of foreign capital was revised to "no less than 25%."

In order to build reputation for CITIC, the State Council deliberately chose to announce the establishment of CITIC on July 8, 1979 to coincide with the promulgation of *The Law of the PRC on China—Foreign Equity JVs*. On October 4, CITIC was officially established. The most challenging task then was to finance Yizheng Chemical Fiber Factory and issue the Japanese Yen private equity bond in Japan. To raise capital for Yizheng Chemical Fiber Factory, Rong proposed to issue bonds worth ¥10 billion in Japan. Though the idea won support from the State Council, it still invited some objection, as the interest rate of the bond was higher than the normal government loan and the loan from the import and export bank. Rong responded in the following words: "The low IR loan often enslaves the debtor to the creditor, with the debtor often forced to buy commodities from the creditor's country. Whereas by issuing a bond, we are free to compare different creditors for the best offer. While the low IR government loan and the loan from the import and export bank have merits, they are not universally feasible. A proper decision should be based on the holistic consideration of timing, location and condition." As a result, the bond issuance was an unqualified success, and the Yizheng Model has become the trend to follow.

Deng reiterated many times that "The introduction of foreign capital and the opening would not lead to capitalism. It is true that some bad things will come but they are not scary." He also addressed foreign businesses: "To facilitate extensive contact, the

China International Trust and Investment Corporation can serve as a window for the opening of China."[1]

4.1.4 Preferential Policies for the Foreign Capital and the Legislation Process

Since the Reform and Opening Up process began, China has been through four stages of development in utilizing foreign capital: The beginning stage of 1979–83, the growing stage of 1984–91, the expansion stage of 1992–2001, and the regular stage after 2002 (Xu Mingqi 2008).

The beginning stage (1979–83). After the third session of the 11th CCCPC, the attitude towards foreign capital changed from repulsion to acceptance, and the Administrative Commission for Foreign Investment was established. Many regulations were published during this period, including *The Law of The People's Republic of China on Chinese-Foreign Equity Joint Ventures* in 1979, *The Income Tax Law on Chinese-Foreign Equity Joint Ventures of the People's Republic of China, Rules on the Registration and Management of Joint Ventures Using Chinese and Foreign Investment, The Interims Regulations on Foreign Exchange Control of the People's Republic of China* in 1980, *The Regulations for the Implementation of the Law of the People's Republic of China on Joint Ventures Using Chinese and Foreign Investment* in 1983, and so on.

At this stage, many policy incentives were offered to foreign enterprises, including the 33% corporate income tax for joint ventures, the tax exemption for the first year and deduction by half for the second year. Flexible and preferential policies were offered to the four SEZs, such as the 15% corporate income tax, the free tariff for imported equipment, and income tax exemption and reduction for reinvested profit for the fifth year onward, and so on.

The growing stage (1984–91). At this stage, the coastal areas were all opened up. In 1984, 14 coastal cities were opened up, economic opening zones were built in the Yangtze River Delta, the Pearl River Delta and the South Fujian Delta in 1985, and the Hainan special economic zone was established in 1988.

Progress was also made with the legislation work, with the promulgation of *The Accounting Regulations of the People's Republic of China for Joint Ventures* in 1985, *The Provisions of the State Council for the Encouragement of Foreign Investment and Law of the People's Republic of China on Foreign-funded Enterprises* in 1986, *The Interim Provision on Guidance of Foreign Investment* in 1987, and *The Law of the People's Republic*

1. Deng Xiaoping, "Our Grand Goal and Basic Policy," in *Selected Works of Deng Xiaoping: Volume 3* (The People's Press, 1993), 79.

of China on Chinese-Foreign Contractual Joint Ventures in 1988, and *The Income Tax Law of the People's Republic of China for Enterprises with Foreign Investment and Foreign Funded Enterprises* in 1991, and so on.

At the same time, China also further liberated the investment policy for foreign business, and offered the preferential policies such as a two-year exemption and three-year deduction of corporate income tax for manufacturing FIEs, free tariffs for imported equipment within quota, and so on. For the SEZs, the policies were even more favorable.

The expansion stage (1992–2001). After the southern tour by Deng Xiaoping in 1992 came some material breakthroughs with the attraction of foreign capital. The regional preferential policies were rolled out to the inland, with the border cities and cities along the Yangtze River opened one after another. In 1999, the State Council made the decision to open the massive west, and offered many preferential policies.

At this stage, attention was given to the industrial direction of foreign investment. In November 1994, *Notice on Tightening up of Control over the Examination and Approval of the Establishment of Foreign-funded Enterprises* was promulgated, and in June 1995, *The Interim Provision on Guidance of Foreign Investment and Catalog for the Guidance of Foreign Investment Industries* was published, dividing the industries into four categories, namely the encouraged, the allowed, the restricted, and the prohibited. The aviation, finance, and retail business, to which the foreign investment had been denied, were deregulated in a gradual way. From January 1, 1997 onward, the FIEs started to receive the joint annual check, which was designed to standardize investment behavior.

The policies at this stage were more inclined to the mid-west region rather than the coastal cities. For instance, it was announced that between 2001 and 2010, the encouraged category of FIEs in west China would be entitled to the 15% corporate income tax, for the FIEs in west China with over 70% of the revenue coming from business operation in transportation, power generation, water conservation, postal service, radio, and TV, upon the 10th year of operation, starting from the profit earning year, the corporate income tax would be exempted for the first and second year, and deducted by half for the third, fourth and fifth year. With the above measures, China absorbed a huge amount of foreign capital and survived the Southeast Asian financial crisis. After the periodical adjustment in 1999 and 2000, the amount of utilized foreign capital picked up again in 2001, bringing China to a new stage.

The regular stage (2002–present). After the accession to the WTO, China began to comply with the international rules and fulfill the commitment of the WTO. On April 1, 2002 the *Catalog for the Guidance of Foreign Investment Industries* took effect, opening the high-tech industry and the monopolized industries. Electronic information, bio-engineering, and aviation were included in the encouraged category, together with energy, transportation, raw materials, and infrastructure. The new catalog also encouraged foreign businesses to utilize adaptable technologies to upgrade machinery, light industry, textiles, and other conventional industries.

According to the WTO commitment, the quota restriction would be gradually removed and the import tariff would be cut down by a large margin. Legal service, tourism, education, and retail business were later opened in succession. The RMB business was opened in Shenzhen, Shanghai and another 16 cities, and policies on the proportion and requirement on foreign shares with the Chinese banks were also loosened. On March 1, 2004, the *Interim Measures for the Management of the Dealings of Derivative Products* took effect, allowing the qualified foreign bank branches to directly engage in the derivatives business in China. On September 1, 2004, the *Regulations of the People's Republic of China Governing Financial Institutions with Foreign Capital* took effect, lowering the market access threshold for foreign banks, and simplifying the examining and approving procedure for such business.

With the above measures, the Chinese market was opened in an all-round manner, but the downside of foreign capital also surfaced.

4.2 Foreign Direct Investment (FDI)

4.2.1 Total Amount and Growth

Since the Reform and Opening Up process began, China has made great progress in attracting foreign capital. According to the statistics of the Ministry of Commerce (MOC), between 1979 and 2006, there were altogether 596,110 projects with foreign capital, utilizing a total of US$1.668069 trillion of foreign capital by contract value, and the actual amount US$882.673 billion. China has become the second-largest receiver of foreign capital. Along with the efforts on the adjustment of economic structure and the change of foreign policy, the attraction of foreign capital went through four stages (Table 4.1 and Figure 4.3).

Stage one: 1979–90. This was the beginning stage with slow growth of investment. There were altogether several thousand foreign invested projects. The total contract value amounted to US$20 billion, and the actual amount used was US$10.5 billion.

Stage two: 1991–93. This was the developing stage with fast growth of investment in both width and depth after the southern tour of Deng Xiaoping. The number of approved foreign invested projects grew from 13,086 in 1991 to 83,595 in 1993, with the contract value growing from US$19.583 billion to US$123.273 billion, exceeding US$100 billion for the first time. The actual amount used also quadrupled from US$1.554 billion to US$38.96 billion.

Stage three: 1994–2000. This was the correction stage with slowing down of foreign investment in both project numbers and contract value. However, the actual amount used rose. The number of approved foreign invested projects dropped from 47,646 in 1994 to 17,022 in 1999, and the contract value dropped to US$52.009 billion in 1999. The actual amount used steadily grew between 1994 and 1997, but due to the Southeast Asian financial crisis, it dropped somewhat in 1998 and 1999.

Stage four: 2001–present. This is the upgrade stage with increase in both the number of foreign-invested projects and the contract value after the accession to the WTO. More attention has been given to the quality of foreign investment. The number of approved foreign invested projects grew from 26,140 in 2001 to 44,001 in 2005, yet dropped to 41,485 in 2006. The contract value grew from US$71.976 billion in 2001 to US$204.663 billion in 2006. The actual amount used grew from US$49.672 billion in 2001 to US$73.523 billion in 2006, and US$82.658 billion in 2007. Though the total amount has not grown much, the investment quality is much better. In particular after 2003, with the overseas IPO of Chinese enterprises, and the arrival of foreign private equity (PE) and qualified domestic institutional investors (QFII), the utilization of foreign capital embarked on a new journey.

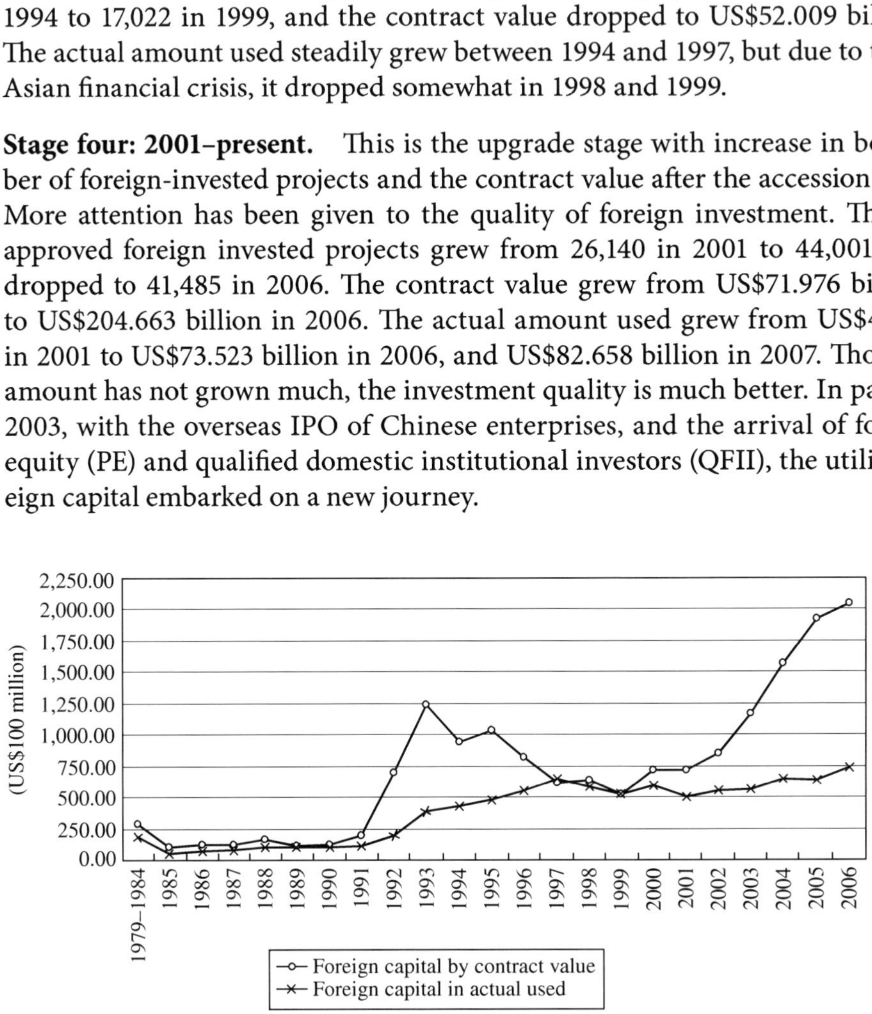

FIGURE 4.1 The total amount of foreign capital utilized between 1979 and 2006

Source: China Statistical Year Book, 2007.

Table 4.3 The utilization of foreign capital in China between 1979 and 2006

Year	No. of projects	Contract amount (US$100 million)	Actual amount used (US$100 million)
1979–1984	3,841	281.26	181.87
1985	3,145	102.69	47.60
1986	1,551	122.33	76.28
1987	2,289	121.36	84.52
1988	6,063	160.04	102.26
1989	5,909	114.79	100.60
1990	7,371	120.86	102.89
1991	13,086	195.83	115.54
1992	48,858	694.39	192.03
1993	83,595	1,232.73	389.60
1994	47,646	937.56	432.13
1995	37,184	1,032.05	481.33
1996	24,673	816.10	548.05
1997	21,138	610.58	644.08
1998	19,850	632.01	585.57
1999	17,022	520.09	526.59
2000	22,347	711.30	593.56
2001	26,140	719.76	496.72
2002	34,171	847.51	550.11
2003	41,081	1,169.01	561.40
2004	43,664	1,565.88	640.72
2005	44,001	1,925.93	638.05
2006	41,485	2,046.63	735.23

Source: China Statistical Year Book, 2007.

The sustainable growth of foreign capital utilization brought more FIEs in. The total number of FIEs grew from 84,300 in 1992 to 274,863 in 2006, and 37,888 more were established in 2007. Up to the end of 2007, there were 312,751 FIEs altogether nationwide.

4.2.2 Structural Features

By the type of foreign capital. Since the Reform and Opening Up process began, there have been three types of foreign capital utilized in China: Foreign borrowings, FDI, and other foreign investment, among which the FDI has been in the leading position, accounting for over 90% of the total. The fast-growing overseas IPO, foreign PE and QFII are included in the calculation.

1. ***Foreign Borrowings.*** Since the foreign borrowings are no longer included in the calculation of foreign capital utilization after 2000 by the China Statistics Bureau, only the foreign borrowings before 2000 are studied here. At stage one (1979–1991), the actual foreign borrowings was the primary source of foreign capital, yet in small amount, with no more than US$10 billion each year. From 1992 on, the FDI has become the major source of foreign capital, leaving foreign borrowings to second place. The actual amount of foreign borrowings has fluctuated between US$7.5 to US$13 billion, and has dropped year on year since 1996 (Figure 4.2 and Table 4.4).

2. ***Foreign Direct Investment.*** Since 1992, FDI has become the pillar of foreign capital with the number of projects and total amount both growing fast, accounting for over 90% of the total foreign capital attracted. From Deng Xiaoping's southern tour in 1992 to now, the actual amount of FDI grew rapidly, hitting US$10 billion in 1992 and US$45.463 billion in 1998. Although the amount dropped somewhat in 1999 and 2000, it still remained above US$40 billion. The contract amount grew from US$69.195 billion in 2001 to US$200.174 billion in 2006. The actual amount grew from US$46.878 billion in 2001 to US$69.468 billion in 2006 (Figure 4.2 and Table 4.4).

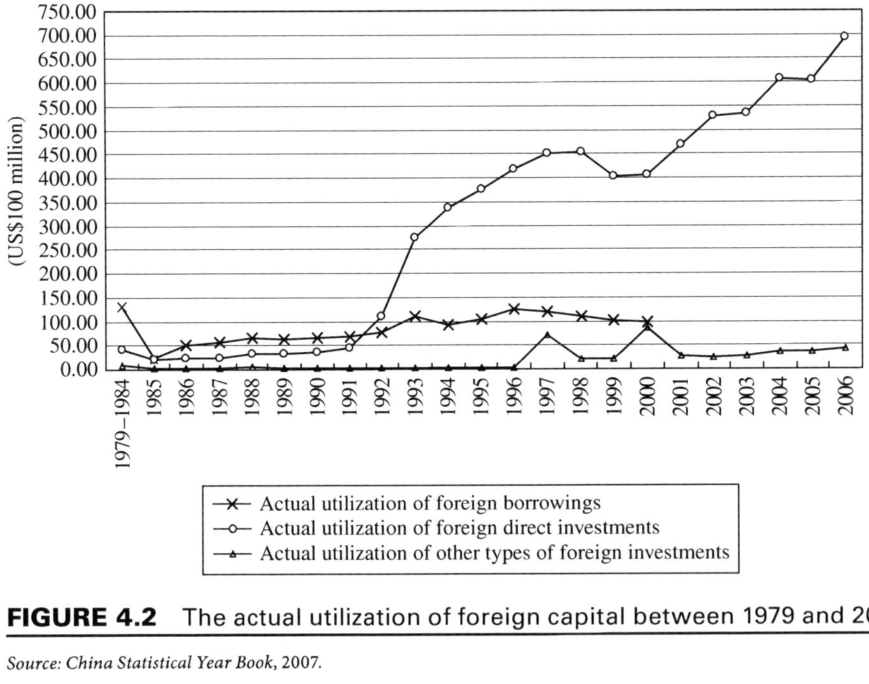

FIGURE 4.2 The actual utilization of foreign capital between 1979 and 2006

Source: China Statistical Year Book, 2007.

Note: Foreign borrowings are not included since 2000.

Table 4.4 The types of foreign capital used in China between 1979 and 2006

	Foreign borrowings			FDI			Others	
Year	No. of projects	Contract amount (US$100 million)	Actual amount utilized (US$100 million)	No. of projects	Contract amount (US$100 million)	Actual amount utilized (US$100 million)	Contract amount (US$100 million)	Actual amount utilized (US$100 million)
1979–84	117	169.78	130.41	3,724	97.50	41.04	13.98	10.42
1985	72	35.34	25.06	3,073	63.33	19.56	4.02	2.98
1986	53	84.07	50.14	1,498	33.30	22.44	4.96	3.70
1987	56	78.17	58.05	2,233	37.09	23.14	6.10	3.33
1988	118	98.13	64.87	5,945	52.97	31.94	8.94	5.45
1989	130	51.85	62.86	5,779	56.00	33.93	6.94	3.81
1990	98	50.99	65.34	7,273	65.96	34.87	3.91	2.68
1991	108	71.61	68.88	12,978	119.77	43.66	4.45	3.00
1992	94	107.03	79.11	48,764	581.24	110.08	6.12	2.84
1993	158	113.06	111.89	83,437	1,114.36	275.15	5.31	2.56
1994	97	106.68	92.67	47,549	826.80	337.67	4.08	1.79
1995	173	112.88	103.27	37,011	912.82	375.21	6.35	2.85
1996	117	79.62	126.69	24,556	732.76	417.26	3.71	4.10
1997	137	58.72	120.21	21,001	510.03	452.57	41.82	71.30
1998	51	83.85	110.00	19,799	521.02	454.63	27.14	20.94
1999	104	83.60	102.12	16,918	412.23	403.19	24.26	21.28
2000	—	—	100.00	22,347	623.80	407.15	87.50	86.41
2001	—	—	—	26,140	691.95	468.78	27.81	27.94
2002	—	—	—	34,171	827.68	527.43	19.82	22.68
2003	—	—	—	41,081	1,150.69	535.05	18.32	26.35
2004	—	—	—	43,664	1,534.79	606.30	31.09	34.42
2005	—	—	—	44,001	1,890.65	603.25	35.28	34.80
2006	—	—	—	41,485	2,001.74	694.68	44.89	40.55

Source: China Statistical Year Book, 2007.

Note: Foreign borrowings are not included since 2000.

3. *Others.* As indicated in Figure 4.2 and Table 4.4, "others" only accounts for a tiny portion of foreign capital. In 1997 and 2000, the actual amount of "others" reached US$7.13 billion and US$8.641 billion. For other years, the numbers were below US$4.1 billion. Before the accession to the WTO, the direct financing from the capital market only accounted for 10% of the total, but recent years saw the coming of PE, IPO and QFII.

PE/VC (private equity/venture capital) is a different form of investment from bank loan or capital market financing. It is a new type of financial capital invested in the upstream part of the investment chain. After accession to the WTO, PE/VC accelerated in China. VC arrived in China earlier than PE. In the Chinese VC market, 80% are from overseas. In recent years, PE has attracted more attention, and VC has also become more PE-like: The proportion of the VC investment dropped from 28% in 2003 to 20% in 2006, leaving more space for PE, and in the bullish market of 2007, a great amount of VC moved towards the PE and IPO market. According to the statistics from the Qingke research center, in Q2 2008, altogether 40 PE/VC funds were set up by 29 PE/VC firms, among which the amount of PE/VC available for investment in China reached US$3.018 billion. A total of 159 enterprises obtained equity investment of US$1.204 billion, a 31.4% increase with the number of enterprises, and a 73.5% increase of the total investment. However, due to the global financial crisis, since the second half of 2008, business has been cornered.

IPO (initial public offering) is the first sale out of the shares of an enterprise in the capital market, which is also a major exit strategy for PE/VC. In recent years, the offshore IPO of Chinese enterprises has become a hot issue, and the Hong Kong main board, the Singapore main board, the NYSE, and the NASDAQ are the top four markets. Through overseas IPO, the Chinese enterprises managed to raise a huge amount of capital from overseas, until the global financial crisis in 2008, which slowed down the pace of IPO (Table 4.5).

QFII refers to the qualified foreign institutional investors meeting the requirements of the CSRC and the investment quota from the State Administration of Foreign Exchange (SAFE), with the money brought in exchanged to the local currency for the purpose of making investment in the local securities market with a strictly supervised account. The capital gains and dividend may be changed to foreign exchange and remitted back to the home country. Since QFII was introduced to China in 2003, up to August 28, 2008, according to the Wind statistics, 65 QFIIs have been approved and 54 have entered the A share market, with a total amount of US$10.67 billion. However, with the collapse of the Lehman Brothers, Fortis, Merrill Lynch, and AIG, QFII subsided in 2008.

Table 4.5 The overseas IPOs for the Chinese enterprises in the past five years

Year	No. of enterprises	Amount raised (US$100 mil)
2003	48	70.00
2004	81	111.51
2005	70	212.30
2006	86	440.00
2007	118	342.00 (the first 11 months)

By the source of foreign capital. Since the instigation of the Reform and Opening Up process, a total of 190 countries and regions, mainly from Asia, have come to make FDI in China. Of the aggregated amount of FDI actually used between 1986 and 2007, the biggest portion came from Hong Kong and Taiwan. Up to the end of 2007, the actual amount of FDI from Hong Kong alone was 57% of the total, while the actual amount of FDI from Japan, the US, and the EU added together only took up 34%, though as an international financial center, the capital from Hong Kong is also international (Table 4.6).

In 2007, for the actual amount of FDI used in China, the top ten countries (regions) were as follows: HK (US$27.703 billion), British Virgin Islands (BVI)

Table 4.6 **The FDI used in China between 1986 and 2007 (US$100 million)**

Year	HK	Taiwan	Japan	US	EU
1986	13.29	—	2.63	3.26	1.79
1987	15.88	—	2.20	2.63	0.53
1988	20.68	—	5.15	2.36	1.57
1989	20.37	1.55	3.56	2.84	1.88
1990	18.80	2.22	5.03	4.56	1.47
1991	24.05	4.66	5.33	3.23	2.46
1992	75.07	10.51	7.10	5.11	2.43
1993	172.75	31.39	13.24	20.63	6.71
1994	196.65	33.91	20.75	24.91	15.38
1995	200.60	31.62	31.08	30.83	21.31
1996	206.77	34.75	36.79	34.43	27.37
1997	206.32	32.89	43.26	32.39	41.71
1998	185.08	29.15	34.00	38.98	39.79
1999	163.63	25.99	29.73	42.16	44.79
2000	155.00	22.96	29.16	43.84	44.79
2001	167.17	29.80	43.48	44.33	41.83
2002	178.61	39.71	41.90	54.24	37.10
2003	177.00	33.77	50.54	41.99	39.30
2004	189.98	31.17	54.52	39.41	42.39
2005	179.49	21.52	65.30	30.61	51.94
2006	202.33	21.36	45.98	28.65	54.39
2007	277.03	17.74	35.89	26.16	67.78
Total	3,046.55	456.67	606.62	557.55	559.31

Source: The database of the United Nations Conference on Trade and Development; *China Foreign Investment of the MOC* 2007; the official website of the MOC.

Note: Between 1986 and 2003, the EU data covered 15 nations, and after 2004, 25 nations.

(US$16.552 billion), South Korea (US$3.678 billion), Japan (US$3.589 billion), Singapore (US$3.185 billion), the US (US$2.616 billion), Cayman Islands (US$2.571 billion), Samoan Islands (US$2.17 billion), Taiwan (US$1.774 billion), and Mauritius (US$1.333 billion). The top ten accounted for 78.84% of the total investment in China in 2007.

By the distribution of investment. Eastern China has been a major recipient of FDI, representing over 85% of the foreign invested projects, and over 70% of actual capital used. Central China accounted for only 5.5% of the national total, and western China still smaller with 2.5% of the actual capital used (Table 4.7).

The eastern coastal area has been a focus of FDI. Guangdong, Jiangsu, Shandong, and Shanghai alone attract over 55% of the total FDI each year. Jiangxi, Hubei, and Hunan in the central region only account for 6% of the actual amount used, with other provinces accounting for an even smaller percentage. Sichuan, Shaanxi, Chongqing, Guangxi, and Inner Mongolia in the western regions account for 3% of the actual amount used, with other western areas accounting for only 1% (Table 4.8).

Although the eastern coastal region has been a focus of FDI, with the rejuvenation of the northeast industrial base, and the west development campaign, a growing number of foreign investors are tempted by the rich natural resources, abundant labor resources, and huge market, and are investing more in the mid-west region. For example, the actual amount of FDI in Jiangxi grew from US$465 million in 1998 to US$1.612 billion in 2003, and Qinghai from zero to US$47 million in 2002, and US$25 million in 2003.

Table 4.7 The distribution of FDI in China between 2002 and 2006 (US$100 Million)

Eastern				Central				Western			
No. of projects	Ratio	Actual amount	Ratio	No. of projects	Ratio	Actual amount	Ratio	No. of projects	Ratio	Actual amount	Ratio
30,001	87.80	457.29	86.70	2,730	7.99	50.09	9.50	1,440	4.21	20.05	3.80
36,159	88.02	459.51	85.88	3,177	7.73	58.31	10.90	1,745	4.25	17.23	3.22
37,978	86.98	522.07	86.11	3,771	8.64	66.80	11.02	1,915	4.39	17.44	2.88
38,439	87.33	535.58	73.97	3,752	8.52	48.26	6.67	1,810	4.11	19.41	2.68
35,538	85.66	569.22	81.94	4,084	9.84	39.22	5.65	1,851	4.46	21.77	3.13

Source: The official website of the MOC: www.mofcom.gov.cn

Note: Eastern area covers Beijing, Tianjin, Hebei, Liaoning, Shanghai, Jiangsu, Zhejiang, Fujian, Shandong, Guangdong, Hainan; central area covers Shanxi, Jilin, Heilongjiang, Anhui, Jiangxi, Henan, Hubei, Hunan; western area covers the Inner Mongolia, Guangxi, Sichuan, Chongqing, Guizhou, Yunnan, Shaanxi, Gansu, Qinghai, Ningxi, Xinjiang, Tibet.

Table 4.8 The FDI used in China in 2002 and 2003 (US$100 Million)

		2002				2003			
Regions		No. of projects	Ratio	Actual amount	Ratio	No. of projects	Ratio	Actual amount	Ratio
Eastern	Guangdong	6,805	19.91	113.34	21.49	7,039	17.13	78.23	14.62
	Jiangsu	5,819	17.03	101.90	19.32	7,182	17.48	105.64	19.74
	Shandong	4,079	11.94	47.34	8.98	5,208	12.68	60.16	11.24
	Shanghai	3,012	8.81	42.72	8.10	4,462	10.86	54.68	10.22
	Fujian	1,826	5.34	38.38	7.28	2,272	5.53	25.99	4.86
	Liaoning	2,147	6.28	34.12	6.47	2,231	5.43	28.24	5.28
	Zhejiang	3,380	9.89	30.76	5.83	4,460	10.86	49.81	9.31
	Beijing	1,370	4.01	17.25	3.27	1,539	3.75	21.91	4.10
	Tianjin	847	2.48	15.82	3.00	957	2.33	15.35	2.87
	Hebei	477	1.40	7.83	1.48	610	1.48	9.64	1.80
	Hainan	235	0.69	5.12	0.97	166	0.40	4.21	0.79
Central	Hubei	484	1.42	14.27	2.70	510	1.24	15.69	2.93
	Jiangxi	592	1.73	10.82	2.05	761	1.85	16.12	3.01
	Hunan	413	1.21	9.00	1.71	509	1.24	10.18	1.90
	Henan	287	0.84	4.05	0.77	304	0.74	5.39	1.01
	Anhui	339	0.99	3.84	0.73	425	1.03	3.67	0.69
	Heilongjiang	197	0.58	3.55	0.67	239	0.58	3.22	0.60
	Jilin	345	1.01	2.45	0.46	340	0.83	1.91	0.36
	Shanxi	73	0.21	2.12	0.40	89	0.22	2.14	0.40
Western	Sichuan	342	1.00	5.56	1.05	326	0.79	4.12	0.77
	Guangxi	279	0.82	4.17	0.79	334	0.81	4.19	0.78
	Shaanxi	203	0.59	3.60	0.68	242	0.59	3.32	0.62
	Chongqing	148	0.43	1.96	0.37	205	0.50	2.61	0.49
	Inner Mongolia	86	0.25	1.77	0.34	89	0.22	2.14	0.40
	Yunnan	150	0.44	1.12	0.21	165	0.40	0.84	0.16
	Gansu	51	0.15	0.61	0.12	59	0.14	0.23	0.04
	Qinghai	31	0.09	0.47	0.09	47	0.11	0.25	0.05
	Guizhou	55	0.16	0.38	0.07	66	0.16	0.45	0.08
	Ningxia	25	0.07	0.22	0.04	28	0.07	0.17	0.03
	Xinjiang	65	0.19	0.19	0.04	86	0.21	0.15	0.03
	Tibet	5	0.01	—	—	49	0.12	—	—

Source: The official website of the MOC: www.mofcom.gov.cn.

Note: The sequence is based on the actual amount used in 2002.

By industry. In the early stage of the reform, foreign investment only focused on certain industries including manufacturing, construction, and a small number of service industries. With the expansion of FDI, the range of investment has also been widened.

Currently foreign investment has covered all the sectors of the three major industries, with the second industry receiving the largest part.

Up to now, the second industry has been the major focus of FDI. Between 2002 and 2006, the actual amount of foreign capital used each year took up 60% of the national total. The first industry attracted little FDI, and between 2002 and 2006, both the actual amount and the percentage of national total declined. On the contrary, the tertiary industry has become more favored by FDI, with the percentage of the actual amount

Table 4.9 The industries receiving FDI between 2002 and 2006 (US$100 Million)

			Primary industry			
Year	No. of projects	Ratio	Contract amount	Ratio	Actual amount	Ratio
2002	975	2.85	16.88	2.04	10.28	1.95
2003	1,116	2.72	22.76	1.98	10.01	1.87
2004	1,130	2.59	32.71	2.13	11.14	1.84
2005	1,058	2.40	38.38	2.03	7.18	0.99
2006	951	2.29	31.99	1.65	5.99	0.95
			Secondary industry			
	No. of projects	Ratio	Contract amount	Ratio	Actual amount	Ratio
2002	25,608	74.94	621.84	75.13	394.65	74.83
2003	30,247	73.63	851.53	74.00	397.10	74.22
2004	31,531	72.21	1,166.21	75.98	454.63	74.98
2005	30,027	68.21	1,344.43	71.11	446.92	61.72
2006	25,517	61.53	1,243.62	64.19	420.46	66.72
			Tertiary industry			
	No. of projects	Ratio	Contract amount	Ratio	Actual amount	Ratio
2002	7,588	22.21	188.96	22.83	122.50	23.23
2003	9,718	23.66	276.40	24.02	127.94	23.91
2004	11,003	25.20	335.87	21.88	140.53	23.18
2005	12,934	29.38	507.85	26.86	269.95	37.28
2006	15,005	36.18	661.67	34.15	203.75	32.33

Source: The official website of the MOC: www.mofcom.gov.cn; *China Statistical Year Book*, 2007.

Note: The first industry: agriculture, forestry, animal husbandry, fishery; the second industry: mining, manufacturing, generation and supplying of power, gas, water, construction; the tertiary industry: transportation, storage, postal service, information transfer, computer service, software, retail and wholesale, hotel and catering service, finance, property, rental and commercial services, technical service and geological exploration, water conservation and public utility, education, health, social security and social welfare, culture, sport, and entertainment, public administration and social organization.

accounting for over 30% of the national total in both 2005 and 2006. Since the 1990s, the focus of FDI was gradually shifted to the service industry, and after the accession to the WTO, with the service industry becoming increasingly more open, it has become more attractive to foreign investors.

By way of investment. Since the 1990s, MNCs slowly moved from green field investment to cross-nation M&A, with the amount of M&A accounting for half of the cross-nation investment.

Since the opening up, green field investment has been the major form of foreign investment. However, in recent years, M&A has become increasingly significant in weight. Though the percentage of M&A is only 10% for the FDI in the manufacturing business, the investment was made on the pillar industries. When the foreign investors acquired the Chinese enterprises, it was the distribution channel, branding, and customer base that attracted the foreign investors. Since these resources cannot be brought in as with capital and technology, or developed in the short term, some MNCs, especially those that came to China late, prefer to adopt the M&A model to win market share in the shortest time. For example, the state-owned Shuang Hui Industrial (Group) Co., Ltd of Henan went public in the Beijing Asset and Equity Exchange in March 2006, with a net asset of RMB 570 million, and was finally acquired through bidding by a Hong Kong company controlled by Goldman Sachs for RMB 2.01 billion. With the gradual opening of the finance sector in China, more foreign investors are inclined to obtain the service network and customer resources through M&A.

4.3 Overseas Direct Investment

4.3.1 The Starting and Developing of Overseas Direct Investment of Chinese Enterprises

Since the Reform and Opening Up policy was announced in 1978, overseas direct investment (ODI) has become an important form of international competition and cooperation. On August 13, 1979, the State Council issued the policy on ODI and since then, many companies have been set up offshore. Up to the end of 2007, there had been over 8,000 Chinese-funded companies offshore as approved by the MOC, with a total investment of US$93.786 billion. Between 2002 and 2007, the amount of ODI grew from US$2.5 billion to US$18.76 billion, climbing from 26th place to 13th place. In Q1 2008, ODI reached US$19.34 billion, an increase of 353% against 2007. With the expansion of investment, the Sino-foreign economic cooperation has also been deepened. Up to the end of 2007, the turnover of the contracted projects overseas amounted to US$206.4 billion, and the contract value amounted to US$329.5 billion; the turnover of the labor cooperation contract amounted to US$47.8 billion, and the contract value amounted to US$52.3 billion; and altogether 4.19 million laborers had been sent abroad. With the direct investment covering nearly 200 countries and regions, China is listed among the top ten countries for contractual projects.

Currently a diversified structure of ODI has been established, with the following features:

Diversified market distribution. China has expanded the direct investment business to over 160 countries and regions including Hong Kong, Macau, Europe, North America, Africa, and Latin America.

Diversified industry. With factory operation, processing, resource development, labor cooperation and project contract, Chinese enterprises have invested in multiple industries including construction, petrochemical, power generation, water conservation, transportation, railway, coal mining, forestry, metallurgy, aviation, and so on.

Diversified operational entity. There are four types of business entities involved in overseas investment: The foreign trade firms and foreign trade group corporations directly under the central government and local government at different levels, such as China National Cereals, Oils and Foodstuffs Import & Export Corporation; the manufacturing enterprises or group corporations, such as Capital Steel Group; the large finance and insurance companies, such as the Bank of China and the other four commercial banks; and private enterprises, small and medium sized state-owned or collectively owned enterprises.

The history of the overseas investment and cross-nation operation of the Chinese enterprises can be divided into four stages:

Stage one: The starting stage of 1979–1986, with few enterprises making investment, few projects abroad, less than US$100 million invested each year, and fewer than 100 overseas enterprises set up each year. The investment was largely made in the aviation, finance, insurance, contractual project, and catering service industries. Between 1979 and 1986, the total amount of direct investment overseas was only US$253 million, and altogether 277 enterprises were established.

Stage two: The developing stage of 1987–1995. Since 1987, the ODI and cross-nation operation entered a fast track, with over 100 enterprises set up each year, and over US$100 million invested each year except for 1990 and 1993. From 1987 to 1995, the total amount of ODI amounted to US$1.693 billion, and altogether 1,651 enterprises were established.

Stage three: The expansion stage of 1996–2002. The acceleration at this stage surpassed the second stage and the scale of investment also came to a new high. Except for 1996, each of the other years saw the set up of over 300 enterprises, and except for 1997 and 1998, all other years saw sharp increases of investment. The amount of ODI reached US$612 million in 1999, and US$983 million in 2002. Between 1996 and 2002, the total amount of ODI amounted to US$3.954 billion, and altogether 2,118 enterprises were established.

Stage four: The upgrading stage of 2003 to now, with ever faster growth. The amount of investment grew from US$2.087 billion in 2003 to US$18.76 billion in 2007. Most of the investment was made in the mining, manufacturing, and commercial service industries in Asia, which took up half of the total. Hong Kong and Macau remained the hot spots of investment. The central government-led enterprises and the ones from the coastal areas have been the main force, and the overseas M&A has also become a trend.

4.3.2 The Trend of Overseas M&A

The fast economic growth and massive market have made China the largest M&A market in Asia for MNCs. Meanwhile Chinese enterprises have also started to acquire mature foreign enterprises. In 2004, Lenovo acquired the PC business of IBM, and Shanghai Auto acquired Korea's Sang Yong. The acquisition of the IBM PC business resulted in Lenovo being known to the world for its manufacturing capability and capital strength. Since 2006, the overseas M&A has become a trend among Chinese enterprises (Table 4.10).

Table 4.10 The representative cases of overseas M&A since 2006

Month/year	Chinese enterprises	Target of M&A	Amount of investment	% of shares acquired
08/2006	China Construction Bank	Bank of America (Asia)	US$9.71 billion	100%
12/2006	Bank of China	Singapore Aircraft Leasing Enterprise	US$965 million	100%
12/2006	ICBC	Bank Halim Indonesia	—	90%
05/2007	China Investment Corporation	Blackstone Group	US$3 billion	10%
06/2007	Chinalco	Peru Copper	US$757.5 million	—
07/2007	National Development Bank	Barclays Group	Euro 2.2 billion	3.1%
08/2007	ICBC	Seng Heng Bank, Macau	US$583 million	79.93%
08/2007	Shasteel	The UK-owned Australian Iron Ore	—	90%
10/2007	Minsheng Bank	United Commercial Bank, US	RMB 2.5 billion	9.9%

Table 4.10 (continued)

Month/year	Chinese enterprises	Target of M&A	Amount of investment	% of shares acquired
10/2007	ICBC	The Standard Bank of South Africa	US$5.46 billion	20%
10/2007	CITIC Securities	Bear Stern	Share swap of US$1 billion	6%
11/2007	BOC HK	Bank of East Asia	HK$ 3.95 billion	4.94%
11/2007	China Ping'an Insurance	Fortis Group	Euro 1.81 billion	4.18%
11/2007	China Metallurgical Group, Jiangxi Copper	Aynak Copper, Afghanistan	US$3.7 billion	—
12/2007	China Investment Corporation	Morgan Stanley	US$5 billion	9.9%
12/2007	Youngor	Smart under Kellwood, US	US$120 million	100%
04/2008	China Ping'an Insurance	Fortis Investment	Euro 2.15 billion	50%
06/2008	China Merchant Bank	Wing Lung Bank, HK	HK$19.3 billion	53.1%
07/2008	Bank of China	Heritage Fund of Switzerland	SF 9 million	30%
09/2008	Bank of China	La Compagnie Financière Edmond de Rothschild	Euro 236 million	20%

According to the data from JP Morgan, the total transaction volume of the global M&A reached US$4.8 trillion in 2007, a 23% increase compared to the previous year, among which China contributed US$140 billion, a 33% increase compared to the previous year. According to the research of Qingke center, in 2007 there were altogether 84 cases of M&A worldwide, among which 37 were related to Chinese enterprises, an increase of 117.6% compared to 2006. Also, in addition to the SOEs and big banks, private enterprises represented by those in Zhejiang also joined the game, such as the acquisition of shares by Youngor, the acquisition of international brand by Aokang, and the acquisition of international advanced technology by WanXiang.

Many more Chinese enterprises are now getting ready to go out and take advantage of the global financial crisis of 2008. Of course, this involves huge risks, not to mention the lack of experience in international M&A. It is highly necessary for China to learn from the "Japanese M&A" in the 1980s.

The trend of overseas M&A manifests the ambition of the Chinese enterprises for global expansion and internationalization. Not each case of M&A brought anticipated return, but the intangible benefits included the negotiation experience, the learning of the local culture for better adaptation, the utilization of the acquired technologies and sales channels, and so on. Even if the efforts may not be rewarded instantly, it is conducive to the long-term globalization strategy of Chinese enterprises.

4.3.3 QDII: The Indirect Investment Overseas

QDII (qualified domestic institutional investors) refers to the system of allowing the domestic institutions to invest in shares, bonds, and other securities in the overseas capital market in a measured approach upon the approval of the competent departments in China when the RMB in the capital account is still not convertible and the capital market is yet to open. In this way, the Chinese enterprises may join the international capital market and earn yields. With the QDII pooling the capital and savings of the Chinese investors together and investing in the international capital market, Chinese investors may engage in overseas investment for profit, and Chinese enterprises may enhance the international competitive power.

With the foreign exchange reserve hitting US$2 trillion, overseas investment might be a good choice for China. However, one year after the launch of QDII, the global financial crisis arrived. With the slump of the US and Hong Kong stock markets, the QDII such as the Hua'an international allocation fund is now in serious difficulty.

4.4 Relative Advantages of the Sino-Foreign Investment Coopetition

4.4.1 The Late Development Payoff of China

The economic growth effect. The introduction of foreign capital is a kind of late development advantage for China. In the early days of the Reform and Opening Up process, the introduced capital helped fill the gap and provided the startup fund for the economic construction. Later, with foreign capital also came advanced technologies and management expertise, promoting rapid economic growth in China through the technical spillover effect. Foreign capital has also provided extensive import/export channels and markets for the Chinese economy, driving the quick growth of foreign trade.

The accumulation of physical capital productive forces. The percentage of FDI in the fixed asset investment has been low, fluctuating around 4%–12% for most years, yet the accumulation of material capital productivity following the coming of foreign capital has been considerable. Take the auto industry as an example. Auto is both a product (consumable) and a tool (capital). After the opening up, the Chinese auto market has been dominated by the Sino-foreign JVs, with the top nine MNCs (GM, Volkswagen, Toyota, Ford, DaimlerChrysler, Renault-Nissan, Honda, Peugeot, and BMW) all coming to China. Many new products have been produced in China with the production equipment and assembling lines moved to the country. After the accession to the WTO, both the output and quantity grew rapidly, with output reaching two million units in 2000, and four million in 2003, ranking fourth in the world. The quantity also increased from 8.17 million in 1993 to 24.92 million in 2003.

The growth of employment and income. The FIEs not only created many job opportunities in China, but also updated the traditional work philosophy and employment system, and promoted the efficient market allocation of labor resources. Since the FIEs are mostly in the labor-intensive industries, they have absorbed a massive portion of redundant rural laborers. Today, with more foreign investment transitioning to the high-tech industries and service industries, more new jobs with higher income have been created. Up to 2006, the FIEs had employed altogether 28 million people, accounting for over 10% of the working population nationwide. Should those employed by the supporting enterprises to the FIEs be counted in, the total number would exceed 100 million. Research shows that for every US$100 million of foreign direct investment received, 2,900 jobs are created.

The upgrading of industrial structure. In the early stage of the Reform and Opening Up process, the economic structure was unbalanced with an illogical weight of heavy industry, light industry, and agriculture. The introduction of foreign capital eased the capital pressure and optimized the economic structure. With most foreign capital invested in the light industry and tertiary industry, it was conducive for the evolution of the industrial structure. From the southern tour in 1992 to 2000, China strengthened its effort in attracting foreign capital, and a huge amount of money was put into the manufacturing, construction, and service industry. A growing number of MNCs started to invest capital and technology in the manufacturing business in China, promoting the upgrade of the manufacturing structure. Since the accession to the WTO in 2001, with the opening of the service trade, the tertiary industry has been leading the growth.

The tax revenue of the government. The Hong Kong, Macau, Taiwan, and foreign invested enterprises have made great contributions (over 25% of the total) to the tax revenue of the Chinese government, mostly in the form of VAT, income tax, and consumption tax. A total of 98% of the foreign tax revenue is generated by the FIEs.

The profit of the Chinese enterprises. It is a simple fact that among the Sino-foreign jointly funded enterprises, the Sino-foreign jointly cooperative enterprises, and the solely foreign funded enterprises, the latter comes smallest in number. As for the former two, the foreign parties are typically minor shareholders, leaving the majority of shares and dividend to the Chinese parties.

The deduction of resources and environment consumption (negative payoffs). For the economic benefit gained from the foreign direct investment, China has also paid a heavy price on resources, energy, and the environment. When the MNCs shifted the highly polluting and resource-consuming enterprises or part of the production to China to set up new factories, they also shifted environmental issues to China. These polluting enterprises are mostly in the rubber, plastics, printing and dyeing, shoe making, leather making, and battery industries, with capital from South Korea, the US, Japan, and Europe. In 2005, the foreign capital invested in the six energy consuming industries—iron and steel, nonferrous metals, power generation, construction material, paper making, and chemical—accounted for 11.28% of the total foreign capital used, and 17.9% of the foreign capital in the manufacturing business. These are the negative gains to be deducted in calculation.

4.4.2 The Early Development Payoff of the Foreign Parties

The profit from capital investment. The foreign investors in China enjoy the early development advantage of capital accumulation. Recently the American Chamber of Commerce (AMCHAM) of China, the American Chamber of Commerce of Shanghai and the American Chamber of Commerce of South China jointly published a white paper on the American Enterprises in China in 2008. This is the 10th annual white paper from the AMCHAM, and also the most comprehensive one so far. Over 800 American enterprises in different industries were covered in the survey, including SMEs and MNCs. The white paper shows that most American enterprises are running well in China with growing revenue. In 2007, 74% of these American enterprises grew in profit, with 10% of them gaining rich profit. Among the 658 enterprises, 88% registered operational revenue growth. Though under the pressure of market cost increase, 89% of the 618 enterprises interviewed expressed their optimism for the coming five years.

Let us review some cases:

Since Motorola entered the Chinese market in 1987, after twenty years of business development, up to June 2004, the company had invested altogether US$3.5 billion in China. Currently Motorola has built 10 enterprises (one solely invested, one share controlling and eight joint ventures) and 24 subsidiaries, employing over 90,000 people (84% of the management staff are Chinese), and is one of the largest FIEs in China.

In 2003, the sales revenue in China reached US$4.67 billion, the export amounted to US$4.09 billion, and the purchase from China amounted to US$3.19 billion in value. Today China has become the third-largest market for Motorola (the first two being the US and Europe), and is becoming one of the world-class R&D centers and production centers of the company. Motorola is also developing new business such as auto electronics and digital integration, while expanding its investment in China and its purchase from China.

As the largest electric and electronics company in the world, Siemens started its business in China in 1972. Gradually the Chinese business became a pillar of its Asia-Pacific business, and an important part of its world business. Currently all the business lines of Siemens have come to China, with the core being the infrastructure construction and industrial solution. Up to September 30, 2006, Siemens had invested over RMB 15 billion in China, with total sales revenue of RMB 50.4 billion. Over 70 operations and 60 representative offices had been established, with a total staff of 43,000, among whom 95% were Chinese, making it one of the FIEs with the largest number of Chinese employees.

Toshiba is one of the earliest MNCs to make investment in China. China is the largest independent market for Toshiba only after Japan and the US, and also the development base for comprehensive business. Up to 2006, Toshiba had established 64 joint ventures and SIEs in China, doing R&D, purchasing, and production businesses. Toshiba has invested over RMB 8 billion in China and employed 23,000 people. In 2006, its business revenue in China reached RMB 68 billion. Toshiba started the China business as early as 1972. After the implementation of the Reform and Opening Up process, the home electronics appliances of Toshiba arrived in China. From 1991 onward, Toshiba has set up a number of enterprises in China, manufacturing products for the Chinese market. Currently China has become not only a production base, but also a development base for comprehensive business including R&D, purchasing, logistics, sales, and so on. While making contribution to the Chinese economy, it has also benefited a lot from China.

The low cost of OEM. OEM (original equipment manufacturer) is a way of production in which the producer, other than doing production, takes responsibility for the design, development, and sales of products, leaving the manufacturing part to its partner enterprises. Microsoft, IBM, and many well-known enterprises have adopted this model for production. Since they don't have to be directly involved in the production of spare parts and components, they may reduce the manufacturing cost, save time, and streamline the supply chain as a result. OEM is the outcome of the refined division of labor in the global economic integration, and can best allocate production resources to reduce the input on fixed assets.

The industrial upgrade effect. Since the 1980s, there has been a new round of evolution of industrial structure in the developed countries, with more energy-saving and high value-added capital- and technology-intensive enterprises established. By controlling the more valuable parts of the industrial chain such as branding, marketing, design, and moving the labor-intensive industry or the lower end of the capital- and technology-intensive industries to the emerging countries or developing countries, the developed countries have managed to upgrade their industrial structure.

As the world manufacturing center, China has helped many MNCs in the upgrade and optimization of the industrial structure, mostly in the manufacturing business, including some high-polluting and energy-consuming industries, unleashing space for the development of the innovative industries.

4.5 Cases of Dongguan, Kunshan, and Dalian

4.5.1 The Story of Dongguan

In the early stage of the Reform and Opening Up process, when Hong Kong started to move the processing industry out of the island, Dongguan, with its rich labor and land resources, grasped the opportunity to host the processing trade. In August 1978, Dongguan brought in capital from Hong Kong to set up the first processing enterprise with supplied material: Taiping Handbag Factory. This started the history of the processing industry in the city. Small workshops could be found everywhere including dining halls, meeting halls, and resident buildings. Today, Dongguan has become the most important base for processing business. In 2007, the GDP of Dongguan hit RMB 315.1 billion, a 120-time increase compared to 1978. With an annual growth of 18%, Dongguan is among the 13 Chinese cities with GDP over RMB 300 billion.

In the early days of the reform, most of the foreign capital in Dongguan came from Hong Kong, and most of the processing business was in the simple labor-intensive industries like textiles, clothes, toys, plastics, and so on. Toward the mid-1990s, the Taiwanese IT industry moved to Dongguan, and this drove the upgrade of the processing industry. Currently, the IT industry has become a leading industry in Dongguan, and the modern manufacturing and high-tech industry is developing fast. With the pouring in of Taiwanese investors, Dongguan has also become a key production base and international processing base for PC components. The PC magnetic head, scanner, driver, AC capacitor, micro motor, computerized refrigerator, and video magnetic head produced in Dongguan account for 10%–40% of the world market share.

The actual amount of foreign capital used grew from US$1.73 million in 1979, to US$1.548 billion in 1998. By the end of 2006, there were altogether 8,344 enterprises engaging in the processing business, among which 816 were joint ventures, 327 were cooperative ones, and 2,047 were solely FIEs (24.53%). In 2007, the actual amount of foreign capital used amounted to US$5.044 billion, and export amounted to US$60.232 billion, ranking fourth among all large and medium-sized Chinese cities. The total industrial output amounted to RMB 664.985 billion, a 1,538 time increase compared to 1978.

Over the 30 years, Dongguan has successfully completed four stages of leapfrog development in the foreign-oriented economy represented by the processing business with supplied materials. The first stage was from 1978 to 1984, during which Dongguan started the business. By 1985, the industrial output exceeded the agricultural output for the first time. The second stage was from 1985 to 1993, during which the industrial output grew by 39% annually and exceeded RMB 20 billion in 1993. The third stage was from 1994 to 2000, during which Dongguan entered the "second industrial revolution," and the number of the provincial level high-tech enterprises grew from 1 to 66. The local fiscal revenue also grew from RMB 770 million to RMB 3 billion. The fourth stage was from 2001 to the present day, during which the processing industry is upgrading from simple manufacturing to the integration of proprietary R&D, manufacturing and distribution. In 2007, Dongguan won the awards of Innovative City, and Safe Social Environment. Today Dongguan ranks the first in Guangdong for comprehensive, competitive power, and the second among all the Chinese cities of the same size.

4.5.2 The Foreign-oriented Economy of Kunshan

Compared to the development model of Dongguan, Kunshan, Suzhou followed a different road in the introduction of foreign capital, focusing more on independent innovation. In 1998, Kunshan started an innovation program on competitive advantages, technologies, system, and industry. From 1999 to 2001, there was a separate three-year program on technical innovation. Within a few years, Kunshan achieved huge progress in the development of high-tech industries, reengineering of old equipment, promotion of technical improvement and upgrade of industries. A number of well-known brands like Giant Bicycle, Kone Elevator, Uni-president Food, Sakura Bath, and Kitchen landed in Kunshan, together with a group of excellent national brands, such as Good Baby, which has applied for 1,922 patents, and led the Chinese market and the US market for six consecutive years. Good Baby is also included in the second group of Chinese enterprises for the program of building international reputation and competitiveness.

In 1978, Kunshan was at the bottom among the six counties under Suzhou with a GDP of only RMB 232 million. Today Kunshan has become a new industrial and commercial city with a foreign-oriented economy. At the end of 2005, Kunshan met its provincial goal to be a "well-off society" ahead of schedule. In 2006, the total output reached RMB 93 billion, the fiscal revenue reached RMB 15.1 billion, and import and export amounted to RMB 42.8 billion. Kunshan has been elected as the most economically developed county (city) for two consecutive years, has won a reputation as the "national eco-city," and was ranked first place among all county-level cities in the assessment on urban innovative capacity organized by the Ministry of Science and Technology and the Chinese Academy of Social Sciences.

The economic development strategy of Kunshan started officially between the mid-1980s and the early 1990s. In January 1985, Kunshan decided to build a new city by attracting foreign capital investment. The FDI filled the technical gap of the township enterprises, and promoted the economic growth of Kunshan. In 1990, the total output reached RMB 2.012 billion, a ten-time increase as compared to 1978. From the 1990s to the beginning of the twenty-first century, on one hand, Kunshan further developed its economy by utilizing the adjacency to Shanghai and the low labor cost to attract foreign investors. Up to the end of 1993, there had been 27 foreign invested projects with a minimum investment of US$10 million each, and many well-known international high-tech enterprises had invested in Kunshan. On the other hand, Kunshan actively brought in the high-tech enterprises and industries from Europe and America, and drove the development of local enterprises by extending product lines. Since the turn of the twenty-first century, with the further expansion of foreign investment and the upgrade of economic structure and the growth of local private business, the economy of Kunshan grew faster. The arrival of foreign enterprises also exerted a profound social impact on the city.

Up to the end of 2006, altogether 4,000 FIEs from 55 countries and regions had moved to Kunshan, and 163 of them had set up R&D centers there, among which 30 were considerable in size. Both the number and capacity of the R&D institutions in Kunshan rank top in Suzhou and Jiangsu. Currently the accredited city level research institutes cover the electronics, chemical, material sciences, pharmaceutical, machinery, and food industries. These foreign R&D centers are rich in capital, advanced in facilities, strong in science. This not only upgraded the industrial structure in Kunshan, but also pushed the local enterprises to set up their own R&D centers, accelerating the independent innovation process. Good Baby is a perfect example of how the R&D center of a local enterprise develops new products and occupies the global market. Currently Good Baby has nearly 1,700 patents, and the R&D people present two new designs each day on average. Another example is Kaigong Machinery, which developed the leading combined drawing and lapping machine and combing machine on its own, and managed to occupy the world market through technology transfer to a German company.

After years of development, the use of foreign capital has reached a mature stage, and great progress has been made with independent innovation. Meanwhile attention has also been paid to the selection of leading industries and the development of independent innovation. Currently IT, electronics, and biology are the leading industries in Kunshan, which has attracted excellent resources domestically and abroad to serve the economic development and independent innovation. Kunshan has also built the mechanism for industry, cooperation, talents, service, and policy to enhance its independent innovation capacity and accelerate development. Also, in the fiber cable industry, with the "Longteng Fiber Cable" as a base, Kunshan has decided to invest US$10 billion to build a complete TFT LCD industrial chain within three to five years, targeting an annual turnover of US$100 billion. The fiber cable industry is expected to become the most robust leading industry in the development zone.

4.5.3 New Dalian Fueled by BPO

On January 18, 2008, according to the latest research of IDC, the most reputable consulting firm in the IT industry, Dalian for the first time beat Shanghai and Beijing for the bargain purchase option (BPO) business. Relying on the offshore software outsourcing business from Japan and South Korea, Dalian has become the new leading city in global outsourcing services, and established itself in software development, call centers, engineering services, and R&D. As the most open and developed city in Northeast China, Dalian is among the five most favored cities by FIEs. Dalian also hosts many of the global 500 companies, such as IBM, HP, Dell, Eccenture, and SAP. The Dalian Software Park has attracted a huge amount of foreign capital, with over half of the world's top ten ITOs and BPOs (ITO covers programming, testing, and other software development work; BPO refers to the trusting of supplementary or even key business to the professional service providers) have business in Dalian, and this has won Dalian the name of Bangalore of China.

In the early 1990s, Dalian was still an old industrial base in Northeast China, and was facing difficulties like decreasing profits, worker layoffs, and a deteriorating environment. The old economic model relying on port business and heavy industry was also in dilemma. In such difficulties, Dalian decided to shift to the software and BPO business. For the geographic advantage and economic heritage, Dalian quickly became a recipient of the software and IT business from Japan. In 1998, Dalian set up the first municipal information bureau in China, to give guidance to the software business. In the summer of the same year, the first "officially organized and privately funded" software park opened in Dalian, marking the first step of the software business.

In the beginning, there were only a dozen IT enterprises and hundreds of IT workers in Dalian, and the annual revenue was merely RMB 170 million. Later Dalian began to take advantage of the geographic location to attract investment from MNCs, and focused on the software outsourcing business. In the early days, business from Japan accounted for 80% of the total. In the autumn of 2001, with the first seminar on BPO held in Dalian, the software outsourcing business moved to a fast track. In 2003, the only national industrial exhibition in China—China International Software and Information Service Exhibition—opened in Dalian, promoting the growth of software outsourcing and its exposure to the world. In 2004, Dalian set up a special fund for the senior IT talents. With the above measures, BPO grew at a dramatic speed. In less than ten years, Dalian Software Park has become the top one in foreign investment, with a huge amount of orders from Japan and South Korea.

Within 10 years, the software and information industry of Dalian experienced dramatic growth. The sales revenue grew from RMB 200 million in 1998 to RMB 2.15 billion in 2007, registering an increase of 100 times and an annual growth rate of 68.2%. The software export grew from US$10 million to 720 million in 2007, an increase of 74 times. By 2007, Dalian hosted 620 IT enterprises, among which 38 were among the global 500. Six of the top ten world BPOs had arrived in Dalian. The total population of IT workers reached 60,000, and over ten enterprises had a staff of 2,000 each. In addition, the software and outsourcing business had made larger contributions to the economic growth. Statistics show that the contribution of software and BPO to the nominal GDP grew from 0.38% in 1999 to 4.81% in 2007, an increase of 4.43 percentage points. Each year, the number of IT enterprises and their employees, sales revenue, export volume, and tax revenue grow by over 50%. According to the latest IDC report on BPO, Dalian ranks first in China and fifth in the world.

The success of the software industry in Dalian also attracted investment from Intel, the largest IC board manufacturer. The phase one investment of US$2.5 billion was to fund the production of the 12-inch, 90 nanometer chips. The LED screen was developed independently by Dalian Luming Group and was used in the 2008 Beijing Olympics, the first such LED (diode) screen in the world, setting seven world records and making the Water Cubic more attractive. Dalian Jiecheng provided the i-MOD series module signal platform for the TV broadcast of the Olympic Games, which was the first digital audio visual editing and decoding platform with network supervision, making China better known to the world. It is fair to say that "Made in Dalian" is a great contributor to the success of the scientific aspects of the Olympic Games. To make Dalian a new leader in global software and BPO services, in July 2008, the municipal government promulgated *The Opinions on the Acceleration of Software and BPO Business,* providing policy support to the upgrade of the industrial structure in Dalian.

CHAPTER

5

The International Flow of Human Capital

As a driver of economic growth, human capital is usually generated in two ways: The general human capital acquired through school education, which may produce the internal effect, and the professional human capital acquired through practice, or learning by doing, which may bring the external effect. The accumulation of human capital enhances the capital yield and accelerates economic growth through technical advancement.

This chapter discusses the reasons behind the fast economic growth from the perspective of human capital. Firstly we discuss the contribution of the accumulated human capital to the economic growth as brought about by labor flow. Then we discuss the school education in China, the international exchange of science and knowledge and the human capital accumulated through learning by doing. Finally we analyze the relative payoffs of China and the developed countries in the flow of human capital.

5.1 The Late Development Advantage of Labor Resources in China

Since human capital is a kind of live technology attached to the laborers, the richness of human capital in one country is determined by the size of the working population. As a large developing nation, China boasts abundant labor resources, and low labor costs as a result of the late development of human resources. Since the beginning of the Reform and Opening Up process, a large number of redundant rural laborers have moved to cities, providing rich human resources for the industrialization and urbanization in China. For the low wage level of this type of laborer, the late development advantage of labor resources is reflected in both the transfer of abundant rural laborers, and the low cost.

5.1.1 The Effect of Labor Transfer

Since the restriction on population flow between cities and countryside was deregulated in 1978 with the start of the reform, the largest ever population transfer began. In particular, after the mid-1980s, China experienced the peak of rural labor transfer. A sample survey conducted by the National Statistics Bureau shows that the number of rural laborers seeking jobs in cities grew from 62 million in 1993 to 120 million in 2004. Should the rural laborers working in the local township enterprises be counted in, the total size of rural labors working outside their hometown amounted to 200 million in 2004, accounting for 41% of the total rural working population. The transfer of rural laborers emerged in a special historical context, and greatly released rural productivity, and accelerated industrialization, modernization, and urbanization in China.

It is undeniable that the transfer of rural laborers contributes to the optimization of industrial structure, yet labor input is only one of the contributors. The commonly agreed motive forces of economic growth are material capital accumulation and technical advancement. According to the report of the World Bank in 1997 on the analysis of the average 9.4% GDP growth in China between 1978 and 1995, capital contributed 37%, labor 17%, and residuals 46% (mainly through technical advancement).

5.1.2 The Labor Cost Advantage

The late development advantage of low labor cost is an important base for the development of labor-intensive industries in China. China is yet to have the international competitive advantage in the capital-intensive and technology-intensive industries. The competitive power of the manufacturing industry in China comes mainly from the late development advantage of low labor cost. According to the statistics, in 2006, the average wage in the manufacturing business was RMB 18,225 per year, or RMB 1,518 per month, and the monthly average wage of the total working population in cities and towns was RMB 1,738, RMB 210 higher than that of the manufacturing business. Also, according to the data from the Boston Consulting Group (BCG), in 2003 the average hourly wage of Chinese workers (including welfare) was US$0.8, which was 40.8% of Thailand, 38.3% of Malaysia, 29.1% of Brazil, 8.0% of South Korea, 4.5% of the UK and France, 4.3% of Canada, 3.9% of Japan, 3.7% of the US, and 2.6% of Germany.

Yet it is worth noting that the investment environment of other developing countries has been improving, and with the economic growth and the development of human resources in China, the labor cost has been constantly increasing. As a result, some investment from MNCs has been transferred to other developing countries, since compared with Vietnam, India, Thailand, and Cambodia, the labor cost advantage in China is no longer such an advantage. Some FIEs originally registered in China have already moved their factories elsewhere. Meanwhile, the Latin American and African countries are also developing their home market and joining the competition. While China still lags behind the developed countries in productivity and technical innovation, the comparative advantage of rich labor and the late development advantage of low cost is diminishing, leaving China on a long and winding road to the goal of "the world manufacturing center."

5.2 Education, Accumulation, and International Exchange of Human Capital

5.2.1 Higher Education was the First Focus of Change in China's Development

On May 24, 1977, Deng Xiaoping said the following when talking to two officials of the central government:

> "The key of modernization is the advancement of science and technology, and to develop science and technology, education is the key. Empty talk won't bring modernization. We need to have knowledge and talents . . . education should go in parallel with science and technology, efforts should be made all the way through from primary school to elementary school and to college. I hope that five years from now, a little progress can be made, and 15–20 years from now great progress can be made. In developing education, both quantity and quality should be addressed. Key primary schools, high schools and colleges should be set up to retain the best talents through rigid examination."[1]

When Deng came back to power for the third time in July 1977, he volunteered to take responsibility for education, and organized the national seminar on the work of science and education, during which a decision was made to resume the college entrance examination system that had been suspended for ten years. On October 12 the same year, the State Council approved the *Opinion on the Student Enrollment of the Institutes of higher learning in 1977* as submitted by the Ministry of Education, marking the official resumption of the system and a turning point in history.

In the winter of 1977, 5.7 million Chinese walked into the examination rooms for the college entrance exam. Later 273,000 were admitted. In 1978, 6.1 million sat for the exam and 402,000 were admitted. The year of 1977 students started college learning in the spring of 1978, and the Year of 1978 students started in autumn the same year, leaving only

1. *Selected Works of Deng Xiaoping: Volume 2* (Beijing: The People's Press, 1994), 37.

six months in between. The total number of 11.8 million examinees for the two exams set the record for China and even for the world in the history of exams. The resumption of the system brought talent training back to a healthy development track. According to the statistics, since the resumption of the exam, over 10 million undergraduate students and 600,000 postgraduate students have entered the job market in succession (Table 5.1).

Before the 1980s, the structure of higher education was unbalanced, with mostly undergraduates, few three-year college graduates and even fewer graduates, which failed to accommodate the need of social development. In 1978, among the 866,900 students at college, 856,000 were undergraduates or three-year college students and only 10,900 were postgraduates, leaving the ratio to 78.5:1. In 1980, *the Regulations of the People's Republic of China on Academic Degrees* was promulgated, dividing academic degrees into three categories: Bachelor, master, and doctorate. It was also proposed that the population of postgraduate students would be enlarged. In 1981, the total number of students at college amounted to 1,279,500, with 21,600 postgraduate students, changing the ratio to 58.2:1. After the promulgation of the *Decision on the Reform of the Education System of the Central Government* in 1985, the structure was further optimized. In 1986, the ratio of postgraduate students, undergraduates and three-year college students was 1:10.4:5.8. Since the 1990s, with the further expansion of higher education in China, the students at college (excluding non-graduating education) amounted to 5,839,000 in 1996, among which 165,000 were postgraduate students (including 35,000 PhD candidates), a 14.14-time increase compared to that of 1978. Since the start of the twenty-first century, graduate education has grown even faster (Figure 5.1).

Meanwhile postdoctoral stations were also set up in China, with the first group of 102 stations from 72 institutions approved in 1985. Today there are over 900 postdoctoral stations in 300 institutes of higher learning, covering 70 level-one disciplines of 12 disciplinary majors including science, engineering, agriculture, and medical and social science. While in 1985 only one postdoctoral student was enrolled, in 2007 there were altogether 7,903 of them. Between 1985 and 2007, 51,768 postdoctoral students were enrolled.

5.2.2 The Rolling Out of Elementary Education

The improvement of higher education and the training of research talents cannot be separated from the rolling out of elementary education. Investment in human capital should first go to elementary education, so that more people may be trained to contribute to general human capital, and gradually move upward to pursue skills contributing to professional human capital. During the Reform and Opening Up process over three decades, China has made brilliant progress in elementary education. On January 1, 2001, the then President Jiang Zemin announced to the world that China had fulfilled the goal of the Nine-year Compulsory Education as planned. The data released from the fifth

Table 5.1 The development of higher education in China between 1978 and 2006

Year	No. of institutes of higher learning	No. of students enrolled (10,000)	No. of students at college per 1 million people
1978	598	40.2	8.9
1979	633	27.5	10.5
1980	675	28.1	11.6
1981	704	27.9	12.8
1982	715	31.5	11.4
1983	805	39.1	11.7
1984	902	47.5	13.4
1985	1,061	61.9	16.1
1986	1,054	57.2	17.5
1987	1,063	61.7	17.9
1988	1,075	67.0	18.6
1989	1,075	59.7	18.5
1990	1,075	60.9	18.0
1991	1,075	62.0	17.6
1992	1,053	75.4	18.6
1993	1,065	92.4	21.4
1994	1,080	90.0	23.4
1995	1,054	92.6	24.0
1996	1,032	96.6	24.7
1997	1,020	100.0	25.7
1998	1,022	108.4	27.3
1999	1,071	159.7	34.3
2000	1,041	220.6	43.9
2001	1,225	268.3	56.3
2002	1,496	320.5	70.2
2003	1,552	382.2	85.8
2004	1,731	447.3	102.6
2005	1,792	504.5	119.4
2006	1,867	546.1	132.3

Source: China Education Statistical Yearbook, 1978–1981; *China Science and Technology Statistical Yearbook*, 1997; *China Statistical Year Book*, 1984, 1997, 2004–2007.

national census on March 28, 2000 also showed that among the citizens in 31 provinces, autonomous regions, and municipal cities directly under the leadership of the central government, as well as the active army, illiteracy decreased to 85.07 million (people who

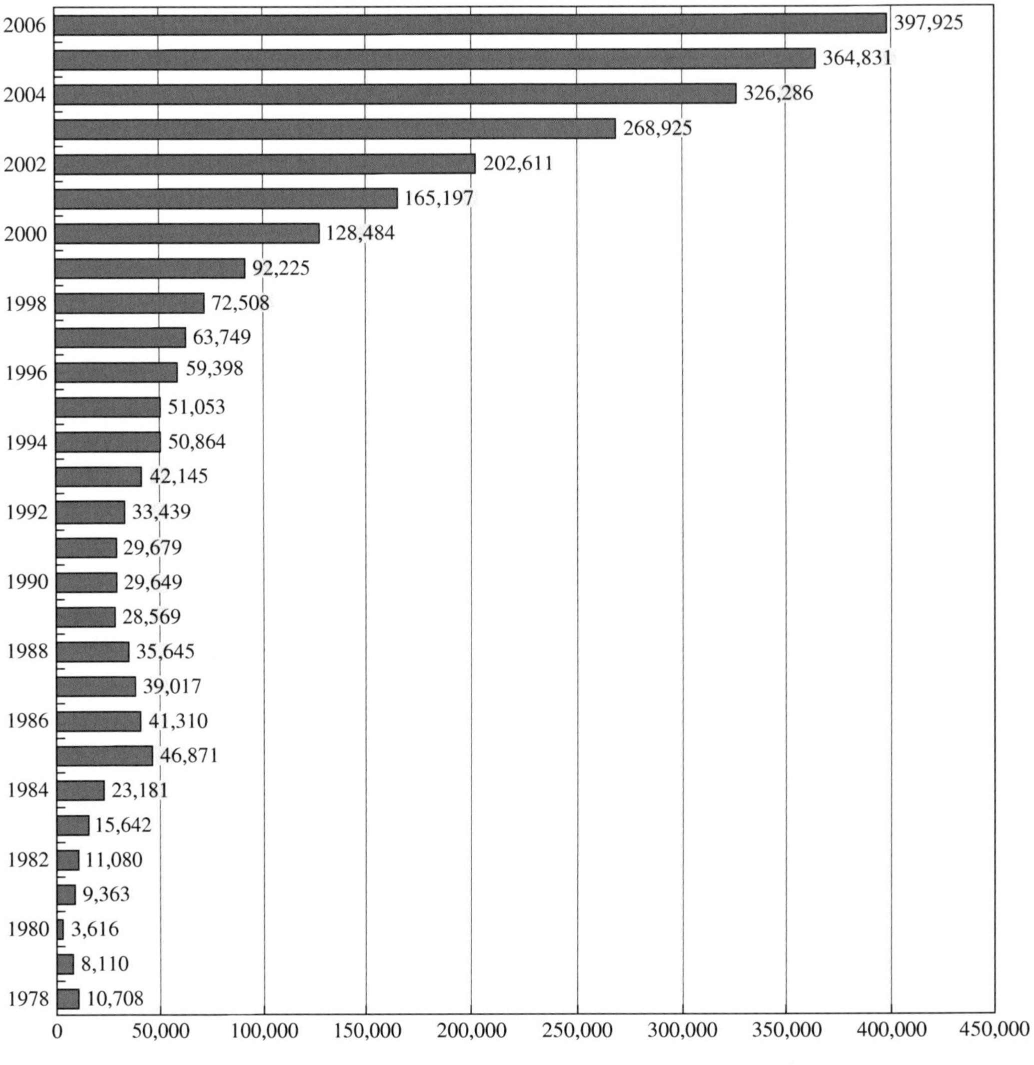

FIGURE 5.1 The size of postgraduate students between 1978 and 2006

Source: China Science and Technology Statistical Yearbook, 1997; *China Statistical Year Book*, 2007.

can read no words or few words at the age of 15 years and above), compared to the number collected in the third national census. The illiteracy ratio dropped from 38.1% to 6.72%, an annual decrease of 1.74%. Moreover, the illiteracy ratio of the young and middle aged has dropped to under 5%, meeting the strategic target of "eradicating young illiterates by the end of the twentieth century" as raised in the beginning of the 1990s.

The rolling out of elementary education and the quick drop in the illiteracy rate can be attributed to the continuous reform on the elementary education system over the last 30 years. In May 1985, it was proposed in the *Decision on the Reform of the Education System,* that "the responsibility of developing elementary education should be passed to the local authorities, to roll out the nine-year compulsory education plan step by step. The local governments at different levels are to take responsibility for the implementation of elementary education." In 1986 *The Compulsory Education Law of the People's Republic of China* was promulgated, giving first priority to the development of the nine-year compulsory education plan. In February 1988, *The Working Statutes on the Eradication of Illiteracy* was promulgated by the State Council, setting the target, mission, and policy measures and providing the legal base for the work. In 1992, the Chinese government formulated the plan on the eradication of young illiterates nationwide by 2000. "By 2000, in places where 90% of the population reside, illiteracy with people aged between 15 and 50 should be eradicated on the whole, raising the literacy ratio for the young and middle aged to 95%, and the sustainability ratio of eradication to 95%." In August 1993, the State Council revised *The Working Statutes on the Eradication of Illiteracy.* In July, 1994, in the *Guidelines on the Education Reform and Development of China*, it was reiterated that by the end of the twentieth century, the illiteracy ratio for the young and middle aged should be reduced to below 5%.

The achievement of the rolling out of the elementary education is considerable. In 2006, 98% of the population was covered by the nine-year compulsory education program. Altogether 2,973 counties (cities and districts, including 205 other county level administrative units) passed the check on the implementation of the nine-year compulsory education plan and the eradication of young and middle-aged illiterates, accounting for 96% of the national total. The rural illiteracy ratio dropped from 20.89% 20 years ago to 6.65%. The net ratio for primary school enrollment reached 99.27% (99.25% for boys and 99.29% for girls), the gross ratio for junior high school enrollment reached 97%. According to the statistics, the implementation of the *Compulsory Education Law* has brought benefit to 150 million rural students, 7.8 million boarding school students from poor families, and 28.21 million urban students. The rolling out of elementary education and the quick drop in the illiteracy rate has guaranteed the quality of the working population in China, and paved the way for the rolling out of higher education and training of senior talents.

5.2.3 The Development of Vocational Education

The major means of acquiring high-profile human capital is through college education for sure, yet in China, not every laborer is entitled to higher education, and vocational education comes up as an effective means of improving professional human capital.

Since the Reform and Opening Up process, vocational education has been growing fast. Figure 5.2 shows the number of students at vocational schools since 1978. As indicated by the figures, in 1978, the total number of students at vocational schools was

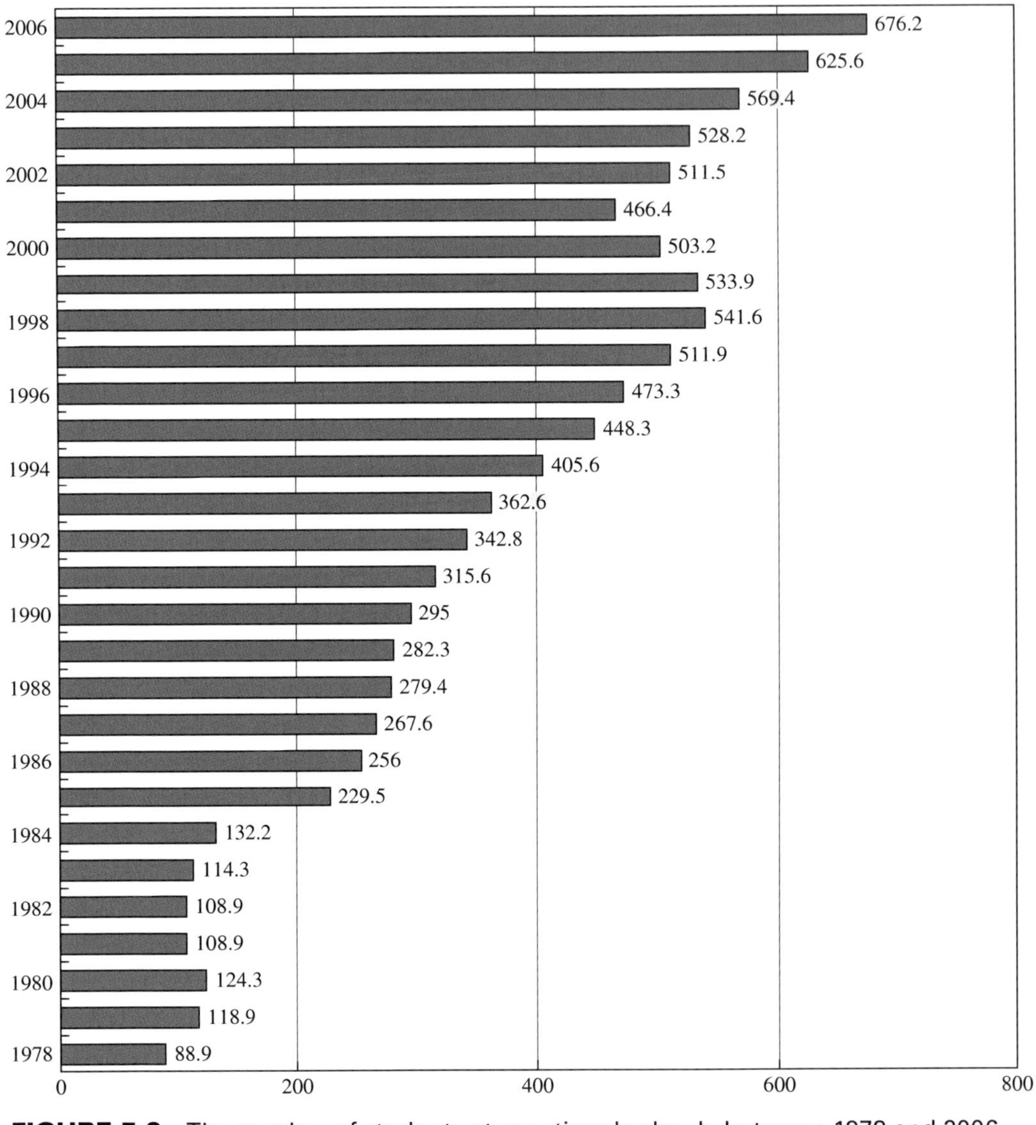

FIGURE 5.2 The number of students at vocational schools between 1978 and 2006 (Unit: 10,000 persons)

Source: China Statistical Year Book, 2007; *China Statistical Year Book*, 1985.

889,000. In 2006, it grew to 6,762,000, an increase of seven times. Over the 30 years, both the number of students at vocational schools and those graduated from vocational schools have been growing. For the two consecutive years of 2005 and 2006, China expanded the size of enrollment of the vocational schools by one million each year. In 2007, the total number of enrollment exceeded eight million, taking the total number of students at school to a record high of 21 million.

As for the higher education for adults, China has established all types of higher learning schools, TV and radio colleges, worker's colleges, farmer's colleges, correspondence universities, night colleges, cadre's colleges, and education schools to cater for the need of people at different education levels and in different sectors to further enhance human capital. In 2006, the total number of adults enrolled by the higher educational institutes amounted to three million, accounting for over half of the total number of college enrollment. Among the total number of 22,637,000 adult students at college, 5,249,000 were in the higher education institutes, accounting for 23.2% of the total. Yet in 1982, the total number of adult students at college was only 1,173,000, accounting for 6% of the total. As for discipline, adult higher education now covers a whole range of subjects including philosophy, economics, law, education, art, foreign language, history, science, engineering, medicine, and management.

5.2.4 Internationl Training and Flow of Talents

China is still a backward developing country, lagging behind in economy and science & technology as a result of backward education. In modern times, China has sent many talents abroad to receive advanced education, and this helped promote the development of the social economy. After the opening up in 1978, a new era of educational exchange and cooperation between the East and West has come.

History has proven that the cross-nation flow of education and human capital benefits the economy of both the source countries and the target countries. For example, the US is the largest beneficiary of the internationalized education and talent flow. According to the statistics, 40% of the technical immigrants worldwide ended up in the US, and most of them were originally from developing countries. Figures from the US National Science Foundation show that in 1995, among the 12 million science and engineering workers in the country, 72% were born in developing countries. Of the 7,000 companies in the Silicon Valley, 2,000 are founded by Chinese or have Chinese CEOs. Another survey shows that one-fifth of Silicon Valley engineers are of Chinese origin. The high-tech industry is well acknowledged as a driver of the US economy in recent years. In the computer industry alone, over 50% of PhDs are foreigners, and 7% of the research and technical staff in IBM and Microsoft were born in countries and regions other than the US, mostly in mainland China, Taiwan, and India. The rise of the US economy after

WWII cannot be separated from the large number of scientific talents and foreign students attracted to the US, among whom a considerable portion from China have made great contribution in the high-tech industry.

The advanced education methodology, the well-developed software and hardware facilities as well as the education system in the US are undeniably attractive to foreign talents. More and more Chinese have chosen to study in the US, and many of them stay in the US to work after graduation. The annual report of the International Education Research Institute shows that in 2006, China topped all countries by sending over 50,000 students to US colleges, an annual increase of 7%. According to the statistics from the Ministry of Education, between 1978 and 2004, altogether 814,000 Chinese went abroad for study, and only 198,000 of them returned. From 1957 till now, seven Chinese Americans have won the Nobel Prize (Yang Zhenning, Li Zhengdao, Ding Zhaozhong, Zhu Diwen, Cui Qi, Li Yuanzhe, and Qian Yongjian). With the exception of Zhu Diwen and Qian Yongjian, who grew up in the US, the other five only went to the US after obtaining their bachelor's or master's degrees in China. The brilliant contributions of the Chinese American scientists not only bring benefits to the US, but honor to all Chinese people as well.

Since the Reform and Opening Up process began, China has sent a large number of students abroad for further study. In early 1978, as advocated by Deng Xiaoping, China resumed the policy on sending students and scholars abroad for study. According to Deng, the main purpose was to bring back new information, new technologies and management expertise to China, so as to modernize the nation and catch up with the Western world. Shortly afterwards, the Chinese government formulated the talents policy accordingly to support studying abroad and encourage return upon graduation. Later, the government adopted the policy of "encouraging returnees to work in the home country or serve the home country in flexible ways." In the report of the 14th Congress, it was proposed that "the returnees are welcome to engage, support or help the modernization construction of the mother country in different ways." The past three decades have seen the largest number of students both going abroad and returning in history.

Table 5.2 shows the variance of students going abroad and returning since the beginning of the Reform and Opening Up process. The exhibit shows that since 1978, both figures grew year on year, and as indicated by the last column, among the graduates with master's degree seeking for jobs in China, a large portion has studied abroad. In 2000, the percentage climbed to a historical high of 18.2%, and then dropped a bit in the following years, mainly because of the expansion on college admission since 1999, resulting in a larger population of postgraduate students after 2001. The absolute increase in number is still evident. Also, according to the statistics published by the Ministry of

Table 5.2 The number of Chinese students studying abroad and the percentage of returnees between 1978 and 2006

			No. of Returnees	
Year	No. of masters from Chinese colleges	No. of people going abroad	Annual figure	% of total graduates
1978	9	860	248	96.5%
1979	140	1,777	231	62.3%
1980	476	2,124	162	25.4%
1981	11,669	2,922	1,143	8.9%
1982	4,058	2,326	2,116	34.3%
1983	4,497	2,633	2,303	33.9%
1984	2,756	3,073	2,920	51.4%
1985	17,004	4,888	1,424	7.7%
1986	16,950	4,676	1,388	7.6%
1987	27,603	4,703	1,605	5.5%
1988	40,838	3,786	3,000	6.8%
1989	37,232	3,329	1,753	4.5%
1990	35,440	2,950	1,593	4.3%
1991	32,537	2,900	2,069	6.0%
1992	25,692	6,540	3,611	12.3%
1993	28,214	10,742	5,128	15.4%
1994	28,047	19,071	4,230	13.1%
1995	31,877	20,381	5,750	18.0%
1996	39,652	20,905	6,570	14.2%
1997	46,539	22,410	7,130	13.5%
1998	47,077	17,622	7,379	13.6%
1999	54,670	23,749	7,748	12.4%
2000	58,767	38,989	9,121	13.4%
2001	67,809	83,973	12,243	15.3%
2002	80,841	125,179	17,945	18.2%
2003	111,091	117,307	20,152	15.4%
2004	150,777	114,682	24,726	14.1%
2005	189,728	118,515	34,987	15.6%
2006	255,902	134,000	42,000	14.1%

Source: Comprehensive Statistical Data on 50 Years of New China; China Statistical Year Book, 2007.

Note: All returnees are counted as graduates. The percentage reflects the proportion of returnees coming back to China for work after completion of study abroad among all graduates seeking for jobs in China in the same years.

Education in 2007, compared to 2006, 2007 saw 10,000 more students going abroad, increasing the total to 144,000. The total number of returnees was 44,000, among which 4,302 were government sponsored, 4,211 were organization sponsored, and 36,000 were self-sponsored. From 1978 to 2007, altogether 1,211,700 people went abroad for study, and 319,700 returned, accounting for 26.3% of the total. Currently 892,000 people are still abroad, among which 657,200 are engaging in the undergraduate, postgraduate, PhD, and postdoctoral study, or conducting academic activities.

Figure 5.3 further describes the variance in the number of people going abroad and returning between 1978 and 2006. As indicated by the figure, from 1978 onward, both numbers rose dramatically, but the former grew faster, particularly after 1999. This reflects the fact that in the early years, most of those going abroad were officially sponsored, making the ratio of return higher. Figure 5.3 indicates that before 1988, the gap between the two numbers was still small. After 1988, especially after 1991, with the number of self-sponsored students exceeding the officially sponsored, the gap between the two numbers quickly widened.

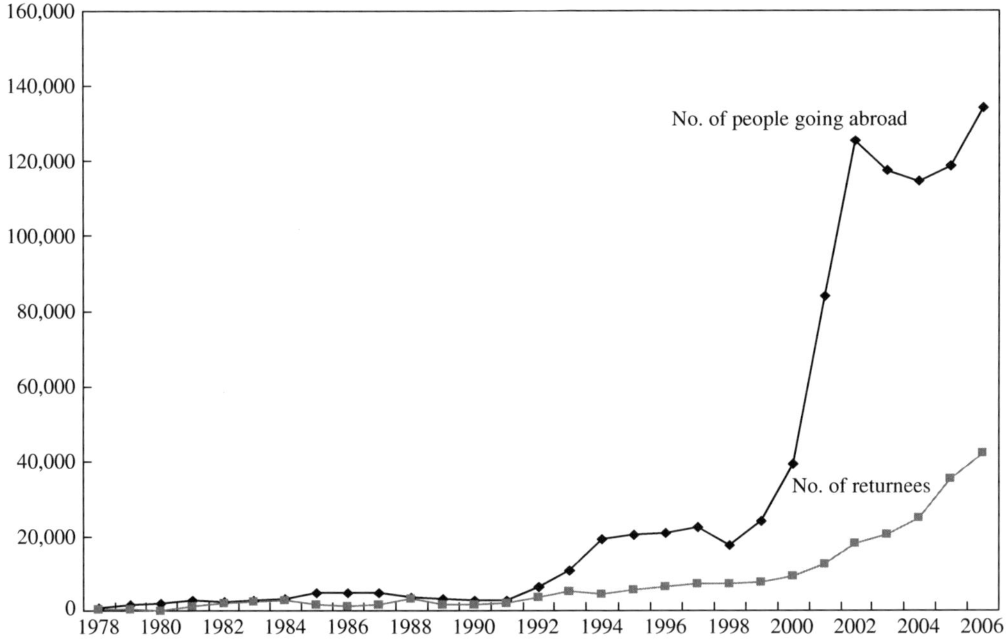

FIGURE 5.3 Distribution of the students returned upon completion of study abroad between 1978 and 2006

Source: Created with the data in Table 5.2.

In such a context, both the central and local government at different levels have been providing supportive policies to encourage students to come back to China to work or start a business. As a consequence, since the mid-1990s, the number of returnees increased considerably. With world-class technologies, resourceful connections, and updated information and knowledge brought back, they are better at attracting funds than those who have never been abroad. It is fair to say that the returnees have higher human capital and are more capable of internalizing the knowledge obtained abroad, and may consequently create greater value.

Upon coming back to the homeland, the returnees have contributed a tremendous amount to the development of the economy in China. According to the statistics, of all the fellows with the Chinese Academy of Sciences, 81% are returnees. Of all the fellows with the Chinese Academy of Engineering, 54% are returnees (excluding the newly elected ones), and of all the chief scientists of the "863 Plan" during the ninth Five-year Period, 72% are returnees. Of all the colleges under the direct leadership of the Ministry of Education, 77.6% of the chancellors on term studied abroad before, and 62.3% of the postdoctoral tutors are returnees. Among the 445 professors of the "Cheung Kong Scholars Program" of the Ministry of Education, 410 are returnees, accounting for 92% of the total. The returnees are not only active in academic circles, but also in business circles, with many successful businessmen either having graduated from prestigious universities in Europe or the US, or worked before in well-known MNCs (see Table 5.3). These experiences have been of great help to businesses, and recent years have seen more returnees starting their own businesses in China: By the end of 2006, over 70 venture parks had been built for the returnees, with over 15,000 returnees from 5,000 companies moving in. The annual output exceeded RMB 10 billion. These people have brought back state-of-the-art technologies, new knowledge, new concepts, and management expertise, and have made great contributions to economic development in China.

5.3 Science Accumulation and International Exchange of Science and Knowledge Capital

5.3.1 Introduction, Learning, and Popularization of Scientific Technologies

The gap between China and the world is still large in terms of science and technology, which is the gap of knowledge reflecting the accumulation of knowledge capital. However, the existence of the gap also implies the late development advantage for China. When China lacks the capability for independent innovation, it may acquire knowledge

Table 5.3 List of the returnee entrepreneurs

Name	Title	Education	Working experience
Ding Jian	Chairman, Aisainfo	MS, University of California	—
Tian Shuoning	President, China Netcom	PhD, Texas Institute of Technology	—
Wu Ying	CEO of UT Starcom	MS, New Jersey Institute of Technology	—
Zhang Chaoyang	President of Sohu.com	PhD, MIT	—
Zhu Min	Vice President of BOC	PhD, Hopkins University	—
Shi Zhengfu	Chairman, Comway Capital	PhD, The University of Maryland	—
Zhu Jia	Partner, Bain Capital	—	10 years in Morgan Stanley
Liang Jianzhang	CEO of Ctrip.com	MS, Georgia Institute of Technology	—
Ding Lei	CEO of Netease.com	—	Engineer of Sybase China
Shi Zhengrong	Wuxi Suntech	PhD, The University of New South Wales	—
Li Ge	President of Pharmatechs	PhD, Columbia University	—
Tang Jun	Ex-President of Snda.com	—	President of Microsoft China
Qin Xiao	Chairman of China Merchant Bank	PhD, Cambridge University	—
Liang Jiaju	Chairman of Ping'an Insurance	—	AIG; Prudential Group

through introduction and learning. Over the 30 years, by translating and importing foreign books and literature, by conducting international exchange and cooperation, and by employing foreign experts and organizing overseas study visits, the gap has been shortened and knowledge capital has been accumulated in a cost-effective way.

The introduction, learning and popularization of scientific knowledge is first of all reflected in the translation and publishing of foreign books. According to the statistics from the Chinese libraries, between 1978 and 1990, altogether 28,500 kinds of books were translated and published, and between 1995 and 2004, altogether 107,500 kinds of translated books were published (excluding the retranslated ones and the ones with multiple editions).The translation and publishing of these books broadened the horizons of the Chinese people.

From the 1980s, China started to import a large amount of the book copyrights. In the early 1980s, a few forward-looking publishing houses started to approach foreign publishing houses. The Science Press, for example, sent groups of people abroad to seek for business opportunities, and to join all types of book exhibitions. With the deepening of the opening up, a growing number of publishing houses began to import books. According to the statistics of the General Administration of Press and Publication, between 1995 and 1999, 20,700 foreign copyrights were traded in China, and between 1999 and 2004, the number grew to 54,100. Figure 5.4 shows the import of book copyrights since 2000. Between 2000 and 2006, altogether 68,716 copyrights were imported. The number increased fast before 2003, and has remained stable at 10,000 per year since then. As for the source, the US, the UK, Germany, and Japan topped all countries. In 2006, the top ten source countries or regions for copyright were: The US, the UK, Taiwan, Japan, South Korea, Germany, France, Singapore, Hong Kong, and Canada, with the US being No. 1 for years. Figure 5.5 further shows the copyrights imported to mainland China from the above countries and regions.

These figures indicate the fact that the industrial and technical books took up the largest portion, with 1,323 in 2005 and 1,258 in 2006. Following were books on science, education and economy. Books from the US, the UK, and Japan accounted for 63% of the total industrial and technical category, most of which were academic books on theory and applied sciences. The mass import of foreign copyrights paved the way for the learning and popularization of scientific knowledge in China.

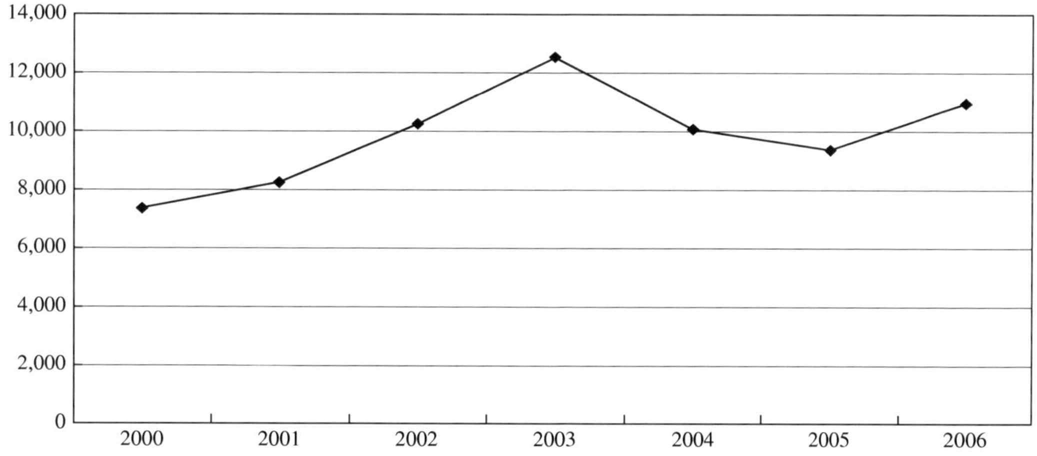

FIGURE 5.4 Number of imported copyrights from 2000 to 2006

Source: The General Administration of Press and Publication, *Report of the Publishing Industry of China* (2005–2006) (Beijing: China Renmin University Press, 2008), 176.

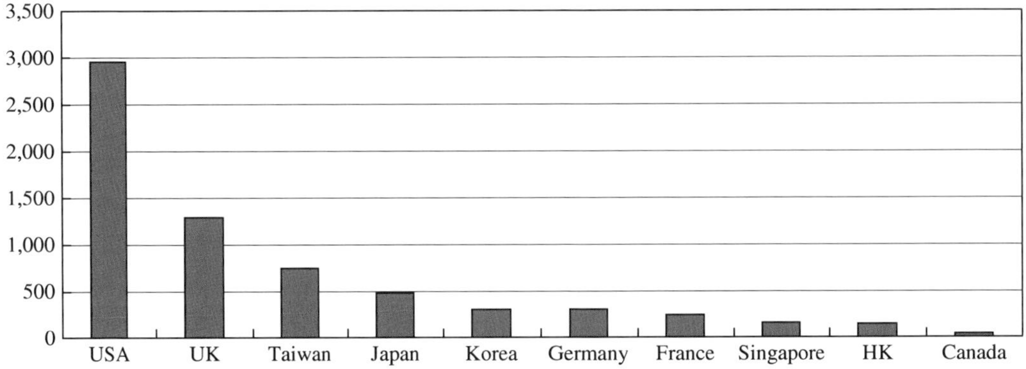

FIGURE 5.5 The top ten source countries and regions for the copyrights imported by mainland China in 2006.

Source: Report of the Publishing Industry of China (2005–2006), 169.

5.3.2 International Exchange and Cooperation on Science and Technology

Before the Reform and Opening Up process, most exchange and cooperation on science and technology was limited to developing countries and a few East European countries, in the form of personnel exchange. In 1983, Deng Xiaoping emphasized the importance of utilizing foreign intelligence, and in the same year, the Chinese government decided to introduce foreign intelligence, and set up a central working team. Over the past 25 years, in the principle of "equality and mutual benefit, fruit sharing, the protection of IPR, compliance with the international practice," the international exchange and cooperation on science and technology boomed, with smooth traffic incoming and outgoing, widened scope for collaboration, growing magnitude, and flexible manner.

Today China has established the exchange and cooperation relationship on science and technology with 152 countries and regions, and has entered into collaboration agreements or economic and trade agreements with 96 of them. Within the framework of the intergovernmental cooperation, various ministries have also signed agreements with international counterparts. For example, the Ministry of Agriculture has established an exchange and cooperation relationship with the FAO and the agriculture departments of over 100 countries, and signed cooperation agreements with over 20 of them. The Ministry of Health has signed health cooperation agreements or MOU with 52 countries. The State Bureau of Quality and Technical Supervision has joined 24 international organizations, and established cooperation and exchange relationships with over 50 countries. China National Nuclear Corporation has signed cooperation agreements on the peaceful utilization of nuclear energy with 16 countries. China is equally active with multilateral cooperation. According to the statistics, there are altogether over 6,000 bilateral, regional, or global cooperation programs on science and technology, as well as hundreds of bilateral or multilateral cooperation funds. China has joined over 1,000 international cooperative organizations on science and technology, and has set up the China-APEC Scientific Technology Cooperation Fund, China-Australia Scientific Technology Cooperation Fund, China-Israel Technical Cooperation Fund, and so on.

With support and encouragement from the government, China has also achieved eye-catching progress in the semi-official and nongovernmental exchange and cooperation on science and technology, with active exchange among research institutes, colleges, academic organizations, enterprises, cities, and individual scientists. According to the statistics, by the end of 2003, the National Natural Science Foundation of China had signed 58 cooperation agreements with related counterparts from 38 countries and regions, with 10%–20% of the total expense earmarked for international exchange and cooperation programs, such as international (regional) cooperation research programs, international academic conferences overseas, international academic conferences in China, and the short-term lecturing of the overseas scholars in China. There were also special funds for the international cooperation with national key labs, and joint scientific research funds with the National Natural Science Foundation-HK United Financial Assistance Bureau. The Chinese Academy of Sciences has established cooperation relationship with over 60 countries and regions. There are over 80 institute level agreements, nearly 1,000 department level agreements, 15,000 inbound and outbound visits, and 100 international and bilateral conferences held annually. Nearly 400 scientists are taking roles at different levels in over 400 international scientific organizations and institutions. Also, the China Association of Science and Technology has established exchange and cooperation relationships with organizations from over 30 countries and regions, and signed over 50 bilateral exchange and cooperation agreements.

Attending international academic conferences and organizing international conferences are also important means of international scientific exchange. The National Natural Science Foundation, the Chinese Academy of Sciences, and many colleges are all supportive financially to the international conferences. In 2002 alone, the National Natural Science Foundation sponsored 1,016 scientists in attending international academic conferences, with a total sum of RMB 10.48 million given. It also sponsored the convening of 271 international conferences in China, with a total sum of RMB 13.24 million given, among which the more influential ones with larger sponsorship were the International Mathematician Conference, the International Rice Conference, the International Macromolecule Conference, the 13th Pacific Nuclear Energy Conference, the Second International Sustainable Agriculture Conference, and so on. In the same year, the China Association of Science and Technology held 236 international academic conferences in China, with 52,000 participants, including 18,960 coming from abroad. A total of 27,060 papers were exchanged during the conferences.

Meanwhile China has also sent many people abroad to partner with foreign research institutes, or set up joint laboratories for collaboration. China is also actively engaging in the major international science programs and is gradually opening its own scientific programs. During the 10th Five-year Plan period, the "Major International Scientific Cooperation Program" was proposed for the first time. The program officially started in 2001, to support the engaging of Chinese scientists in major international research programs in areas of space technology, high energy physics, exploration, and development of the polar region, life science, biotechnology, biodiversity, resources, environment, and human health, and cooperation with developed countries and scientific powers in the field of information technology, life science technology, new material technology, energy science technology, high-tech agriculture, advanced manufacturing technology, automation technology, ocean technology, and environment technology. In 2002, China officially started the opening of the high-tech development plans and major basic research plans to the outside, extending the area of scientific research and cooperation, and boosting the existing cooperation to a new high. Up to now, the sixth framework program of the EU has been fully opened to China, and a number of projects are now in the verification process. The national 863 high-tech development program and the 973 basic research program are also open to the EU.

5.3.3 Engaging Foreign Technical/Management Experts

Shortly after the People's Republic of China was founded, China invited a large number of technical and management experts from the former USSR to assist 156 major projects in China, and this unveiled the import of intelligence to new China. The size of foreign experts has been growing all the time. Over the 30 years, China has established an all-round, widely ranged, and multichanneled structure for the import of foreign intelligence. While the Chinese government has been active in bringing talents in, the rapid economic growth has also attracted increasingly more expatriates to come voluntarily. Recent years saw a growing number of Americans (including Chinese Americans) and Europeans moving to the Chinese mainland.

The investment and operation of MNCs in China has created a huge demand for overseas talents. With the extension of such demand, many foreigners have found their places in the administration, education and research, legal consulting, wealth management, and other professions. For those coming to China, quick modernization and internationalization is the biggest attraction. Local enterprises have also become aware of the significance of bringing talents, and have enhanced their efforts on the import of technical and management experts.

Up to 2002, the State Bureau of Foreign Experts Affairs alone had established talents exchange and cooperation relationships with 320 governmental organizations, social bodies, universities, and international organizations of 54 countries. In addition, some well-known civil organizations such as the China Association for International Exchange of Personnel, the Chinese People's Association for Friendship with Foreign Countries, the Chinese Association of Science and Technology, and the China International Center for Economic and Technical Exchanges have also set up working relations with international counterparts, diversifying the channel for talents import. Also, with the gradual opening of the talent market in China, a group of international agencies have come to the Chinese market through joint investment, providing new options for importing overseas talents. With the healthy interaction between government, civil organizations, agencies, and enterprises, a solid foundation has been built for the import of talents.

According to the statistics from the China Association for International Exchange of Personnel, between 1978 and 1999, China imported altogether 824,000 foreign experts, and since the twenty-first century, each year over 400,000 foreign talents come to work in China. According to the statistics, in 2001, China had altogether 440,000 experts coming from Hong Kong, Macau, Taiwan, and other countries, among which 249,000 were from other countries, accounting for 56.6% of the total. The top five source countries, excluding Hong Kong, Macau, and Taiwan, were Japan, the US, South Korea, Germany, and Russia. In 2003, the number dropped somewhat due to the SARS outbreak, with 390,000 experts arriving for the whole year, among which 205,000 were on short-term contract and 185,000 on long-term contract. In 2005, altogether 480,000 experts were employed, including 340,000 from other countries, accounting for 70.83% of the total. Besides, the central fiscal budget set aside a special fund of RMB 3 billion for the employment of foreign technical and management experts as well as the sponsorship to the locals for overseas training. In 2006, 2,649 graduates with master's or doctoral degrees from overseas started research work in China via research projects, and 314 senior experts were employed to enhance the international cooperation in some specific research programs. The overseas talents not only brought advanced technical and management experiences to the enterprises, but also helped to build the technical tracking and R&D systems worldwide, enhancing the competitive power of enterprises in the overseas market with bidding, sales, and after sales service.

To give honor to those foreign experts with excellent contribution to the economic and social development of China, the Chinese government set up the "Friendship Award" of the paramount honor. Each year about 50 foreign experts are chosen for this award. Since the first award was given in 1991, 999 experts from 58 countries have won this honor.

In recent years, the international exchange and cooperation of talents has come to a new stage. The China Association for International Exchange of Personnel alone has established regular exchange relationships with 370 agencies from home and abroad, and built 19 international talent markets. The range of talent import has also been further widened. For example, to address the "Three Rural Issues," many groups of agriculture experts have been brought in; to balance the regional development and implement the project of importing overseas talents to the western region, 150,000 overseas experts were employed to work in western China and 30,000 people from western China were sent abroad for training between 2002 and 2007. To construct an innovative society, the "Scientific Innovation and Intellectual Introduction Program of Institutes of higher learning," the "Overseas Teachers Program," and the "International Partnership Program on Scientific Innovation" were established. To build social harmony, the program called "Light of Harmony" was adopted to raise the proportion of foreign experts in the medical health, community construction, social security, and cultural sectors.

5.3.4 Visits and Investigation Trips Abroad

China follows a parallel way of bringing in foreign intelligence and sending out locals for study. While promoting the international scientific exchange and cooperation by employing foreign technical and management experts, more Chinese scientists have been sent abroad to conduct site visits and investigations. Take the Chinese Academy of Sciences as an example. Over the 30 years, more than 10,000 scientists and researchers have been sent to the US for study. Among the officials and elite of the research institutes under the leadership of the Chinese Academy of Sciences, most have overseas working or studying experience. In 2008, the Foundation College of China Scholarship Council sent notice to all colleges, enterprises, government organizations, and research institutes on the selection of visiting scholars (including postdoctoral researchers) nationwide. Key disciplines such as energy, resources, environment, agriculture, manufacturing, and information, as well as the strategic disciplines including life science, space, ocean, nanometer, and new materials were covered in the program.

Table 5.4 shows the number of overseas visits, trainings, and exhibitions attended and the number of participants since the mid-1990s. The table indicates different trends for the three types of activities between 1995 and 2006. The number of overseas visits reached a peak in 1996, with 11,115 visits, and the number of visitors reached a peak in 1997, with 30,499 visitors. After 1996, while the number of visits dropped occasionally, the total number of visitors grew moderately, revealing a twofold fact: While the desire for studying abroad remained strong, with the development of the economy, China has trained a large number of local talents within the country. Also the localization strategy of MNCs in China presented the opportunity to learn advanced skills within China.

Table 5.4 Visits, trainings, and exhibitions abroad between 1995 and 2006

	Visit		Training		Exhibition	
Year	No. of visits	No. of participants	No. of training sessions	No. of participants	No. of exhibitions	No. of participants
1995	6,133	21,578	2,687	12,127	496	3,729
1996	11,115	29,338	2,796	11,852	374	3,661
1997	8,984	30,499	2,909	10,733	482	3,809
1998	5,222	19,322	1,754	6,754	407	2,296
1999	6,167	20,833	2,410	8,912	491	3,545
2000	5,825	20,568	1,836	6,425	293	2,023
2001	5,903	21,574	1,834	7,218	224	1,447
2002	7,104	27,605	1,794	6,826	292	2,983
2003	4,796	20,061	1,339	5,690	267	2,392
2004	5,695	25,365	1,340	6,022	450	2,493
2005	6,218	23,335	1,593	7,520	577	3,086
2006	6,603	27,300	1,945	2,300	571	3,754

Source: China Science and Technology Statistical Yearbook, 2001, 2007.

Since the mid-1990s, both the number of exhibitions held abroad and the number of participants have grown, indicating the fact that the progress in science and technology has provided us the qualification and opportunity for more exhibitions abroad.

5.4 "Learning by Doing" in the International Processing Trade

5.4.1 The Learning by Doing Effect in the International Processing Trade

Since Guangdong province took the first order of processing trade with supplied materials in 1978, the Chinese processing trade has been developing over 30 years. After 1993, with the deepening and enlarging of the opening up process, MNCs from Europe, the US, and Japan started to bring mature technologies and working procedures into China. Since the first bonded zone was established in Waigaoqiao, Shanghai in 1990, 15 more bonded zones have been built in Dalian, Tianjin, and other places. With the operational environment improving, FIEs quickly became the dominant body of the processing trade. Meanwhile the product structure has also shifted from the labor-intensive type to the labor/technology/capital-intensive type, with high-tech products and machinery products becoming the major products processed. With the competition among

MNCs getting fiercer, more of the noncore production, marketing, logistics, and R&D and even some of the noncore design work are outsourced to local Chinese enterprises or specialized companies, accelerating the diffusion and transfer of knowledge from MNCs to local processing enterprises. Through learning by doing, the Chinese processing enterprises have translated the knowledge to competence, and enhanced both the enterprise human capital and individual human capital.

The "learning by doing" effect is initially reflected in the transfer of knowledge. With the products processed getting increasingly sophisticated, more advanced technologies and management expertise are transferred. Also, when the processing enterprises become more capable with knowledge acquired, the more competent ones may transfer knowledge to the less competent ones, so the human capital of the latter can also be enhanced. In practice, since China is already a key base for the global manufacturing business, MNCs are transferring purchasing, processing, assembling to China as driven by cost, and bringing technologies, management expertise, and capital to China as driven by market. With the market competition in China also getting fiercer, MNCs are now forced to move their regional R&D centers, operation headquarters, and regional logistic centers to China. As a consequence, Chinese enterprises have become more competent through learning by doing.

A typical example is Suzhou, Jiangsu. In the 1990s, the IT assembling enterprises from Taiwan started to invest in Suzhou and Kunshan in the form of KD (knocked down), CKD (completely knocked down), and SKD (semi-knocked down). After that, FIEs became the new point of growth for the local economy. After 1993, many MNCs came to Suzhou to build production bases, with the finished products delivered directly to the international market. The foreign investors not only brought in capital, technologies, management expertise and information through "learning by doing," but also helped the local processing enterprises with resource allocation and productivity enhancement. The product structure has also changed from textiles and hardware to machinery and high-tech. Today, exports from Suzhou are mostly computers and telecommunications equipment (like desktop PC, laptop PC, mouse, keyboard, CD driver, LCD, automatic digit processing component, and so on). On the basis of "learning by doing," local enterprises have improved innovation capacity, and are now shifting to the high end of processing such as IC, software development, and so on.

Unlike Suzhou, the international trade in Ningbo, Zhejiang still follows the traditional model with mostly normal trade and little processing trade. Though located in the Yangtze River Delta with favorable conditions for developing processing trade, by the end of 2002, there were only 911 processing trade enterprises in Ningbo, lagging behind the national average, not to mention the developed region. Today most of the processing businesses are still processing with supplied material for traditional products. By comparing the trade gains of Suzhou and Ningbo, it is easy to see that the contribution of processing trade to the local economy in Suzhou is much larger. As for the reasons behind this, on one hand, Suzhou has benefited more from the "learning by doing" effect in the operation of processing trade. On the other hand, Suzhou has brought in the advanced technologies and management expertise through operation, with knowledge later transferred from one industry to many other industries. In recent years, Ningbo has also strengthened the effort on developing processing trade.

5.4.2 The Learning by Doing Effect in the Garment Industry

The garment industry as a major branch of the textiles industry represents well the international processing trade in China. The general rule of industrialization and economic development indicates that the textile industry has always been a leading industry in the early stage of industrialization of a country or region, with textile products and garment becoming the major exported goods afterwards. With the globalization of the economy, and the upgrade of economic structure in all countries, the garment industry is gradually changing from a labor-intensive industry to a capital-intensive one, and the worldwide pattern of garment production and sales is changing with the joint force of capital/technology advantage from developed countries, and labor cost advantage from developing countries. After 30 years of development, a comprehensive industrial structure has been established for the garment industry, from the simple processing with supplied materials to the sophisticated production of ready-to-wear. Since 1994, China has become the largest garment manufacturer and exporter of the world, with products exported to Italy, Hong Kong, Germany, France, Turkey, India, Indonesia, South Korea, and Thailand.

As the industry with the longest history of opening up, the Chinese garment industry has already been integrated into the world system of labor division. Since the 1980s, the garment enterprises from Hong Kong and Taiwan have slowly moved the processing business to the mainland, especially the Pearl River Delta. Advanced technology and management expertise pushed the development of the local garment industry. Between the end of the 1980s and the beginning of the 1990s, with the improvement of product quality, operation, processing technology, and management expertise, many international players chose to outsource the processing business to China, and the overall processing and quality management of the Chinese garment industry moved closer to meeting international standards. Demand in the international market also provided space for the further development of the Chinese garment industry. Since China's accession to the WTO in 2001, its garment industry has accelerated its integration into the global division of labor, and enhanced its position in the global manufacturing network. Currently seven of the top ten men's brands are processed and exported from China. Through "learning by doing," the Chinese garment enterprises have been improving the production technologies and almost represent the top world level today.

The interviews and questionnaires on 86 garment processing enterprises in Kunshan and Dongguan reveal the optimization and upgrading of the processing business in many dimensions (Liu Dexue 2006). Since the Reform and Opening Up process, products processed in China have become more diversified in category and brand, covering the simple designs such as underwear, T-shirt, shirt, and the more sophisticated designs such as suit, coat, and dress. Of all the enterprises under investigation, 70.9% adopt the OEM model for processing, and 19.8% adopt ODM, leaving very few enterprises adopting the simple processing model. Also, a few enterprises with years of experience with OEM and ODM have started to establish their own brands and test the international market. The fact that most of these enterprises had been on close working terms with the top brands indicates that more contact with leading manufacturers brings more chance to learn the core technologies. Most enterprises have mastered the common technologies of the foreign companies, and some have even mastered the international leading technologies. On the whole, the processing capacity of the Chinese garment enterprises has been boosted, and the basic techniques have been improved. Almost all the sizable enterprises have adopted the modernized and standardized assembling line production, and normative management. Finally through continuous learning, Chinese enterprises have managed to upgrade in the network system, and created international competitive power in the processing part of the value chain, and built a foundation for independent design and branding.

Take Youngor as an example. Started with RMB 20,000 in 1979, it has grown into a big modern group company with net assets of over RMB 3 billion, and has been the leader of the Chinese garment industry over the 30 years of development. In 2007, the *Global Entrepreneur* and Roland Berger jointly organized the election of "the Most Competitive Chinese Companies of the World in 2007," and Youngor was shortlisted among the top 25.

The story of Youngor is a typical Chinese success story of diligence, innovation, and hard work. In the start-up days, Youngor was only a workshop with ten workers and a few sewing machines. Compared to other garment enterprises, there was no competitive edge at all. It was the Reform and Opening Up process that brought opportunities to this small workshop. In the 1980s, the Chinese garment enterprises started to take orders of processing with supplied materials, and Youngor grasped the opportunity to learn the technologies and management expertise from abroad to expand business. The late 1980s and the early 1990s was the time when the whole industry moved closer to the international standard in processing technology, product quality, operation philosophy, and management expertise. Youngor also managed to improve technology, craftsmanship, quality, and management through practice, and started to embark on the OEM road. In this way Youngor quickly integrated into the global market, and mastered the manufacturing technologies and development trend of the international brands through

OEM. Meanwhile Youngor continued to bring in advanced manufacturing technologies and management expertise to expand the production scale. Since the mid-1990s, Youngor has been growing fast as an industry leader and successfully changed its position from a manufacturing enterprise to a marketing enterprise.

Over the 30 years, the "learning by doing" effect has been fully reflected in the development of the enterprise. In the early ODM stage, Youngor learned a great amount of advanced technologies, craftsmanship, management expertise, marketing experiences and branding management from the international players, with which Youngor developed its own brand, own products and own marketing network. With this approach, Youngor gradually becomes a name with international reputation, and created a miracle in the history of the Chinese garment industry.

5.4.3 The Learning by Doing Effect in the IT Industry

While the low-tech processing trade is represented by the garment industry, the high-tech processing trade is represented by the computer industry. For the extensive association of computer/periphery equipment with both the upstream and downstream industries, it is the most representative high-tech industry in China. Statistics in 2007 shows that in 2006, the total value of processing trade amounted to US$245.82 billion, accounting for 87.3% of the total export, among which the computer and telecommunications products accounted for four-fifths of the total export.

As for the development of the computer industry, before the Reform and Opening Up process, the industry went through a hard journey with rigid policy and limited domestic resources. Since 1978, the cheap and abundant skilled workers in China have attracted avalanching orders from MNCs, most of which were from Taiwan. The worldwide price drop of computers and periphery equipment, together with the cost increase in Taiwan, pushed manufacturers to transfer the production of mature products like keyboard and mouse to Fujian and the Pearl River Delta. The operation of the Taiwanese enterprises not only drove the development of the computer processing business in China, but also equipped Chinese enterprises with technologies and the capability to take orders from the global buyers as low-end suppliers. Between the late 1980s and mid-1990s, with more attention given to R&D and marketing, MNCs expanded the efforts on outsourcing, and China became the recipient of capital, technologies, and industry from developed countries. Also, with the achievement of the Reform and Opening Up process becoming noticeable, the development of the domestic market made China more attractive. Enterprises from Japan, the US, South Korea, and Western Europe placed more ODM orders in China, and Taiwanese enterprises further expanded operation by moving production to the Pearl River Delta and the Yangtze River Delta. The transfer of the production enterprises also gave rise to the collective move of the enterprises producing supporting goods. With the accumulation of capital and technology, some private enterprises in Shenzhen, Kunshan, and Suzhou gradually became the suppliers to the global leading manufacturers of computers and periphery equipment. The scope of ODM has also been extended from periphery equipment to complete computers, network products and high-tech components, with the product line moving from the low-end components to the high-tech semi-conductors. By then China had displayed huge potential as a production base of computers and periphery equipment, and its position in the global production network had also been enhanced. Since the 1990s, the Internet craze has further promoted the expansion of the Chinese computer industry. Especially after the accession to the WTO, the huge domestic market of China has attracted players from around the world, with Intel, NEC, Samsung, and other international manufacturers all coming to invest in China, bringing advanced technologies and management expertise. In 2004, most of the IBM notebooks were produced by the Great Wall Computer Corporation, whose manufacturing facilities in Shenzhen became a major base for IBM notebooks. The fast development of the trade boosted the position of China in the global production network.

From the processing of a single product to the emergence of many upstream and downstream enterprises, a complete production network has been formulated in China, and the industrial conglomeration effect as driven by knowledge and technology has surfaced, represented best by the Taiwanese computer enterprises in China. Currently a conglomeration with specialized division of work and collaboration among enterprises has already been established with the Taiwanese computer enterprises in Dongguan, Guangdong, and the conglomeration generated production capacity has attracted manufacturers from the US, Japan, and South Korea, who have been moving both capital and operations to China. The Taiwanese enterprises in Suzhou and Kunshan have also displayed similar effects. Currently more than 500 Taiwanese computer enterprises have invested in Suzhou, forming a complete industrial chain covering R&D, manufacturing, and sales. Meanwhile, with the establishment and extension of the production network in China, and through purchasing and staff flow, these computer enterprises have been providing the desired technologies and human capital to the local players.

5.5 Relative Advantages of the Sino-Foreign Talent Coopetition and Flow

5.5.1 The Late Development Payoff of China

Should the inbound and outbound flow of human capital be viewed as a whole, the late development advantage of China is reflected as follows: Firstly, the learning of advanced scientific knowledge of the developed countries saves time for China in acquiring such knowledge; secondly, the receiving of advanced education overseas or the employing of foreign experts saves education input for China; thirdly, the attraction of foreign capital, technologies or "learning by doing" improves the technical and management level in China; and fourthly, the joint R&D with developed countries promotes technical advancement in China.

Accumulation of knowledge. As one of the four ancient civilizations of the world, China was quite developed in science and technology in the Qin Dynasty and Han Dynasty, and reached a climax in the Song and Yuan dynasties. However, due to the closed-door policy in the feudal society, China isolated itself from the world and gradually lagged behind in science and technology ever after. Meanwhile, since the late sixteenth century, Western countries made huge progress in astronomy, physics, chemistry, math, and philosophy. As a result, an industrial revolution based on modern science took place in the 1760s. After the Reform and Opening Up process began, with huge enthusiasm, China started to learn the advanced science and technologies from the West, and managed to bridge the knowledge gap within a mere 30 years. The late development effect thereof is remarkable.

Contribution made by international talents. The returnees have been playing significant roles in many industries, and even those yet to come back are acting as a bridge of international exchange. For instance, many Chinese students abroad are using the overseas network to help Chinese enterprises to develop the international market. Others are introducing foreign enterprises to China, or doing business with China representing foreign capital. The high-tech projects brought back have promoted the upgrade of the industrial structure in China. The foreign experts and technical people working in China have also made great contribution to the economic construction and social development in China, especially with the key projects such as the Daya Bay Nuclear Station, Baosteel, and the Three Gorges project.

Enhanced corporate and individual capacity through "Learning by Doing." For example, after 30 years of development, the processing enterprises have improved productivity dramatically and moved towards the high end of the value chain. Take the handset business as an example. In the early stages, China was only a manufacturing base for the production and exporting of Nokia, Samsung, and Motorola. Later China started to develop its own brands such as TCL, Bird, and so on. Today these Chinese handset enterprises are competing with foreign players in the market, with the market share of the domestic handsets exceeding 50% in China in 2003.

Technical advancement through joint R&D. Since HP set up the first R&D center in China back in 1990, many MNCs have set up R&D centers here. In particular, in 2002 after the country's accession to the WTO, over 100 R&D centers were set up in China by MNCs. According to the territorial principle, the enterprises set up in China by MNCs are Chinese enterprises, and the R&D centers of MNCs are therefore an organic part of the technical innovation system in China. MNCs also recruit local researchers and integrate China into their global research network. While MNCs obtain the research resources from China, China also brings the R&D and innovation resources of MNCs into the state system of innovation. The multinational R&D centers set examples for the local enterprises, who have been stimulated to input more in R&D.

5.5.2 The Early Development Payoff of the Foreign Parties

China is not the only beneficiary of the coopetition and exchange of human capital. With the existing early development advantage, developed Western countries may benefit even more. Take the education industry as an example. Chinese students studying abroad pay much higher tuition fees than if they study in China. Also many Chinese talents choose to stay abroad after graduation, making remarkable contributions to other economies. In addition, many foreign companies investing in China benefit from the rich and inexpensive local labor and intelligence.

Benefit of the education industry. The money spent by Chinese students abroad is typically composed of two parts: Tuition fees, and living expenses. As for the destination of the Chinese students, the US and the UK are the top two, and also represent the greater proportion of tuition fees. According to the statistics, a Master's degree (1.5 years) costs between US$20,000–40,000 in the US, plus RMB 80,000–100,000 of living expenses each year, and US$500–1,000 of compulsory insurance. An average Chinese student spends RMB 220,000–38,000 in the US a year (based on the current exchange rate). If not lucky enough to get a scholarship, most students would have to take part-time jobs to survive. Statistics from the American International Education Research Institute shows that most overseas students live on financial support from their home countries, which amounts to over US$12 billion each year. Of the tuition fees paid by overseas students, three-quarters comes from places outside the US. The US Department of Commerce has already made higher education the fifth-largest industry for the export of services. The tuition fees of the UK are the highest of all European countries, with an average overseas student paying RMB 170,000 each year. In recent years, many Chinese students have chosen to study in New Zealand, Singapore, and Russia, where tuition fees are lower, but it still costs RMB 80,000–120,000 each year to study in New Zealand, and RMB 80,000–90,000 each year to study in Singapore.

Economic benefit and human capital acquired from the senior Chinese immigrants. Take the US, the biggest receiver of technical immigrants as an example. According to the statistics of the UN, 40% of the technical immigrants worldwide are attracted to the US. Between 1960 and 1987, altogether 825,000 professionals emigrated to North America. Figures from the US National Science Foundation show that in 1995, 72% of the 12 million technical people were immigrants from developing countries. In the 7,000 companies in the Silicon Valley, there are 2,000 Chinese bosses or CEOs, and altogether 250,000 Chinese staff. Another survey shows that one-fifth of Silicon Valley engineers are Chinese by origin. The US does not attract talents from the developing countries only. In 1997, 98,000 Canadians flowed to the US, mostly to the medical, education or high-tech industries, and about 400,000 European senior talents are working in the US. The US has made the attraction of senior talents an important part of its scientific strategy, and has been constantly revising the immigration laws to accommodate the talent flow.

Cost saved by the MNCs (including the R&D centers) through the localization of talents. Rich and inexpensive labor resources (including intellectuals) are a great attraction to foreign enterprises. The BCG data shows that in 2003 the average hourly wage of Chinese workers was US$0.8 (benefits included), which was 8% of South Korea, 4.5% of the UK and France, 4.3% of Canada, 3.9% of Japan, 3.7% of US, and 2.6% of Germany. While the pasting of micro chips onto printed circuit board requires the use of costly machines in Japan, it only takes a young female worker with a monthly wage of RMB 500 to do the same job manually in China.

CHAPTER

6

The International Transfer of Technical Advancement

The scope of technical advancement is extensive and hard to be classified and measured. The UN once categorized the import of technologies by developing countries as the following eight types:

- importing books, journals, and other publications;
- organizing international personnel exchanges through study visits;
- sending students and technical people abroad for learning and training;
- conducting information and talent exchanges through technical cooperation;
- employing foreign experts and consulting services;
- importing machinery equipment and attached documents;
- conducting licensing trade concerning technical know-how, patents, and trademarks; and
- accepting foreign investment and joint operation.

By referring to this categorization, I divide technical advancement into two types: The technical advancement of human capitalization, including the living skills attached to people and some soft skills in the form of knowledge; and the technical advancement of physical capitalization, including hard skills in the form of production equipment and tools, and some soft skills in the form of intelligence (like patents). With the first type already discussed in the previous chapter, this chapter focuses on the second type. The point of departure is the two types of mechanism for the emergence of technical advancement. Analysis would be conducted on some typical industries, with the aim of exploring the relative benefit gained through the transfer of technologies.

6.1 Two Mechanisms for Promoting Technical Advancement

6.1.1 The R&D Innovation Type

The first mechanism is what we call the endogenous R&D innovation type, which is the innovation of technologies through independent R&D. For the forming and development of any technology, R&D innovation is always the starting point. However, because of the huge amount of capital, facility, and human resources required for technical innovation, it is always the developed countries with rich financial and material resources that enjoy the advantage in such technological advancement. When the technologies developed by developed countries become mature, these countries may either apply them in the production in their home countries for direct economic benefit, or transfer them to the late movers for indirect economic benefit. Therefore, developed countries always dominate international transfer as technology providers.

After overtaking the UK in the twentieth century, the US created for itself a role model of R&D innovation and technical advancement. According to statistics, the R&D expenditure in the US accounts for 44% of the total expenditure of the OECD countries. Table 6.1 lists the R&D expenditure of some countries in both amount and percentage of the GDP between 2002 and 2006. From the table, we notice that the US topped all countries between 2002 and 2006. With R&D expenditure higher than the total sum of the other G7 countries, the US left China, Brazil, and India way behind. Between 2002 and 2006, US R&D expenditure accounted for 2.6% of its national GDP (except for 2004, when it was 2.59%), a lot higher than other developed countries, excluding Japan. Meanwhile, the US GDP figure is always the highest in the world. With a GDP of US$13.98 trillion in 2006, it was 2.6 times the size of Japan.

It is universally acknowledged that the US is the only superpower today, controlling the world economic and political situation, due to its advantage in scientific innovation. In recent years, with the changing of the global competition pattern, and especially the emergence of China and India in the economic and technical domain, the US government has increased its input on technical innovation and R&D by introducing a series of strategies and policies. In education, the US continues to focus on talent training with ever growing investment. In science, the US continues to support elementary research and improve research infrastructure so as to maintain its leading position in major scientific fields. In technology, the US government continues to strengthen ties with enterprises to promote new productivity growth. Over the years, the input of enterprises accounted for two-thirds of the total input of the society. The input of government accounted for 30%. The strong R&D power has won the US the absolute early development advantage in the global competition.

Table 6.1 R&D expenditure of some countries

	2002		2003		2004		2005		2006	
	Amount (US$100 mil.)	Percentage of GDP	Amount	Percentage of GDP	Amount	Percentage of GDP	Amount	Percentage of GDP	Amount	Percentage of GDP
US	2,770.55	2.66	2,897.22	2.66	3,010.16	2.59	3,244.48	2.62	3,437.48	2.62
Germany	502.22	2.49	615.54	2.52	682.51	2.49	693.17	2.48	730.50	2.51
Japan	1,240.27	3.17	1,352.80	3.20	1,458.76	3.17	1,512.70	3.33	—	—
France	324.95	2.23	390.16	2.17	442.85	2.15	455.89	2.13	476.49	2.12
UK	288.18	1.83	324.90	1.79	373.43	1.73	395.71	1.78	—	—
Canada	149.99	2.04	173.71	2.01	199.87	2.01	224.25	1.98	249.98	1.97
Italy	137.40	1.13	166.69	1.11	189.39	1.10	193.99	1.10	—	—
China	155.56	1.07	186.01	1.13	237.57	1.23	298.98	1.33	376.64	1.42
Brazil	43.60	0.95	48.95	0.97	55.98	0.93	73.41	0.83	—	—
India	35.47	0.82	39.47	0.8	45.26	0.78	48.01	—	—	—

Source: Chinese Science & Technology Statistical Data 2008, 35.

With the capital advantage in technical innovation, which includes both physical capital and human capital, the early development countries boast abundant financial, physical, and human capital for R&D and innovation. Traditionally, technical innovation occurs first in the developed countries. According to statistics, DuPont of the US alone has 2,300 researchers in its own labs, with the annual research budget as high as US$1.2 billion. Today the company has developed over 40,000 new products and obtained 25,000 patents. Once technical innovation succeeds, developed countries can enjoy the technical edge and early development benefit. They may also gain larger benefit by transferring technologies to the developing and emerging countries.

However, technical R&D and innovation requires huge input, and in terms of success, it is risky. According to statistics, 95% of investment brings no yield at all, and even for the technically successful achievements, only a small portion can be translated later into commercial value. This is also why most developing countries cannot afford to own their own R&D and innovation system. Also many of the newly innovated technologies can be easily imitated by other countries, so the first movers would have to be innovative all the time to maintain the edge, which brings both economic and technical pressure.

6.1.2 The Importing and Learning Type

Unlike the mechanism of the early development countries, the endogenous importing and learning type is more popular among the late development countries. History of the world economy shows that late development countries all have to go through a process of technical import and digestion before conducting independent innovation. In catching up with developed countries, many late movers chose to import mature technologies for leapfrog development so as to accelerate technical advancement and economic development, and to boost their international competitive power. The quick rise of Japan and South Korea after WWII could be attributed to the import of foreign technologies, which nurtured the independent innovation of the two countries later on.

Experience shows that though late development economies are backward in technology, management, and institutions, through the import of technologies, the late developers may obtain considerable advantage as well. For example, the cost for importing technology is much lower than the cost for innovation. Research shows that the cost for learning technologies is about two-thirds of technical innovation. Also, technologies imported are all proven ones with existing commercial value, saving the late developers the potential economic loss of R&D failure. It is also time- and trouble-saving to import. Therefore, many late development economies choose to import and learn existing technologies. The four-decade high growth of Japan between the 1950s and the 1980s, and the four-decade high growth of the four Asian Tigers in the same period, which were miracles in economic history, could be attributed to the import of technologies.

Compared to the US and Europe, Japan used to be a backward country in the twentieth century. The road Japan chose for economic development was a typical one of import and learning. From the Meiji Reform to the beginning of the twentieth century, it only took Japan forty years to complete the major part of the industrial revolution. Shortly after the end of the WWII, Japan was 20–30 years behind developed Western countries. In 1950, Japan began to import advanced foreign technologies and established the Japan External Trade Organization in 1958, which was later named the Economic CIA by the Americans, to take responsibility for collecting, analyzing, and disseminating economic and technical intelligence worldwide. Through different means and channels, Japan managed to absorb a huge amount of advanced technologies from the US and other countries in a short time. In the 1950s, 233 technologies were imported each year on average, in the 1960s, 1,090, and in the 1970s, 2,091. By 1988, the average personal income of Japan was already on the same level with the US. Following the learning path, Japan saved decades of time for modernization.

South Korea as one of the four Asian Tigers imitated Japan in technical development and has been equally successful. Like Japan, South Korea created the Han River Miracle through the import of technologies. Data shows that within 20 years, South Korea imported 4,090 foreign technologies, among which 50% were in mature stage, 37% were in growing stage, and 5% were in early stage. As for the business sector, manufacturing business accounted for 58% of the total import. As for the application of technologies, 64.4% were applied in the production of domestic consumables and 35.6% for the export market. The technologies imported were also perfectly compatible with the pace of industrial upgrade. In the 1960s, the technologies imported were mostly used in the labor-intensive industries such as textiles, construction materials, iron, and steel. In the 1970s and 1980s, the technologies imported were mostly in the heavy industries and new technical industries such as ship building, chemical, electronics, and automobile. In the 1990s, imports were in new materials such as in the fine chemicals, bioengineering, and information industries. By 2000, the production value of semiconductors amounted to US$12.67 billion, accounting for 8.14% of the world total. In 2004, it further grew to US$20.42 billion, accounting for 10% of the world total. In 2006, South Korea ranked 11th in the world with the total GDP of US$992 billion. Today the iron/steel industry and microelectronics industry of South Korea is world-class.

Of course the late economies need the ability to digest technologies imported. To begin with, it is not feasible to imitate each and every technology. For the existing big gap between the developed countries and the developing countries, the later economies need to be careful in selecting the technologies within their digestion capacity. Secondly, the digestion of technologies requires high-profile human capital, so that technologies imported can be translated into real value later on. Also, with the continuous improvement of the economic level of the late developers, the technical gap would become narrower gradually, leaving fewer and fewer technologies to import, and making imitation harder and harder. Finally with the upgrade of the industrial structure of the developing countries, the building of independent innovative capacity would emerge as the new priority in the post-importation time.

6.2 Technology Import and Learning in China

6.2.1 Purchase of Key Complete Sets of Equipment

Technical import in China started with the purchase of complete sets of equipment. Between 1950 and 1978, complete sets of equipment accounted for over 90% of technical import. In the early days of the reform, the production facilities for home electronic appliances were largely imported. Between 1985 and 1987, altogether 115 color TV production lines, 73 refrigerator production lines, and 22 IC production lines were imported, and China soon became a big power of home electronic appliances. Afterwards the mere import of complete sets of equipment was replaced by the combination of technologies and equipment together. The purpose of import also shifted gradually to the optimization of product structure, and enhancement of product added-value and innovative capability. Since the twenty-first century, technical consulting services and patent rights have been imported along with complete sets of equipment.

The import of complete sets of equipment and key equipment has played a significant role in the economic development in China, especially in the machinery sector. Since the beginning of the 1980s, China has imported a series of complete sets of equipment and technologies to support the construction of national key projects, such as the 500kv high voltage power transmission and transformer equipment, the 300kw and 600kw thermal power equipment, the metallurgy equipment for Baosteel, and so on. To support the national key scientific projects, some advanced manufacturing technologies and cutting-edge products were imported in a measured approach, such as the digital machine tools, and the milling and boring tools imported by Weihai Precision Machine Tool Works from the US during the seventh Five-year Plan period. Also, to improve the manufacturing technology and facilitate enterprise reengineering, three kinds of basic (basic machine, basic spare parts, and basic materials) manufacturing technologies, alloy steel casting technology, and negative pressure EPC technology were imported.

With the complete sets of equipment and key technologies imported, China started the process of digestion and independent research. Since 1983, through joint production, and joint design and research, China conducted simulation and independent research on 12 key technologies including the 300kw and 600kw thermal power machine units, metallurgy equipment with Baosteel, and a 20-million-ton mining system for open pits. By the end of 1993, altogether 40 plus sets of equipment had been developed and put into operation for over 50 key projects, among which 15 were fully localized and applied in 30 projects, making a great contribution to the national economic development. Since the 1990s, the five-million-ton underground mine equipment, and the 300kw and 600kw subcritical thermal power machine units have been localized. The localization ratio in the petrochemical, metallurgy, and mining industries has been improved to 85%–90%. With the import of complete sets of equipment and technologies, the equipment manufacturing industry in China has maintained a growth rate of 17.6% annually, promoting the fast growth of the iron and steel, power, oil, and coal industries.

6.2.2 Development of Technology Trade

With the import of complete sets of equipment, China also saw the growth of technology trade. 1979 to 1996 was the first stage of such development. With the implementation of the Reform and Opening Up policy, and the dramatic change with the political, economic, and social environment, increasingly more developed countries and regions started technical exchange and cooperation with China. During this stage, guided by the thinking of "Opening up to Foreign Capital," China started to import technologies in all dimensions. License trade, technical service trade, and compensation trade appeared. According to the statistics, by 1983, of all the technical import, software technologies accounted for 46.3% and hardware 53.7%. By 1984, the percentages further changed to 59.9% and 40.1%. Between 1980 and 1990, altogether 4,000 plus contracts were signed on technical import with a total value of US$22.8 billion, among which license trade, consulting services, and technical services accounted for 21% of the contract value. At the same time, economic and legal consulting services related to technology trade also became available in the market.

With the technical exchange between China and the world becoming more frequent, enterprises also demand more imported technologies. The conventional import of complete sets of equipment and key equipment was replaced by the import of patent technology, know-how, and technical consulting services. Innovative practices such as technologies and license swaps also appeared in the market. According to the statistics from the Ministry of Commerce, in 2006, altogether 10,538 technology import contracts were filed, with the total contract value reaching US$22.02 billion, a 15.6% increase year on year, among which technical fees amounted to US$14.76 billion, accounting for 67.0% of the total. In 2006, the value of know-how license contracts reached US$7.28 billion, a 42.8% increase year on year, accounting for 33.0% of the total, among which technical consulting and technical services amounted to US$5.18 billion and US$4.29 billion,

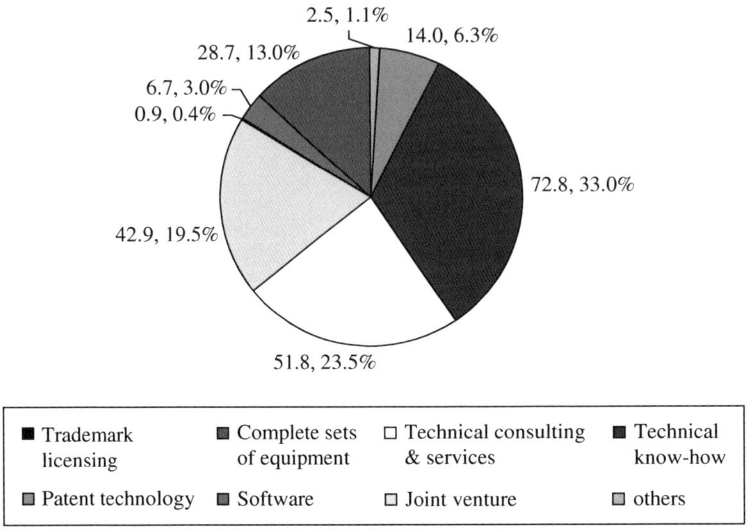

FIGURE 6.1 The major means of technology import in China in 2006

Source: China Scientific Statistical Yearbook, 2007.

Note: The first figure for each item refers to the contract value in US$100 million and the second figure the percentage in the total.

respectively, accounting for 23.5% and 19.5% of the contract value, and registering second and third place in the rankings (Figure 6.1).

Since the 1980s great progress has been made in technology trade in China. Through the import of advanced equipment, manufacturing technologies, and engineering technologies, the R&D, designing and manufacturing capacity of some industries has become closer to the world standard. For example, in the beginning of industrialization, the ship building industry relied heavily on foreign design and joint design. Later it turned to the purchase of patents and licenses, with more than 50 crucial manufacturing technologies imported. After that, China developed 191 technologies, imported 47 foreign technologies, and restructured 44 technologies, narrowing the technical gap between China and the world. Currently, ships built in China have been exported to more than 50 countries and regions including Japan, Germany, Britain, Norway, and the USA. China has successfully become the No.3 shipbuilding country in the world through the digestion, absorption, and re-innovation of imported technologies.

6.2.3 Technology Spillover of FDI

The spillover effect of FDI brought by the MNCs in terms of technology, knowledge, talent, ideas, and management is an essential means of innovation capacity building, industrial upgrade, and leap-frog development for developing countries. First, FDI brings about advanced technology and management philosophy in the localized production, and sets good examples for local firms. Secondly, in order to improve the skills of the local staff to serve the production purpose, MNCs often provide trainings of all kinds, which improve the quality of local human resources. When the local staff has mastered the technology, knowledge, and managerial skills, technology is transmitted and established in the host countries. Thirdly, along with technology, FDI has also brought competition. With greater market share resulting from advanced technology, MNCs impose pressure on local enterprises, forcing local players to keep improving techniques, optimizing product structures, and raising product quality and independent innovation capability in order to survive the competition. Moreover, FDI has played an important role in the upgrade of the industrial structure of the host countries through technology diffusion in the industrial chain.

Ever since China's first move to invite FDI in 1979, the technology spillover effect from FDI has given a big boost to the Chinese economy. Data shows that up to 2007, the cumulative paid-in foreign investment reached US$965.32 billion, making China the largest receiver of FDI among all developing countries for 14 consecutive years, and one of largest receivers of the world. In recent years, many MNCs have established R&D centers in China. According to statistics from the Ministry of Commerce, over 1,000 R&D centers have been established in China by MNCs, among which 400-odd were newly built up in recent years. GE alone has over 60 R&D labs in China, with 1,200-odd researchers and over 200 claimed patents. By 2007, Microsoft had 1,200 staff researchers and 1,500 contractual researchers in China. The R&D input in 2006 reached US$100 million. Of all the 2,000 plus patents Microsoft has obtained, 10% are from the R&D team in China. Through research and development on new technologies in China, MNCs have enhanced the magnitude and speed of technology transfer, which contributes to the technology import and innovation system in China.

The technical advancement driven by FDI technology spillover is represented by the growth of the new high-tech industry and upgrade of the industrial structure. The influx of foreign capital helped boost the infant and high-tech industries such as home electronic appliances, automobile, telecommunications facilities, electronic information, and so on. In 2007, the export volume of high-tech products reached US$347.83 billion, representing 28.6% of total exports, among which computer and telecommunications products registered four-fifths of the amount. US$161.2 billion of foreign exchange was earned for the export of high-tech products. Also, to cut cost, some foreign-funded enterprises purchased more from the Chinese suppliers, which promoted the development of the upstream and downstream enterprises, and the formation of industrial chains in China. For instance, over 100 supporting enterprises to

Volkswagen have come to invest in China in order to assist the production of Shanghai Volkswagen. Forty-four spare parts producers came to China when GM made the first investment here, bringing a total investment of US$2.23 billion. Up to now, Shenzhen has formed a complete industrial chain by taking advantage of the technology spillover effect, which covers electronics, computer, telecommunications facilities, optical communication components, and optoelectronic display technology. In addition, with the driving force of the FIEs, a group of local high-tech enterprises, such as ZTE, Huawei, and Lenovo have been established. As in the auto industry, by bringing in investment from the world-leading MNCs, a number of proprietary brands like Geely and Chery have been established in China.

The technology spillover effect is also manifested in the cultivation of a group of management talents for modern enterprises. To carry out the localization strategy, most MNCs have talent training programs. For example, IBM trained 100,000 software staff for China in three years. HP China spent US$18 million in total on staff training between 1989 and 2000. Nestle has been running its on-going training program since 1998, covering every Chinese staff. Since Siemens founded the management school in Beijing in 1997, it provides training to 6,000 staffs each year.

All these MNCs have helped fill the gap of high-tech talents and encouraged the reversal of the brain drain. In recent years many postgraduates and PhDs from prestigious universities in Europe and the US came back to China to establish their own businesses, many of whom had previous working experience in the Silicon Valley or well-known MNCs, and are in possession of state-of-art management expertise, which enables them to access the international market in a short time. A few examples are Huawei, Baidu, ZTE, and UTStarcom. The backflow of overseas talents has laid a solid foundation for the development of the high-tech industry in China.

6.3 Technical Advancement in Some Representative Industries

6.3.1 Technology Import in the Auto Industry

From 1953 to 1983, China isolated itself from the world automobile market and was slow in development. In 1984, Beijing Jeep was founded as the first auto joint venture in China, which triggered a hot wave of auto joint ventures. In 1985, the Sino-German joint venture—Shanghai Volkswagen—was set up; in 1986, the Sino-French joint venture Guangzhou Peugeot was established; in 1991, FAW-Volkswagen was opened; in 1992, the DPCA jointly developed by Dongfeng and French Citroen launched their business; in 1997, the Sino-US Shanghai GM was founded; then came Guangzhou Honda in 1998,

Chang'an Ford in 2001, Tianjin Toyota in 2002, and Guangzhou Toyota and BMW Brilliance in 2003. Leading overseas auto manufacturers came to invest in China one after another, in the aim of beefing up their global strategy by building up joint ventures in China. The Chinese auto market took the opportunity and established itself as one of the fastest-growing and most potential auto markets in the world. In particular, after the accession to the WTO, the Chinese market surfaced as a point of profit growth for MNCs. At present, the top nine auto groups all have multiple joint ventures in China: 11 for GM, 5 for Volkswagen, 12 for Toyota, 6 for Ford, 13 for DaimlerChrysler, 5 for Renault-Nissan, 5 for Honda, 2 for Peugeot-Citroen, and 1 for BMW. China has become a hot-spot of investment for the auto MNCs.

While the auto sector has attracted a huge amount of foreign investment, it is still uncertain whether the practice of "market for technology" may sustain. However, I believe that through joint investment and joint operation, the Chinese auto manufacturing industry has benefited a lot in technology. Motivated by shared profit, both parties must ensure technological superiority as well as quality, so as to expand their market share in both local and international markets. Therefore, MNCs had to share the latest technologies with their Chinese partners. Also, to raise efficiency and cut costs, MNCs would usually outsource the production of spare parts and components to local manufactures, during which the production technologies of the MNCs are passed to the local manufacturers, accelerating the technical progress in China. Moreover, it leads to the upgrade of technical and product structure, benefiting the industry as a whole.

Take GAIG (Guangzhou Automobile Industry Group Co., Ltd) as an example. After the strategic restructuring in 1997, Guangzhou Peugeot was taken over by Honda, and a Sino-Japanese joint venture was established under the name Guangzhou Honda Automobile Co., Ltd. Hence, Guangzhou Honda embarked on a fast track of development. Since the completion of the first Accord on March 26, 1999, Guangzhou Honda boasted an output of 10,000 cars that year, 32,000 in 2000, 59,000 in 2002, 117,000 in 2003, and over 200,000 in 2004. Product lines were also expanded from Accord to New Accord, Odyssey MPV, and Fit, the economic type. Since China's accession to the WTO, GAIG has deepened its cooperation with its international producers, and launched more new series. Thanks to the import of advanced technologies through cooperation with foreign giants, GAIG has been growing fast, with products selling well in the market.

However, the innovation of auto manufacturing cannot sustain with sole dependence on cooperation with overseas auto enterprises. So far, the key technologies of auto making are still in the grip of foreign parties, and the infiltration effect is also limited. Though China has the ambition to import advanced technologies through joint investment, and develop its own cars one day, producing auto parts is far from independent production. The key point is, the quality of finished products is usually embedded in the long-term accumulation of ever-developing technology, knowledge, and skills, which are the essential assets of those MNCs, and beyond the reach of the Chinese auto producers. Still, R&D is the most important link within the whole system, and the key of IPR. Only with the possession of IPR is learning feasible. Nevertheless, the Chinese auto makers have little chance to obtain the R&D know-how, other than following the finished design. Apart from that, since the domestic private auto makers are still at the growing stage, they are yet able to rival the multinational auto makers. The Chinese auto manufacturing industry is still in the middle between technology import and independent innovation.

With decades of joint venture experience, China has turned itself into a big auto manufacturer and achieved dramatic breakthroughs in creating local brands upon the digestion and absorption of modern technologies. A group of local private companies represented by Chery and Geely are developing fast. Those manufacturers started from scratch and accessed the market through learning and simulation. Though they are still not comparable to the overseas brands for technology and quality, they are successful in getting market share with the product lines fitting the market condition and price concern. Chery and Geely registered on the OICA name list of 50 leading automobile manufacturers for two consecutive years of 2004 and 2005. Chery ranked 43rd and 29th, and Geely 41st and 32nd. In 2005, the sales volume of Chery and Geely reached 189,200 units and 151,400 units, respectively. Though these figures were still away from 200,000, which is the generally accepted benchmark for auto industry, both companies are growing at full speed. In 2006, their production volume surpassed 200,000, 302,500, and 204,400, respectively, and soared to 380,800 and 219,500 in 2007, an increase of 25.86% and 7.38% against the previous year, ranking 7th and 10th in the Chinese market.

Take Geely, China's first private automobile producer, as an example. Mr. Li Shufu, the chairman of Geely, began his business with the production of fridge parts. In 1997, through the acquisition of a state-owned auto enterprise in Deyang, Sichuan Province, he entered the auto manufacturing industry. Since the beginning, Geely has attached great importance to international cooperation. From 2002 on, with Project CI 1 with Italy, Geely has mastered the technologies for modeling and sampling. By carrying out Project CK 1 with one Korean instructor tutoring two Chinese technicians, Geely acquired the standard vehicle designing techniques, which include three parts: The development of punch mold and detecting tool part for new models; the design of welding wire and components; and project synchronization. Through cooperation with Germany on Project CG 1, Geely managed to design an auto chassis on its own. To raise funds for further development, Geely went out to the overseas capital market for financing. In 2003, Geely set up two joint ventures with Guorun Holdings Ltd., and launched six models including Merrie, Uliou, Huapu, Beauty Leopard, and so on, as well as four motors of 1.3L, 1.5L, 1.6L, and 1.8L with matching gearboxes.

On the basis of cooperation, Geely made great efforts in independent innovation and R&D. On January 14, 2008, Geely Group announced at a press conference during the North American International Auto Show (NAIAS) in Detroit that it had made a breakthrough in the security control of tire blowouts. The adoption of this technology would sharply reduce the number of accidents caused by the sudden blowout of tires at high speed. This was a remarkable invention of the Chinese automakers, and a significant contribution to global security technology. On January 30, 2008, Geely announced in Detroit the technology of BMBS (blowout monitoring and brake system), which won Geely the special prize of innovation of the NAIAS, and moreover, honor for the Chinese auto business as a whole. The successful story of Geely reflects the progress made by the Chinese auto industry in less than 20 years, which has shifted from technology laggard to leader with independent R&D and innovation. In May, 2007, Geely announced its strategic transformation from price competition to technology, quality, and service orientation, with the new development strategy featuring, following the international trend while leading in some areas, building synergies with focus, inviting talents, and catching up.

Chery is another key local player which chose the same road as Geely in the early days. The initial technology strategy was to imitate and transcend in three phases: Imitation, cooperative R&D, and self-R&D. Imitation is still going on while cooperative R&D and independent R&D is advancing rapidly. Today, Chery has caught up from behind in the trade.

6.3.2 Technical Breakthrough in Express Rail

In 2004, the State Council approved the first "Medium and Long Term Plan on the Railway Network" in the Chinese railway history, and worked out the policy on the import of modern technology and joint production to promote the modernization of railway facilities. After many rounds of research and comparison, the Ministry of Railways announced the program on railway modernization, which included the digestion and absorption of key technologies imported, the active utilization of the huge domestic market, the control of cost through alliance with domestic enterprises in scientific research, design, and manufacturing, so as to boost the national industry and fulfill the requirement of expanding railway capacity within three to five years. In this way, a campaign on railway technology modernization was launched in an all-round manner.

Compelled by the saturated market at home and attracted by the unique market in China, world express rail giants like Alstom, Siemens, Kawasaki Heavy Industry, and Bombardier had to agree to the transfer of technologies to China, which was the victory of "market for technology." By playing the role of "strategic buyer," the Ministry of Railways decided that only Sifang Holdings and Changchun Railway Vehicles CO., Ltd were to negotiate with the overseas players. In the bidding of 2004, since Siemens offered an extremely high price and accepted nothing else, Alstom, Kawasaki, and Bombardier were given the chance to work with China. For the failure in this round, the stock price of Siemens slumped and the CEO was forced to resign. In 2005, Siemens came back, offering a price of RMB 250 million for every carriage and EUR 80 million for the transferring of key technology. For this project alone, China saved about RMB 9 billion for the motor train unit, which was 14% lower than that paid by Spain, 20% lower than that paid by Korea, and 40% lower than that paid by Taiwan. Moreover, according to the purchase agreement, Germany was to provide overall training to the Chinese staff on top of the designing, commissioning, and manufacturing documentation given, which laid a solid foundation for further independent innovation.

With three years of digestion and absorption, China has mastered the nine key techniques and 10 supporting technologies for the production of a motor train unit. Over 70% of the bullet trains with speeds up to 200 km/h are now produced solely by China. Of the total 160 trains, only six were imported as complete trains, 12 were assembled in China, and the remaining 142 were all produced by domestic companies with technologies imported. On April 18, 2007, China witnessed speed increases at the largest scale ever, with the Bohai Sea Region, the Yangtze River Delta, the Pearl River Delta and other trunk lines operating the homemade CRH Harmony. It took 30 years for Japan to accomplish the development of a bullet train with a speed of 200 km/h to 300 km/h, ten years for the European countries like France and Germany, but only three years for China to materialize the bulk production of homemade CRH since the initial technology import. On April 11, 2008, just one year later, the homemade CRH3 Harmony of 350 km/h made its debut in Tangshan, Hebei Province. From then on, China has become one of the few nations worldwide that are capable of manufacturing bullet trains with a speed of 350 km/h. The CRH3 Harmony leads the world for the traction system, brake system, high-speed bogie, carriage aerodynamics, and so on.

In just a few years, China has made great achievement in project construction, locomotive design, and operation control. In addition, China has formed a technology system with independent IPR, including the technology of producing express trains with speed of 350 km/h, and the operation of the Beijing-Tianjin intercity rail. Opened on August 1, 2008, the Beijing-Tianjin intercity rail operates as the first high-speed railway with independent IPR in the Chinese rail history—the CHR3 Harmony—with a speed of 394.3 km/h in the trial run on June 24, 2008. On April 18, 2008, one year after the sixth speed increase of the Chinese rail system, the Beijing-Shanghai high-speed rail project was launched. This will be the largest construction ever since the founding of the new China, with the length of 1,318 km between Beijing South Railway Station and Shanghai Hongqiao Railway Station. Construction will take five years with a total investment of RMB 220.94 billion.

Meanwhile, progress has also been made with the Maglev train. In fact, China started with research on the Maglev train in the 1970s. At the end of 2002, through partnership with Germany, a Maglev line of 31 kilometers and with a maximum speed of 430 km/h was put into operation in Shanghai. At the beginning of 2007, the "National Key Technology R&D Program" was initiated in Beijing. On February 9, 2007, the program defined the "High-speed Maglev Transportation" as a key project. The program also called for the localization of transportation control system and the IPR for the suspension guidance control, traction control, operation control, system integration, and other key technologies, as well as a 30-km Maglev pilot line for conducting qualitative experiments. The "High Temperature Super-Conduction Trail Train" project jointly carried out by Southwest Jiaotong University and other institutions has been included in the "National 863 Project." Tongji University and Zhejiang University have also acquired some Maglev IPRs.

6.3.3 Technical Innovation in Equipment Industry

Founded in July 1959, China XD Group is a perfect example of the equipment industry in China with proprietary R&D and innovation based on modern technologies imported. Its success also inspired the revitalization of the equipment industry nationwide. According to statistics, during the 9th and 10th Five-year Plan period, China XD Group imported altogether 11 advanced technologies, and localized over 70% of these technologies through research and redevelopment. On top of that, it has developed 296 new products all by itself, out of which 78 are of international level, and 36 are with national patents. XD Group has also accomplished 51 national scientific projects, with the scientific input taking up about 4% of the business revenue (Wang Zhile 2008).

Before 1985, SHIKY, a high-voltage switch company under China XD Group conducted little improvement in its technology for 26 years. In 1985, SHIKY imported the switch producing technology from Mitsubishi, including the GIS, dead tank circuit-breaker and live tank circuit-breaker. With the adoption of new technology and the training of technicians, XD Group got a good grasp of all the innovative technologies from Mitsubishi within 15 years. The ratio of self-made products jumped from 5% in the beginning to 100% finally. Between 1994 and 1995, the key technologies for ten switches developed by China XD Group all passed national accreditation, and the output grew by 30% for three consecutive years since 1995. A subsidiary of SHIKY further deepened the scientific research on top of the Mitsubishi technology and invented the single-break switch of 330 KV and 500 KV in 2002. The insulated switchgear of 750 KV to 850 KV made in 2004 has also passed national accreditation.

XD Transformer, another subsidiary under China XD Group, imported technologies from Mitsubishi Electric and ABB. Today, XD Transformer is able to produce a whole series of transformers including 750 KV and ±500 KV DC transformers. Cooperation and communication with ABB has also played a crucial role in R&D. In recent years, all the affiliated companies of XD Group have imported the ABB technology through the "Three Gorges Project." With both hardware and software imported, technicians are able to simulate the circulation space in electric, magnetic, and air flow field, speeding up the process of new product development.

The progress made by XD Group since the twenty-first century is even more remarkable. The 126–252 KV/40 KA self-extinguish switch with spring mechanism, the 550 KV/63 KA GCBT with pneumatic spring, the 550 KV/50 KA single break GCBT, and the 252 KV/550 KV/63 KA high-capacity GIS were successfully developed through independent research. The technology involved is in line with the international standard, filling the gap for China. The star product-converter station flat-wave reactor enjoys independent IPR; and the flat-wave reactor, converter transformer, and 750 KV single-phase on-load transformer lead the domestic trade. During the period, XD Group took the responsibility of 30 national key projects, and has delivered the 720,000 KVA three phase circuit transformer, the 600,000 KVA generator transformer, the 330 KV/500 KV live tank circuit-breaker, hydraulic and spring units above 252 KV, and other products to projects like: The 750 KV pilot project of power transmission in the Northwest, the ±500 KV HVDC Project, the Northwest-Mid China DC Back-to-back Project, the Transformer Station Project ("Three Gorges" Project), the North China Grid, the East China Grid, the Northwest Grid, and so on.

In the meantime, XD Group has also become more competitive at home and abroad. During the 10th Five-year Plan period, the Group achieved an increase of 18% in sales revenue from RMB 2.61 billion in 2001 to RMB 6.07 billion in 2005. The total profit soared from RMB 75 million to RMB 135 million. The tax paid grew by 24% to RMB 1.85 billion. The total foreign exchange earned grew by 42% to US$4.15 billion. This has made China XD Group the only producer in China with a full range of transformation equipment covering transformer, switchgear, electroceramics, capacitance, and so on. XD Group now owns over half of the market share for insulated switchgears beyond 360 KV, one-third market share for breakers above 330 KV, and one-third market share for transformers over 550 KV.

The success of XD Group is not only built on the localization of the imported technology, but also on the re-innovation, which serves as a foundation for the on-going access to new technologies. Only in this way can the company enhance its innovation and R&D ability.

6.3.4 Technical Advancement in the Service Industry

The opening up strategy in China was adopted first in the manufacturing industry and then in the service industry. After China's accession to the WTO, foreign investment in the trade in services grew fast, with increasingly more service-type MNCs marching into China, providing services inr finance, insurance, securities, circulation (logistics, wholesale, retail, foreign trade), telecommunications, law, accounting, public relations, project management, and consulting. In the *Guiding Opinions on the Work of Attracting Foreign Investment* of 2007, the Ministry of Commerce gave policy encouragement to investment in the modern service industry and outsourcing industry. The technology spillover effect of MNCs has benefited all trades from manufacturing to the service industry. According to the research report of CCID Consulting, software outsourcing undertaken by China in 2005 amounted to US$920 million, and is estimated to reach US$7,028 million by 2010.

To collect cases of technology import in service industry, Mr. Wang Zhile (2008) carried on an investigation between October 2006 and March 2007 on 80 design companies for outsourcing business. Among those 80 enterprises, 50 were local and 30 were foreign-funded. The survey shows that as an essential part of the modern service industry, the design industry reflected a significant spillover effect with the outsourcing business, which played an active role in the fast growth of the local design companies that have approached the international market with own brands and international best practice. The spillover effect has also made a grand contribution to the strengthening of competitiveness in both the design and manufacturing industries.

The spillover effect is first of all reflected in business expansion and profit growth. By taking outsourced business from MNCs, the local designing enterprises are able to approach international clients by operating worldwide. Besides, the price offered by overseas companies are normally higher than that offered by local companies, and since most MNCs enjoy a good reputation, there exists higher profitability and reliability.

The second benefit is the improvement on learning and design. The results of the questionnaire conducted by Mr. Wang Zhile indicate that 74% of the companies involved have received new knowledge and skills from the outsourcing business. It is commonly deemed that cooperation with world-leading companies provides access to the most updated expertise, notion, and management practice. For instance, E-Madesign owes a lot to its cooperation with Flextronics, whose top cell-phone designers are senior technicians with Siemens. By learning from Flextronics, E-Madesign has come up with better cell-phone designs.

The third benefit is the advancement of service through specialization. MNCs usually have stricter requirements for technology, forcing domestic counterparts to deepen specialization. In addition, local designers are exposed to new information, techniques, and modern designing concepts by communicating with the experienced designers from MNCs. Progress can also be made in design management and service philosophy. All the improvement would bring about better service to the domestic enterprises.

The fourth benefit is the extension of the business chain toward the high end on account of improved technical and service quality. Some enterprises have embarked on the more sophisticated outlook design; some have shifted from design to general business; some have turned to consulting, planning, and ODM service; still others start to serve the large MNCs instead of the SMEs. Before 2005, Newplan, an industrial design consultancy in Shenzhen, ran only a single designing business and earned revenue of RMB 17 million. Since the adoption of the OEM model in 2006, its revenue has climbed up to RMB 75 million, up by over four times in one year.

The fifth benefit is the acceleration of internationalization. The mastering of global standards and norms through the outsourcing business paved the way for future access to the global market. Extensive contact with overseas companies, chances to present design works in the global market, and rich experiences acquired are among the few. A good example is ARTOP Industrial Design in Shenzhen, which developed its own model in four steps: Local operation, outsourcing business, domestic service providing, and global operation.

Finally, the spillover effect is manifested in branding. On one hand, local enterprises have more exposure to the international stage by taking outsourcing business from MNCs. On the other hand, with equally powerful influence on the local market, these enterprises may also attract outsourcing business from local companies who would otherwise turn to overseas players. For example, ARTOP has attracted business from domestic giants like Changhong, Huawei, Haier, and so on, after taking outsourced business for Motorola, Sanyo, and so on.

6.4 Relative Advantages of the Sino-Foreign Technological Coopetition

6.4.1 The Late Development Effect of China

With technology import, the first gain is technical advancement. Since China lagged behind the developed nations in technology, there exists space for learning and simulation, which is what the late development advantage is about. Guided by the philosophy of "In China, For China," GE Healthcare has transferred a variety of modern technologies to China through its localization strategy, and has trained a group of top management talents for China. Currently, GE Health China R&D center is capable of developing helical CT with single, double, four, eight, and sixteen layers. It is also the largest R&D and manufacturing center of common CT machines, and shared part of the production of high-end CT. Generally speaking, the more powerful the learning ability, the larger the technical advancement. Since Haier developed the new product line Qindao-Liebherr by adopting the German technology in 1984, it has always focused on its learning ability and has acquired independent R&D ability in a short time. By 2004, Haier had taken part in the formulation of 86 national standards and two international standards. With 5,469 patents applied for, it is the enterprise with the most patents in China

The second gain is the improved productivity of Chinese enterprises from the imported technologies. Judging from the TFP, the labor productivity and technology level of FIEs are much higher than the domestic ones. In 2001, the labor productivity of the SOEs in the chemical industry was RMB 38,432.74 per capita, productivity of the electronics industry was RMB 99,743 per capita, and the productivity of the machinery industry was RMB 44,770.46 per capita, while the productivity of FIEs was 3.3, 1.25, and 2.32 times higher, respectively. Fortunately, with strong learning ability, domestic enterprises have witnessed a quick upswing of productivity by digestion and absorption of the modern technologies imported. Take Guangdong Province for example. With technologies imported in basic industries like energy, transportation, telecommunications, and raw materials, Guangdong Province managed to overthrow the outdated image with upgraded technology and productivity. The fastest-growing industries, such as machinery, paper making, textiles, building materials, electronics, and so on, were the ones that imported the most technologies. From 1979 to 1991, Guangdong Province purchased up to 30,000 pieces of advanced agricultural equipment, and imported 1,200 excellent animal and plant species, which largely boosted the productivity and foreign exchange earning capacity of the agricultural industry.

The third gain is the saving of R&D expenditure by importing advanced technologies from abroad. The importers always pay far less than the inventors. As the developed countries already possess the most advanced technologies, they can only count on themselves for further invention. Yet for developing countries like China, the cost of import is way lower than independent R&D. The "Asian Tigers" imported a huge amount of technologies in the catching-up phase, and China has also relied heavily on technology imports in the past 30 years of the Reform and Opening Up process.

The fourth gain is the saving of time in catching up with the developed countries. The later one country takes off, the more options there are for technology adoption and the less time is needed to catch up. Ever since the 1980s, there has been an increasingly rapid dissemination of new technologies. With the abundance of advanced technologies, developing countries have enough to choose from, and since they are situated at the technical frontline in a flat world, they may even overtake the old timers. There are three cases of how the developing nations and regions caught up with the developed ones: It took the US 43 years to overtake the UK, it took Japan 40 years to catch up with the US, and it took the Asian Tigers 30 years to catch up with Western Europe. We have already mentioned that it took China only three years to produce the motor train units with a speed of 200 km/h to 300 km/h. The time consumed was only one-tenth of that of Japan, and one-third of that of France and Germany.

Last is the imitation-and-innovation effect for enterprises on the medium level in the trade. Those enterprises may have some R&D ability, but not enough to stand out. Arca Technology, and BYD are among those. Applying the strategy of innovation on the basis of imitation, these enterprises keep a close eye on the latest development of new technologies and the potential influence on the market. By conducting analysis on the integration of new technologies with present products, they have managed to bring about new products competitive in performance, quality, and price.

6.4.2 The Early Development Effect of the Foreign Parties

In the Sino-foreign technical coopetition, China enjoys late development benefits, and the foreign parties enjoy early development benefits, which are reflected in three aspects: Revenue from technology export; monopoly profit from royalties; and innovation revenue from founding R&D centers in China.

First let us take a look at the revenue earned from technology exports. Although the sources of technology imports have been increasingly diversified, they still remain highly concentrated on some developed nations and regions as measured by contract value. China has paid a huge amount for the technology brought in from those developed countries and regions such as the US, the EU, Japan, South Korea, and so on. Table 6.2 lists the top 15 nations and regions with the highest contract value in 2006. South Korea received US$5.24 billion for technology exports, out of which US$3.19 billion was technical fees; the US got US$42.30 billion, out of which US$3.44 billion was technical fees. Among these 15 countries and regions, seven were from the EU, namely, Germany, France, Sweden, Italy, Holland, Denmark, and Austria. They altogether registered a total contract value of US$7.40 billion, with US$3.96 billion being technical fees. Japan earned US$1.31 billion, out of which US$1.23 billion was technical fees.

Another part of revenue comes from the monopoly royalties through technology trade. With the technology import becoming regularized in China since the twenty-first century, foreign parties have earned a lot from transferring patent technologies to China. Table 6.3 reveals the total contract value of the transferred patent technologies since 2001, which amounted to US$5.83 billion, out of which US$5.81 billion was technical fees. It can be inferred from the exhibit that the proportion of technical fees has been growing while that of the equipment cost has been declining.

Table 6.2 Top 15 nations and regions in terms of their contract value of technology exports to China in 2006

		No. of contracts	Contract value (US$10,000)	Fee for technology transfer (US$10,000)	Percentage of the total
1	South Korea	3,068	524,485	319,500	23.82
2	US	1,436	423,059	344,530	19.21
3	Germany	1,140	259,725	149,402	11.80
4	France	364	220,964	65,055	10.03
5	Sweden	70	155,802	77,610	7.07
6	Japan	723	131,585	123,652	5.97
7	Switzerland	161	30,361	23,547	1.38
8	HK	1,122	82,806	75,736	3.76
9	Finland	34	58,094	40,849	2.64
10	Singapore	331	48,328	48,251	2.19
11	UK	301	37,921	32,758	1.72
12	Italy	193	33,916	22,510	1.54
13	Holland	143	26,130	25,598	1.19
14	Denmark	54	22,386	10,516	1.02
15	Austria	100	21,224	12,929	0.96

Source: China Statistical Yearbook, 2007.

Table 6.3 The transfer of patent technologies to China between 2001 and 2006

Year	No. of contracts	Contract value (US$10,000)	Fee for technology transfer (US$10,000)	Equipment cost (US$10,000)
2001	164	48,176	43,349	4,827
2002	195	583,160	581,319	1,841
2003	259	132,545	128,715	3,829
2004	361	102,633	100,052	2,580
2005	320	127,838	118,143	9,695
2006	405	139,843	139,288	555

Source: China Statistical Yearbook, 2002–2007.

In recent years, many MNCs of developed nations have started to move their R&D centers to China. Altogether 800 R&D centers have been set up in China by MNCs, with half in Beijing, and the other half in Guangzhou, Shenzhen, and so on. Still many MNCs are moving their Asia-Pacific R&D centers to Shanghai. These centers not only contribute to the technical advancement in China, but also bring innovation revenue to the MNCs themselves. For instance, GE Healthcare R&D center in Beijing is now the global R&D center for CT machines, with its newly developed economic CT machines selling well in both China and Japan, bringing huge profits to GE.

It is for both reasons of cost and gain that MNCs choose to build R&D centers in China. In terms of cost, China enjoys a relatively low cost of labor, infrastructure, and land. In terms of gain, MNCs have access to excellent Chinese scholars and technicians, whose different cultural background contributes to innovation in the cross-cultural context. MNCs may also be easily inspired in this green market of China.

CHAPTER 7

Management Learning and Institutional Evolution

Technical advancement is a broad concept which includes both hardware technologies such as equipment, instrument, and craftsmanship, and soft technologies like management. Management is an experience type of technology or even an invisible art. Standardized and rule-based management is also a form of institution. This chapter analyzes the learning of management and the evolution of the institution at the micro level (enterprise), the macro level (government), and the institutional level, and discusses relative payoffs of Chinese-foreign coopetition on management institutions.

7.1 Learning Enterprise Management Experience

7.1.1 Chinese Enterprises Learning from Equity JVs and Contractual JVs

Since the beginning of the Reform and Opening Up process, equity JV and contractual JV have become the major forms of strategic alliance and also the major platform and channel whereby China learns from foreign countries. Over the past 30 years, more than 300,000 foreign-invested enterprises have been established in China. Except for a small number of solely foreign-owned ones, most are Sino-foreign equity JVs or contractual JVs. At different stages, Chinese enterprises have a different focus in learning.

In the early stages, learning was focused on production technologies and production management from the Chinese merchants in HK and Taiwan. Before the mid-1990s when China was in the shortage economy, supply failed to meet demand in the market, making the expansion of production the priority. Therefore, in the equity JVs and contractual JVs, the introduction of production equipment (assembly lines) and the learning of advanced manufacturing technologies became the major focus. As for the type of industry, home electronic appliances, food, textiles, footwear, and headwear were among the few.

The targets of learning at this stage were the Hong Kong enterprises and enterprises run by the overseas Chinese, and also some Taiwanese enterprises arriving in China via other places. As a service center, Hong Kong started to shift some of its labor-intensive industries such as beverages, food, apparel, footwear, headwear, and toys to the Pearl River Delta in the 1980s. Those Hong Kong enterprises moving to the mainland later were mostly in the import and export business or financial brokerage business. Taiwan is known as a manufacturing center. Since the 1990s, groups after groups of Taiwanese enterprises came to the mainland to run processing businesses, especially in the IT industry. Both Hong Kong and Taiwan are successful economies. Since the opening up, especially in the early stages, investment from Hong Kong and Taiwan accounted for two-thirds of total foreign investment. Though they were relatively small in scale and not so advanced in technology, they brought both technologies and management to local enterprises. Having both the heritage of Chinese culture and the modern Western management philosophy, they served as examples of the perfect match. From the 1980s to the 1990s, the Hong Kong and Taiwanese enterprises served as role models for the mainland enterprises, which first started among the JVs in the Pearl River Delta and the southeast coastal areas before spreading throughout the country. The impact was not just in the economic field, but also in the social and cultural fields.

In the later stages, focus was shifted to the learning of management expertise from the US, European, and Japanese enterprises. In the late 1990s, with the deepening of the Reform and Opening Up process, great changes took place in the Chinese market environment, with the buyer's market coming into existence. Chinese enterprises accordingly shifted their focus of learning to marketing and management along with technologies. Especially after the accession to the WTO, with competition becoming fiercer in the market, Chinese enterprises shifted the focus of learning to the upper part of the value chain, that is, R&D of core technology, branding, marketing, quality management, and strategic management, to enhance their core competitive power.

The targets of learning at this stage became large enterprises from Europe, the US, and Japan. In addition to the equity JVs and contractual JVs, there were also strategic alliances with no equity involved. As for the type of industry, auto, iron and steel, chemical, machinery, telecommunications equipment, finance, and information technology were among the few. A good example was Haier. As early as 1984, Haier (the former Qingdao

Refrigerator Factory) introduced the production line from Liebherr Germany, and in 1993, the air conditioner production line from Mitsubishi, Japan. In addition, in July 2008, it entered into a strategic alliance partnership with Mercedes-Benz in Qingdao to learn lean management. According to the alliance agreement, Mercedes was to transfer the production system into the washing machine production of Haier so as to optimize production procedure, improve efficiency, develop a lean philosophy, and enhance product quality. To raise the competitive power in the international market, Haier has set up 48 project-based R&D centers with well-known MNCs and research institutes.

Among the over ten enterprises that I served as consultant or independent director over the years, a Sino-Japan listed apparel JV and a leading cable enterprise both learned the organizational structure and management model from Japan, and have been highly successful so far.

After accession to the WTO, the proportion of investment from Hong Kong, Macau, and Taiwan dropped from the peak 67.15% in 1991 to 37.37% in 2004. Meanwhile more and more American, European, and Japanese enterprises came to China for equity and contractual joint cooperation. Compared to the Hong Kong/Taiwanese enterprises, they were larger in scale and more advanced in technology and management. Today, learning is no longer limited to the manufacturing industries. For instance, the Bank of Communications, the Bank of China, and China Construction Bank have all introduced strategic investors from the US and Europe, or set up partnership alliances in the last few years. In 2006, the Industrial and Commercial Bank of China (ICBC) signed a strategic investment and cooperation agreement with the joint investment group composed of Goldman Sachs, Allianz, and American Express, starting cooperation in corporate governance, risk management, asset management, staff training, and so on.

7.1.2 The Internationalized Learning and Growth of Huawei

On July 9, 2008 Huawei published its fiscal report of 2007: Total revenue amounted to US$12.56 billion, an increase of 48% from 2006, overtaking Nortel as the fifth largest telecommunications equipment provider.

The full name of Huawei is Huawei Technologies Co. Ltd, which was founded in Shenzhen in 1988 as a telecommunications network solution provider. The business scope of Huawei covers mobile, broadband, IP, fiber network, value added communications services, and terminal services. Huawei aims to become a world-class telecommunications solution provider, and adopts the strategy of learning and following before leading. In the early days, Huawei attributed its quick growth to headhunting (Wu and Ji 2006).

After overcoming the internal crisis in 1993, from 1995 to 1998, following the path of "countryside first city next," Huawei managed to establish its leading position in the telecommunications equipment market in China and reached the most important interim objective. Huawei impressed the domestic competitors as a technology-centered and R&D-focused enterprise, with over 10% of the annual sales revenue put into the R&D of new products, and 40% of staff involved in R&D. By the end of 2007, among the 81,000 staff, 35,000 or 43% were involved in R&D.

However, Ren Zhengfei, the founder, noticed hidden dangers. With the R&D expenditure growing or even doubling each year, efficiency was decreasing, leaving Huawei far below the international level in R&D return. The success of Huawei in market share lay on acute market sense and quick release of new products as well as service on demand. However, as Gao Ruibin, the regional president of Motorola put it, quick reaction is not always positive. With too many changes came too many versions, making the system upgrade a total mess. While quick reaction was possible for a smaller customer base, considering the future global market, it might not work as it did within China. The company was in need of reform.

Reform started with learning. At the end of 1997, a group of people led by Ren Zhengfei visited the US and selected four representative enterprises—IBM, HP, Hughes, and Lucent—to study. Among the four, Ren learned the most from IBM, especially the six-stage R&D management model including conceptualization, planning, developing, verification, releasing, and life cycle. Also, the integrated product development of IBM was the weakest link for Huawei. Ren was impressed by IBM's ability to maintain flexibility and speed as well as consistency for an enterprise of such magnitude, which was exactly what Huawei was looking for in addressing the conflict between quick expansion and current capacity. In the transition from a telecommunications equipment manufacturer to a total solution provider and service provider, the knowledge and experience of IBM was exactly what Huawei could learn. Therefore, Ren was determined to learn management expertise from IBM.

In order to learn in an effective manner, Ren spared no effort in inviting the instructors home to teach knowledge and methods, and to give guidance in real projects. In August, 1998, the "IT Strategy and Planning" program between Huawei and IBM was officially launched to plan the business procedure and supporting system for business development in the coming three to five years, focusing on integrated products and supply chain management. With 50 IBM experts teaching in Huawei, earning a consulting fee of US$200,000 per year, more than US$50 million was spent in five years. As the finance department calculated later, over RMB one billion was spent for the five-year business reform.

The Integrated Product Development emphasizes market and customer orientation. Product development is seen as an investment, which is evaluated from both commercial and technical perspectives at each step to ensure returns on investment and avoid risk of failure. Over the years, the technical people of Huawei focused largely on the development of functions, neglecting reliability and service quality, which resulted in heavy wastage of material due to R&D failure and high travel costs incurred in order to solve problems that arose. Yet, for enterprises like IBM, efforts are not only made to accelerate product development, but also to advance product release dates without compromising quality.

The Integrated Supply Chain includes purchase, inventory management, production, delivery, and after sales service. Through designing, planning, and controlling of the logistic flow, information flow, and capital flow, the intention was to increase customer satisfaction and decrease cost.

Given the high tuition fee spent, Huawei staff were not motivated to learn. Since the procedure reform took place in the summer months, there was no sense of urgency. The students didn't pay much heed to the training schedule and often came late or left early. Some present even dozed off in class. Ren was serious about addressing the training problem and said: "I hate most those who think themselves to be smart. You ought to understand how IBM made it. We will give exams after the training course and anyone who fails will be laid off, even if he thinks himself smarter than IBM. We are against the Chinese-style management and Huawei-style management. Managerial innovation at this point is the digestion of the mature management expertise of the Western world." With iron-fisted advocacy and by linking the procedure of reform to the staff compensation scheme, the apathy toward learning was corrected.

In November 1999, with the conceptualization stage coming to an end and the promotion stage started, Ren raised the three-step process for the procedure of reform, namely "ossification, optimization, and solidification." By the end of 1999, the development of integrated products came to the local implementation stage. The R&D center was given to the product development teams, which performed like a small start-up company. Each team took responsibility for the entire process of a particular product including conceptualization, R&D, product development. During the development process, the marketing staff, finance staff, customer service staff, and purchasing staff were all involved in conceptualization so that the cost factor and future market trend could both be taken into consideration.

Yet, resistance came naturally as the procedure of reform deepened. Many expressed doubt about the speed of market reaction after the release of the integrated products. After the reform, customer requirements would need to be prioritized at the headquarters and deliberated by the integration team at their monthly meeting. Even when accepted, over four technical evaluations would have to be conducted by the product development team before anything could be done. In the short run, market reaction slowed down. As some Huawei people believed, IBM as a market leader was in a position to notice market trend and could afford to take action after the emergence of new products, whereas Huawei as a follower may lose market share, should reaction slow down. Yet, Ren stuck to the three-step process—ossification before optimization and solidification. Sure enough, as time went by, people came to realize that though speed was compromised at the early stage, with customer need taken into greater consideration at the R&D stage, quick reaction was no longer necessary. In this way, after the smooth operation of the integrated products, the R&D cycle was shortened and risks mitigated.

In 2007, the Patent Cooperation Treaty (PCT) Report of the World Intellectual Property Organization (WIPO) showed that with 1,365 PCT applications published in total, Huawei ranked fourth among all enterprises in the world. By the end of 2007, Huawei had joined 83 international standard organizations. The total number of patents applied for amounted to 26,880, among which 4,256 had been authorized.

7.1.3 The Internationalized Learning and Growth of the CEIBS

The China Europe International Business School (CEIBS) was founded in 1994, and is today among the top 100 business schools in the world. In May 2003, the CEIBS was listed among the top 100 for both graduating and non-graduating courses in the rankings conducted by the *Financial Times.*

The leapfrog development of the CEIBS is a miracle of internationalized learning and a reward for the continuous learning of advanced experience and successful operation models of foreign business schools, as well as the effort to innovate as the environment changes. At different stages, the CEIBS focused on one or two learning methods, and gradually established an all-round learning capacity (Yang and Ulrich 2005).

In 1992, with the reform entering a new stage, China was in demand of senior business administration talents with global vision. Though MBA courses were offered by a few universities then, none was able to meet the market demand in scale, level, and internationalization. In such context, Mr Jan Borgonjon, who later became the vice president of the CEIBS, noticed the business opportunity and discussed with the then standing deputy dean of the Management School of Shanghai Jiaotong University to set up an international business school with financial aid from the EU.

In September and October 1994, the Chinese government and the EU signed the *Financial Agreement of the CEIBS*, authorizing the independent legal person status and independent operation rights to the school. Later, Shanghai Jiaotong University and the European Management and Development Foundation as the designated executing bodies of both governments signed the contract, bringing the management committee under the board responsible for the school's operation.

At first, the school lacked capital, hardware facilities, knowledge, and management expertise. To address these issues, the CEIBS decided to learn from world-class business schools. Some staff were sent to the top business schools for study visits and internships so as to learn marketing, professor recruitment, classroom decoration, promotion material preparation, and so on. In the first five years, the CEIBS learned marketing from IMD, Switzerland and Michigan University, US, customer relation management from Insead, France, and curriculum management from IESE, Spain. The CEIBS also opened some joint classes with top business schools, and learned by doing. The resourceful students of the CEIBS also contributed a lot to the school after class. Such learning models helped the school to turn education into a product which could be marketed, promoted and sold. In addition, the school also learned management service from hotels by inviting seasoned tutors to give training. As a result, the service quality on each link improved tremendously.

As for student recruiting, a commercial operation model was borrowed in approaching candidates and promoting courses. The practice of "Global Breakfast Meeting" was borrowed from Wharton and Insead, and the practice of "Road Show" was adopted for promotional activities, during which professors were invited to give demo classes, and participants were invited to discuss management theories and methods. The value of the CEIBS was delivered to potential students in this way. Later, presidents from both the Chinese and European side were also invited to the road show and alumni activities, which added to the publicity and attraction of the school.

Within a couple of years, the CEIBS had established its own organizational learning ability. Weekly meetings were set up by the school leaders, during which the management staff would review work of the previous week and discuss tasks ahead. With an all-round management team available, mistakes in decision-making could be minimized. After five years of study and development, in October 1999, the MBA course of the CEIBS was rated No. 17 in Asia by *Asia Business*, marking the first tier ranking position in Asia.

Meanwhile the market had also been changing. A large number of prestigious universities started to partner with foreign business schools and opened MBA and EMBA diploma courses, posing a competitive threat on the CEIBS in terms of student leads, school facilities and faculty. To maintain the leading position in China, since 2000, continuous improvement has been made in the following ways: Holding promotional meetings in big cities in a planned way with professors giving demo lectures; inviting students to evaluate all courses and professors to improve lecturing quality; building a customer database and customer visiting system to strengthen customer ties; setting up career development centers and alumni offices to improve service; opening new programs and courses such as the 18-month, on-the-job diploma course for business management and hospital management to fill the market gap and differentiate itself from other business schools. In January 2002, the CEIBS was rated third in Asia and listed among the top 100 of the world by the *Financial Times*, marching another step forward.

The following target was to create a world brand for China in the education industry, and provide a CEIBS model for the development of MBA education in China, which definitely required innovation. By then, though 71% of the faculty members were internationalized, with the professors coming and going, and teaching mostly Western-style management, it was hard to satisfy market demand. To address this issue, the CEIBS focused on the staffing of fixed-term professors so that its professors may settle down in China. Attention was also paid to the scientific research facilities, and high-profile research centers like the Behavior Science Research Institute, and the SME Research Institute were set up accordingly. An alumni club was also organized for better utilization of the precious fellow resources. With information provided by the school fellows, the MBA graduates have been given more opportunities in the job market.

All the hard work was rewarded. In 2007, the MBA course was rated No.11 in the world by the *Financial Times*, marking the accession of the school to the first-tier ranking.

7.2 Learning Government Administration Policy

7.2.1 Learning Macro Policy: Research and Consultation before Formulation and Implementation

Before the Reform and Opening Up process, decision-making in China was highly experimental, with many decisions made as a result of the sudden will of certain officials, resulting in frequent policy errors. Since the beginning of the Reform and Opening Up process, scientific and democratic decision-making methodology has been introduced. Research and consulting is usually done ahead of policy formulation and implementation, which has greatly reduced policy errors. The research and consulting process is itself a learning process in which both successful experiences and failed lessons are examined.

For instance, in 1987, the State Commission for Restructuring the Economic System conducted research on the "Reform Plan on the Economic System in China for 1988–1995," dividing the period into three years (1988–1990), five years (1988–1992) and eight years (1988–1995). This was known as the "358 plan". The State Commission for Restructuring the Economic System organized the State Planning Commission, the Development Research Center of the State Council, the People's Bank of China (PBOC), the CASS, Peking University, Renmin University, and Shanghai municipal government for the research. Nearly all the best economists were called upon to engage in the research, and finally over ten plans were submitted. All plans reflected the fact that experts in different topic groups had studied both the positive experiences and the negative lessons of reforms at home and abroad when preparing the innovative ideas. When all the plans were gathered in Beijing, the State Commission for Restructuring Economy held a two-day seminar, during which "price reformists" and "enterprise reformists" had a heated debate. As someone put it later, it was somewhat similar to the collision between "Washington Consensus" and "Beijing Consensus." The result of the debate was later passed to the top decision-makers of China.

Another example is the World Bank, which not only provides funds to developing nations but also advice and policy recommendations. Over the past 30 years, cooperation between China and the World Bank has been highly successful. Each year, the World Bank publishes reports on the policy research of this largest developing nation and interacts with Chinese leaders, who not only attach great importance to the opinions of the World Bank, but also meet well-known foreign scholars on a frequent basis to listen to their suggestions. Those who have been received by the top leaders of China include the Nobel Prize winners Tobin, Friedman, Stiglitz, and Mundell. The "release price and control currency" suggestion provided by Friedman, the representative figure of liberalism, aroused active response during his visit to Beijing together with Steven N.S. Cheung in the late 1980s.

Case 1
The Bashan Liner Meeting: Inviting Foreign Experts

The fourth quarter of 1984 saw loss of credit control, overinvestment, overconsumption, and price inflation (over 10%). In 1985, the Chinese economy reached a critical point. The top priority of the government was to adopt proper measures to cope with the chaotic macro economy.

It was in such context that the "International Seminar on Macro Economic Management" was convened by the Economic System Reform Commission, the CASS, and the World Bank between September 2 and 7, 1985. The meeting took place on a liner named "Bashan" sailing from Chongqing to Wuhan, and was later known as the "Bashan Liner Meeting." A number of well-known scholars, experts, and leaders from the economic sector conducted some in-depth discussions on the major issues which arose in the economic reform process.

CASE 1 *(continued)*

For example, to address the problem of inflation, quite a few local reformists regarded it as something unavoidable in economic takeoff, which was an issue concerning economic structure rather than total volume, so was not something for the government to react to. Should tight macro policy be carried out, that was no other option than to reverse the reform.

However, after the participating economists studied the figures from the World Bank, they unanimously agreed that excessive demand, investment, and consumption as well as economic overheating did exist, and China was in inflation as a consequence of demand drive and cost increase. In 1985, a survey conducted by the Economic System Reform Institute showed that in 1984, labor productivity grew by 7.8%, national income grew by 12%, salary income of urban residents grew by 22.3%, overall residents income, with farmers included, grew by 25.3%, and administration expenditure grew by 38%. The increase by a large margin of urban consumption, rural consumption, and social group consumption indicated inflation.

Foreign economists were inclined to adopt a credit crunch policy to restrain demand. During the meeting, the 1981 Nobel Prize winner Professor Tobin of Yale University suggested the adoption of tight fiscal, monetary and income policy. After the meeting, four provincial governor-level meetings were held to implement the proposal raised on the Bashan Liner Meeting, and to curb excessive investment and consumption.

Another legacy of the "Bashan Liner Meeting" on decision-making was the formulation of reform targets and strategies. Most foreign economists thought the market coordination mechanism with macro control should be the target model for the economic reform in China. However, there was a long way to go. As for the manner of transition, "a basket of reform" was agreed on. It was agreed also to introduce supporting reform centered on price reform, followed by capital market reform, and foreign exchange reform.

The "Bashan Liner Meeting" was indeed successful and seven reports on specific topics were written afterwards, including The Target Model and Transition Steps, The Fiscal Policy and Macro Management, The Monetary Policy and Reform of Financial System, The Income Policy and Macro Management, The Economic Growth and Investment, The Inflation and Price, and The Important Precondition for the Indirect Control of Macro Economy. The meeting brought the high-profile officials in the Chinese government to a deeper understanding of the macro economy, the formulation of macro policy goals, and the path to success in the market economy.

Case 2
Collective Learning of the Politburo of the CCCPC

After the first plenary session of the 16th CCCPC, the system of collective learning was introduced to the Politburo, with experts lecturing the standing members. On December 26, 2002, President Hu Jintao pointed out, when presiding over the first collective learning session, that officials at different levels should understand that with the vast change of the society in all dimensions, and the successive innovation of the people, the lack of learning, or lack of consistency in learning, or lack of serious learning would leave officials lagging behind and unable to shoulder responsibilities. To become a qualified leader and administrator, one should give more attention to learning, and enrich oneself with knowledge provided by society.

The collective learning of the Politburo has several features: First, all members of the Politburo attend the learning, and experts, scholars, and other high-ranking officials are invited to discussions. Second, learning is related to practical work, with the topics of learning related to current economic development. Careful selection and preparation was made before each learning course to improve efficiency.

Altogether 44 collective learning sessions were organized by the Politburo of the 16th CCCPC, and eight by the Politburo of the 17th CCCPC. The learning of the Politburo ensured rational decision-making on the macro level, and is a kind of innovation for decision systems (Appendices 1 and 2).

Not only are experts and scholars invited to the decision-making consultation, members of democratic parties and nonaffiliated people are invited as well. The decision makers—the governing officials—have become better informed. Among the new generation leaders, more have professional backgrounds (Appendix 3).

7.2.2 The Learning of Local Governments

As I was an advisor working for the Governmental Decision Making Consulting Group of Shanghai for three terms between 1997 and 2002, and the Economic Development Commission of Yunnan Government, and have provided decision-making advice to the local governments of Suzhou, Nantong, and Zhenjiang, I may be in a position to say that the learning of local governments at different levels has been open and international.

Take Shanghai as an example. In the 1980s, Mayor Wang Daohan attached great importance to the consulting opinions of experts and scholars, and Jiang Zemin and Zhu Rongji, who served this position later had maintained the heritage. A "Decision-making Consulting Group" was established by the Development and Research Center of the Shanghai Municipal Government with each term lasting two years. A "Development and Research Foundation" was also set up to sponsor a number of key research programs and hot topics. Seminars on topical issues in economic and social development were frequently organized by the municipal officials to invite opinions from experts. For example, the "Consulting Conference between Mayor and International Entrepreneurs" has become a regular activity.

In the late 1980s and early 1990s, Shanghai was in a critical time of development, with a number of issues happening at the same time, including the SOE reform, market development, economy transformation, and urban transition. To address these issues, the municipal government decided to solicit opinions from different channels.

In 1988, the then Shanghai mayor Zhu Rongji took advice from Jing Shuping, the then standing director of China International Investment and Trust Corporation, to establish the "Consulting Conference between Mayor and International Entrepreneurs." The then president of Anderson (Hong Kong) helped by inviting 12 presidents from well-known MNCs to sit on the board. In October 1989, the first Mayor Consulting Conference was held as a preparatory meeting for the adoption of the Articles of Association.

Between 1989 and 2008, altogether 20 conferences were held to discuss the construction of Shanghai, such as the construction of Shanghai as an international financial center, trade center, and shipping center, the construction of infrastructure, industrial coordination, environment management, cooperation mechanism, and the deepening of social system reform, the improving of industrial added-value, and the development of the SMEs amid the revitalization of the SOEs, and the development of telecommunications, aviation, and urban planning (Table 7.1).

Table 7.1 shows that the agenda in the 1990s was more specific, focusing on such aspects as the measures to improve the industrial added-value, factors impacting the foreign investment environment, revitalization of the SOEs, re-employment training, telecommunications and aviation, urban planning, and human resource development. Since the twenty-first century, more attention has been given to the macro and strategic issues, such as the building of Shanghai as a world-class city, building of international competitiveness, acceleration of the service industry, building of the innovative capability, and so on. Among all these, finance and innovation are the two most frequently discussed topics, indicating the importance attached to them.

Manufacturing and service also appear in turn in the conferences as hot topics. A close look at the agenda would bring you to the conclusion that focus has gradually

Table 7.1 Topics of the meetings of International business leader's advisory council for the mayor of Shanghai

1989:	Preparatory meeting, aiming for the adoption of the AOA
1990:	How to build Shanghai as a trade and logistics center and improve the industrial value added, factors impacting the foreign investment environment in Shanghai
1991:	How to build Shanghai into a financial center
1992:	How to set up SMEs and rejuvenate SOEs
1993:	Telecommunication, aviation transportation
1994:	Urban planning, developing human resource
1995:	A second talk on building Shanghai into a financial center
1996:	Making Shanghai an international trade and business center and reemployment training for the laid-off workers
1997:	How to face the twenty-first century
1998:	Management of financial risks, consumer psychology
1999:	Innovation and the development of new industries
2000:	Urban management
2001:	The opportunities and challenges of Shanghai after the accession to the WTO
2002:	How to make Shanghai a world-class city
2003:	How to organize a successful World Expo
2004:	How to enhance the international competitiveness of Shanghai
2005:	Accelerating the modern service industry
2006:	Enhancing the innovative capacity of cities
2007:	Building a resource-efficient and environment-friendly city
2008:	Review & Prospect—Shanghai in globalization

shifted from the revitalization of the SOEs to new industries and modern enterprise management, from telecommunications and aviation to international competitive power. Innovation accompanies every step of the development.

In addition to the discussion on development trend and specific action plans, attention has also been paid to the direction of the world economy and the role of China in the international economic environment. After the outbreak of the Asian financial crisis, the topic for 1998 was risk management. In the heyday of the new economy, the topic for 1999 was "innovation and development of new industries," and at the eve of China's accession to the WTO, the topic for 2001 was opportunities and challenges of Shanghai after the accession.

The participating entrepreneurs are rich in experience and good at referring to successful stories elsewhere. With deep understanding of the Chinese market and

Shanghai, they make each conference fruitful. The wisdom of entrepreneurs has become a driving force for the progress of Shanghai. Many pertinent suggestions have been adopted to guide the work of the government. The conference has become a bridge between Shanghai and the world, focusing on innovation and future vision. With this, Shanghai has managed to present the world a new image every two or three years, which has caught wide attention.

7.2.3 The International Coordination of Economic Policy

Policy learning is the first step toward policy innovation, which leads to the marginal innovation of institution. The internationalized learning and coordination of policy may promote the opening evolution of the management institution, which is reflected in the Sino-US Strategic Economic Dialog (SED) in recent years.

On September 20, 2006, the then deputy Premier Wu Yi announced, together with the then Treasury Secretary Henry Paulson, that the SED system had officially started. This mechanism was initiated by President Bush and was readily accepted by President Hu Jintao. The SED is conducted twice a year in Beijing and Washington in turn. Madam Wu Yi and Secretary Paulson, as special representatives of President Hu Jintao and President Bush, jointly chaired the SED. The first SED took place in Beijing at the end of that year.

Since the two countries set up a diplomatic relationship in 1979, bilateral trade has grown rapidly. In 1979, Sino-US imports and exports amounted to US$2.45 billion. By 2005, the figure had grown to US$211.63 billion, an annual growth rate of 20%. By 2005, the US has become the second-largest trading partner of China (the first being the EU), the largest export market and sixth-largest import source; China has become the third-largest trading partner, the fourth-largest export market and the second-largest import source. However, the Sino-US economic and trade relationship has undergone ups and downs as well. Since the 1990s, with rapid development of bilateral trade, the surplus on the China side grew fast, and trade protectionism on the US side became stronger. Data from the US shows that in 2003, the US trade deficit against China exceeded US$100 billion, and the US Manufacturing Association attributed this to the undervaluation of the RMB. In 2004, Senator Schumer and Senator Graham raised the Punitive Tariff Act, the real target of which was to force the appreciation of the RMB. The economic conflict between the two countries was also reflected in other issues like economic safety, Intellectual Property Rights (IPR), and energy supply.

The visit to China by Secretary Paulson in September 2006 and the following SED were of great significance. Before that, there had been at least nine bilateral or multilateral committees such as the Joint Economic Committee, and the Joint Commission on Commerce and Trade, taking the form of dialog mechanism, cooperation mechanism, and forum, all for the purpose of addressing the trade policy and energy issues. Yet the SED is different in scope and depth. It tackles the economic framework of two countries in a macro, all-round, and long-term view. The SED is so far the most senior consultation mechanism between the two countries, and is also the exchange activity of top economic leaders of both countries.

On December 14 and 15, 2006, the first SED took place in Beijing, with the theme of "The Development Road of China and the Economic Development Strategy." Five sessions were held and 11 topics were covered, including the balanced development of city and countryside, sustainable economic growth, trade promotion, investment, energy, environment, and sustainable growth. Four orders were placed, including the purchase of US$550 million worth of airplane engines and airport fire engines by China, the acquisition of chain stores of construction materials by the US, and the joint construction of an Internet analysis Web site with China Netcom. The fruits of the dialog included the establishment of a representative office of New York Stock Exchange (NYSE) and NASDAQ in China, and China's accession to the Pan-American Development Bank. An agreement facilitating the export financing from US to China was also concluded. China would join the government guidance commission of the "Power Generating Plan of the Future," and the aviation dialog was to restart.

On May 22 and 23, 2007, the second SED took place in Washington. Before this dialog, the trade protectionism on the US side was strong, and the US was exerting continuous pressure on issues like trade deficit, opening of the service industry, IPR, RMB exchange rate, and so on. During the SED, both sides conducted some frank and in-depth discussions on issues concerning the service industry, investment, transparency, high-tech trade, energy and the environment, balanced economic growth, and innovation. Consensus was reached on financial service, energy and environment, aviation, and so on. The fruits of the dialog were as follows: China resumed the examination and approval for the establishment of securities companies in the second half of 2007, the gradual expansion of the business scope of the qualified joint securities companies, the provision of technical assistance from US to China in financial markets, and the signing of the MOU on the IPR law enforcement.

On December 12 and 13, 2007, the third SED took place in Beijing, during which both sides discussed the future development of the Sino-US economic and trade relationship. Centering around the theme of "Grasping the Opportunity of Economic Globalization and Coping with Challenges Thereof," both sides conducted some in-depth discussions. During the SED, a number of agreements including the *Agreement on the Safety of Food and Feed,* and *MOU on the Safety of Medicine and Medical Equipment* were signed, and 31 consensuses in eight areas including financial service, product quality and food safety, energy and the environment, transparency, investment, market position of China, and balanced economic growth were reached. The fruits of the SED were as follows: The US would actively promote the high-tech trade to China for civilian use, the ten-year cooperation plan for energy and environment, the launching of the enterprise cooperation mechanism, the status of tourist destination country of US for group tourists from China, and commitment on the effective governmental supervision on export.

On June 17 and 18, 2008, the fourth SED took place in Annapolis, Maryland. Vice Premier Wang Qishan and Treasury Secretary Henry Paulson co-chaired the dialog. During the SED, both sides emphasized free trade and investment facilitation, and committed to improving the investment environment. Both sides conducted in-depth discussion on major issues including the subprime crisis, financial market turmoil, and global food safety. Both sides agreed to strengthen the communication and coordination on policies on public investment and macro economy so as to cope with economic globalization. Both sides agreed to discuss the IPR issue on a strategic level and construct an innovative society. During the SED, the U.S-China Ten-Year Energy and Environment Cooperation Framework was signed, contributing to the sustainable development of the world.

China is the largest developing country and the US the largest developed country. With different state conditions, economic structure and development status, friction is unavoidable in building win-win economic and trade relations, which calls for solutions on a strategic level. The SED mechanism is a symbol of the skillful handing of the economic and trade issues, and the promotion of bilateral relationships.

7.3 Institutional Learning and Innovation

7.3.1 Imitation of the Planned Economy of the Former USSR

Upon the founding of new China, the top priority was to industrialize the nation and reduce poverty. The starting of industrialization required primitive accumulation, which is always time consuming. To catch up with the developed nations, administrative compulsory measures were adopted to invest the agricultural surplus in the industrial construction through the "scissors gap" of prices between the industrial products and agricultural products, and to nationalize and levy heavy tax on the industrial and commercial enterprises.

This compulsory accumulation mechanism could only function in the planned national economy, that is, the centralized mandatory planned economy. The merit of the USSR-originated system was the quick gathering of limited human, financial and material resources for major construction. After WWII, the USSR continued to adopt the planned economy system, and gave priority to heavy industry. This development strategy worked at the beginning stage of industrialization. Between 1951 and 1982, the annual growth rate of GNP was 7.2%, the average growth rate of industrial output was 8.4%, annual growth rate of social productivity was 6.8%, and the average growth rate of industrial productivity was 5.5%. In the same period, the above four indexes in the US were only 3.2%, 3.6%, 2.3%, and 2.7%, respectively.

The fast economic development in the USSR could be attributed to the gap between itself and the US in economic volume, which is what we call the "late development advantage," as well the fact that low consumption generated high accumulation, which provided capital to reproduction, and the highly centralized management system, which endorsed centralized resource allocation.

For the special political status and economic achievement of the USSR after WWII, most socialist countries followed the USSR model and adopted the planned economy system, and China was no exception. In 1957, the first Five-year Plan was completed ahead of schedule and the industrial infrastructure was basically established. The total industrial output grew by 1.3 times compared to that of 1952, an annual growth of 18%. During the first Five-year Period, priority was given to heavy industry. In 1957, the production value of heavy industry grew by 2.1 times compared to that of 1952, or an annual growth of 25.4% on average. The weight of production material jumped from 35.6% in 1952 to 48.3% among the total industrial production value. During the first Five-year Period, the average growth of the major industrial products was as follows: 31.7% for steel, 25.2% for pig iron, 14.4% for crude coal, and 21.6% for electricity, far above the growth of most capitalist countries.

7.3.2 Learning of the Market Economy System

The downside of the planned economy is the low efficiency of resource allocation amid fast growth. With the industrial foundation established, information became more fragmented, and the relationship between supply and demand became more complicated. The huge labor division system called for the market allocation of resources. Should the mandatory planned economy continue, economic structure would become unbalanced, economic efficiency would be lowered, and productivity would be retarded. There had to be a restructuring or transition of the economic system as industrialization deepened and productivity developed further.

When the reform started in 1978, the goal and target for system reconstruction was not clear, which forced China to learn from abroad, mostly from the reform trials in East Europe, including the reform of Hungary, Poland, and the former Yugoslavia. Later the target of learning changed to East Asia, including Japan and the Asian Tigers (South Korea, Taiwan, Hong Kong, and Singapore) and other emerging economies and regions. Finally the target shifted to the developed countries in Europe and the US.

The early reforms in East Europe. Reform in the East European countries started much earlier than in China. Market reform on a trial basis began in the 1950s and 1960s, in the aim of breaking through the traditional planned economy. For the concern of common ideology, in the early stages of the reform, China learned market reform from the East European nations. Through visiting abroad and inviting experts in, some basic ideas of reform were borrowed. Some theories of the East European scholars became the source of the Chinese scholars. For example, economists Ma Hong and Sun Shangqing of the Chinese Academy of Social Sciences (CASS) and the Development Research Institute of the State Council led many delegations to the East European nations, with literature brought back and research reports compiled upon return having huge impact in China. Sun Yefang, the first one to talk about price rule and profit, was influenced by Liberman from the USSR. The early reform economists, including the founder of the Market Socialism Theory, Oscar Lange, and the founder of the Economics of Shortage, J Kornai, combined the Marxist economics and the Western Neoclassic Economics, and had a huge impact on the Chinese reform economists and policy-makers in the 1980s. It was not until the 1990s that Western Economics was introduced and started to dominate economic theories and policies in China.

Then what measures and practice of reform did China learn from Eastern Europe?

The autonomy-oriented reform of the former Yugoslavia. From the 1950s, Yugoslavia started the autonomy-oriented reform, and by the mid-1960s, a worker autonomy system was established. Rather than the USSR-type, state-owned system, social ownership was adopted for the autonomy. Each enterprise had a worker committee and a management committee directly elected by workers as the decision-making body and the enforcement body, to be responsible to all workers.

The economic system reform covered the following: Firstly, the centralized administrative plan was replaced by the autonomy social plan for the management system. Other than giving mandatory command to enterprises, the new system only set the basic ratio for production and distribution, leaving specific items to the discretion of enterprises whose decision was based on the basic ratio, market demand and production capacity. Secondly, the unitary administrative pricing system was replaced by a combination of administrative price and economic price. The market price in Yugoslavia in the 1970s was determined by the domestic supply—demand, price of the international market, and the average productivity of all sectors. Thirdly, a new budget law was adopted in the early 1950s to replace the highly centralized old system with lump sum collection and lump sum spending. In the mid-1960s, the national infrastructure fund was replaced by bank loans, signaling the fundamental change of the centralized fiscal system. Fourthly, since 1953, a new salary system with clear reward and punishment was adopted instead of the standard salary system formulated by the government. Yet the enterprises were still not given the right to distribute individual income. After 1958, enterprises were able to determine salary rules, and pay differentiated salary according to different performance and contribution. Fifthly in 1953, the governmental monopoly on foreign trade came to an end, with some qualified enterprises obtaining foreign trade rights. The management on foreign exchange also changed from complete governmental administration and disposal to a new structure in which enterprises may retain 20% of the foreign exchange.

The combination of planning and market in Hungary. In 1968, Hungary started its overall economic system reform, the core of which was to build a system combining plan and market to optimize resources allocation without changing the existing ownership system. The economic system reform and achievement of Hungary was eye-catching, and a Hungarian model combining plan and market was created.

The essence of the reform was the combination of the leading of the central government with the liberty of enterprises, and the combination of the administrative measures with more economic measures. Reform measures included the following: Canceling the mandatory quota on enterprises and introducing economic means for regulation; replacing the centralized allocation of production materials and distribution of products with market trade; combining the state pricing and enterprise pricing; replacing budget financing with bank loans; replacing the unitary salary system with a differentiated floating salary system.

The "planned commodity economy" thinking in the early stages of the reform in China as an attempt to combine plan and market was borrowed from Hungary.

The power delegation reform of Poland. Between 1956 and 1959, a power delegation reform was carried out in Poland to expand the power of local authorities and enterprises. Mandatory plans from the government were reduced, giving more decision-making power to enterprises in planning and operations. In 1958, the central administration bureau was dismissed, and the united companies were set up as economic units. A large number of SMEs were given to the local authorities for management. Yet, as a local reform against the existing system, it was terminated when conflict became tense.

The new economic system was tried in 1973 among 27 large economic units, which was called the "New Economic and Finance System" or "Large Economic Organization," referring to the merger of enterprises, the establishment of united factories, united enterprises, and united companies of the same trade. Much liberty was given to these units, such as the exemption of the annual plan. With more power in investment, salary, employment, and pricing, the administrative command system remained unchanged. Internally, the grass-root level enterprises were subject to the higher level of economic organizations, limiting the fruit of the reform.

After the crisis of 1980, Poland started to seek for the fundamental change of the economic system, in the aim of replacing the mandatory system with the combination of central plan and market regulation. The purpose of the central plan was to define the development goal and qualification of the economic organizations, rather than directing tasks. The formulation and enforcement of plans were open to society for participation and supervision. As for the enterprises, gains and losses would be borne by enterprises themselves through a system of self-ruling and self-governance, and staff would be involved in decision-making for major issues. The economic reform policy proved somewhat effective, with the economy warmed up since 1983, yet the whole situation remained largely the same. The ups and downs in Poland served as a negative example for China, saving China much trouble in reform.

In conclusion, the economic reforms in East European countries stand as both experiences and lessons for China. The effort to break through the bottleneck of the highly centralized planned economic system of the former USSR, and the exploration on the transition from planned economy to market economy served as model and reference to China in the economic transition.

Learning from the East Asian Model. After WWII, the fast growth of Japan, the Asian Tigers, and the ASEAN countries attracted global attention, and won the name of the "East Asian Miracle." The geographic adjacency and cultural similarity made the East Asian Model a new target of learning.

Market mechanism and a strong government. Take Japan as an example. In the modernization process of Japan, government played a major role. The Japanese government has always been authoritative in history, and the accord of government and industry contributed to the economic growth. The government intervenes in the economy through the market-oriented guidance plan. Government plans were built on the basis of thorough communication with citizens and aimed at the enhancement of competitive power of industries. Intervention on such basis worked better for the long-term interest of the country. For instance, when government auctioned land for construction purposes, it was the more promising enterprises rather than the one offering the highest price that were more favored by the government. The Ministry of International Trade and Industry (MITI) limited the enterprises with excessive market share to prevent possible damage to the competition mechanism. The government was also active in importing advanced technologies and selling to key enterprises with affordable price. The market economy in Japan is considered, therefore, "development oriented," with pro-market government backing.

The four Asian Tigers are unique in different ways. They more or less borrowed experience from Japan. Both South Korea and Singapore started the market economy with a strong government, which also formulated a series of guidance plans that are close to the world trend and flexible to market change.

Since the 1980s, with the rapid development of Malaysia, Thailand, and Indonesia, Southeast Asia became one of the most vigorous regions in Asia Pacific. The government-driven market economy was a key source of growth. The ASEAN countries engaged directly in the reproduction of materials using state capital, and conducted macro control on the national economy through regulations on production, distribution and circulation by means of pricing, taxation and credit, and so on.

The fast economic growth of East Asia indicated that the catching up of late movers was not possible without strong government-issued guidance plans. Since the reform, by referring to the East Asian model, China shifted from mandatory plan to guidance plan, which was much less administrative and much more market oriented. The market has since played a fundamental or key role in resource allocation.

Industrial policy and group enterprise. Industrial policy originated in Japan. In the revival stage after WWII (1945–1960) the industrial policy in Japan was highly flexible and adaptable to the international economic situation and the domestic economic environment. In stage one, the industrial revival policy with the core of "inclining production method" was formulated to give priority to the coal and iron steel industries, and to fully utilize the limited resources for industrialization. In stage two, the industrial rationalization policy was adopted to give guidance to industries through indirect means such as fiscal investment loan, special taxation measures, FX quota, and rationalized Cartel. In stage three, trade protectionism was adopted to boost industry. A rigid approving system on the import of material and technologies was adopted in time when Japan was in shortage of FX to ensure that priority be given to the most desirable industries. High tariffs and quotas on imports were also adopted, creating a barrier to entry for foreign goods. All this saved Japan from the strong impact of the international market, and Japan managed to revive its economy and industry between the end of WWII and the late 1950s.

In the high growth stage in the 1960s, to enhance international competitive power and occupy a favorable position in the international labor division system, an industrial organization policy was adopted to encourage merger and centralization of enterprises by providing low interest loans. Entrance barriers were also set to discourage the entrance of new enterprises under a certain size.

In the industrial correction period from 1971 to 1982, in the face of pollution of the eco-environment brought by high growth, and congestion in cities and insufficiency of public facilities brought by centralized production, the government corrected its industrial policy in a timely manner by shifting to the energy-saving industries and the "high processing level" industries. The industrial structure changed from the capital-intensive heavy industry and chemical industry to the knowledge-intensive assembling and processing industries. Later, favorable policies were released to encourage the IC and PC industries.

The industrial policies of Japan helped the country define goals and grasp opportunity at each stage, upgraded the industrial structure, and rationalized the industrial organizations in a gradual way. In 1989 China launched its industrial policy by referring to Japan, and the result has been positive so far.

Organizing large group enterprises is another feature of the East Asian model. Both Japan and South Korea organized some giant groups in industries with increasing returns to scale such as the auto industry and electronics industry to maintain competitive position in the international market, For instance, limiting car imports and the cross holding of legal persons, particularly the holding of banks, provides stable financial supply to the auto industry. Efforts were also made to squeeze the small enterprises out, and to inhibit excessive competition so that a few auto oligarchs could be beefed up to join the international competition. When the government departments in charge of enterprises were dismissed in China in the 1990s, many group enterprises were set up, following the Japanese and South Korean model.

The foreign-oriented development and export oriented strategy. A modernized country needs an internationalized economic system and structure. With insufficient natural resources in East Asian, integration into the international labor division is highly necessary. In 1955, the first Five-year Plan was formulated in Japan to subsidize enterprises and control import, making the boosting of export an economic goal. The "import substitution" strategy was adopted then to assist some competitive enterprises with the protection of the "infant industries." When the substituted import was saturated in the domestic market, the "export oriented" strategy was adopted to further develop the economy.

In the early and mid-1960s, the four Asian Tigers also experienced a shift of strategy from "import substitution" to "export orientation." The continuous expansion of foreign exports promoted the economic development of the Asian Tigers. To promote exports, the governments and authorities of these countries set up specific institutions and export-processing zones, adopted favorable export policies, and organized information collection. The growth of the Asian Tigers was also related to abundant foreign investment, which was attracted to these countries by their safe investment environment, modernized infrastructure, favorable policies, and efficient economic systems and facilities. The opening up of China, in particular the development of southeast coastal regions, largely followed the foreign-oriented economic model of East Asia.

The learning from the US and Europe in terms of market economy development. The market economy in the US and Europe is featured by the clear definition of property rights, minimum government intervention, and a large reliance on the market for resource allocation.

The modern enterprise system. The modern enterprise system refers to the new enterprise system, which is based on the comprehensive legal person system, guaranteed by limited liabilities, and takes the form of enterprise with clear property ownership, division of rights and responsibilities, separation from government, and scientific management. It includes the enterprise legal person system, sole responsibility for profit and loss, limited liabilities for capital contributors, scientific leadership, and management system. The limited liabilities companies and shareholding limited companies are the two most representative forms largely adopted in the US and Europe.

The 14th Congress has made the building of a modern enterprise system with "clear property rights, division of rights and responsibilities, separation from government, and scientific management" the direction for the SOE reform, to make enterprises the legal person entities and main bodies for competition. This was obviously borrowed from the US and Europe.

Market transaction rules and market price system. The market economy requires the function of the market price mechanism, which definitely requires fairness of transaction, and standardization of transaction. The main responsibility of government is to formulate and maintain rules.

Since the 1990s, the Chinese government has gradually stepped away from competitive industries. In the course of reform, the government has been making the market and exiting from the market at the same time, that is, dismantling the old framework and building a new market system, including the nurturing of the market mechanism, the construction of market form, and the formulation of market rules. While bringing the economic entities to the market, it gradually retired from the market through power delegation. In changing its role from the sole boss in the planned economy to the organizer and leader in the market economy, many practices were borrowed from elsewhere.

Macro control. The Great Depression of the 1930s put the "Smith Doctrine" to an end. In such context, Keynesianism gave a prescription to the economic crisis, changing the role of state in market economy ever since. The Keynesian theory was adopted in the New Deal of President Roosevelt, by investing heavily in infrastructure and driving the revival of Europe and the boom of the US after the war. From then, all Western countries turned to the state regulation of the economy.

Since the 1990s, the Chinese government has become more skillful with macro control. From the combat on inflation to the prevention of depression, the Chinese economy has registered steady growth for over ten years, manifesting the power of macro control.

7.3.3 The Evolution and Innovation of the Socialist Market Economy System: Innovation by Learning.

The target of learning in the economic reform has changed from the East European nations to the East Asian ones then to the developed nations in America and Europe. All the experiences and models have been of reference value to China, but for the different condition of each country, the successful experiences of other countries still need to be modified before being adopted in China, requiring China to be innovative and adaptive in learning.

China has been learning and innovating over the past 30 years to move closer to the goal and direction of the reform, which is the socialist market economy with Chinese characteristics.

On December 18, 1978 the third session of the 11th CCCPC unveiled the Reform and Opening Up process in China. Shortly afterward, discussion on the "relation between plan and market" among scholars loosened the bondage on the conventional way of thinking for the first time. In September 1982, during the 12th Congress the principle of "planned economy as the mainstay and market economy as the supplement" was proposed, introducing the market as a means of resource allocation to the socialist construction. In October 1984, the third session of the 12th CCCPC defined the socialist economy as "planned commodity economy" on top of the public ownership system, moving one step forward. The 13th Congress in 1987 defined the economic system as "state regulating market and market guiding enterprises." Yet the planned commodity economy was still subject to the plans on the commodity economy. In this sense the planned commodity economy was not fundamentally different from the planned economy, and was only a provisional target in the economic reform. The goal of reform was only confirmed when the concept of "socialist market economy" was put forward in an explicit way during the 14th Congress in 1992.

Institutional evolution in China and Russia: A comparative study. The market economy is a general form of economic system adopted by most countries, and China is no exception. Yet China has never abandoned socialism while adopting the market economy. China adheres to the four basic principles, socialism, and the ruling of the communist party all the time, which is different from the case in Russia. The reform in Russia followed the fully liberal "Washington Consensus," in adopting the radical "shock therapy," turning Western overnight. The reform in China followed the "Beijing Consensus" in adopting the gradual marginal method, with a different goal and different means to the goal.

As a consequence, the reform in Russia led to a serious economic slump. When the "shock therapy" was adopted in 1992, GDP dropped by 14.5% in one year, the national income by 16.2%, industrial output by 18%, and agricultural output by 8%. The economy was in negative growth until the end of 1998, and only weakly picked up in 1999. The GDP dropped again by nearly 50% in the 1990s. Whereas in China, with learning, evolution, and innovation, China managed to find a suitable road, emancipated productivity and promoted high growth. The GDP has maintained double (or near double) digit growth for 30 years, presenting to the world a "China Miracle."

7.4 Relative Advantages of the Sino-Foreign Coopetition in Management Institutions

7.4.1 The Late Development Effect of China

China as a late development country is backward in economy, technology, and management system, the last of which is reflected in the competitive disadvantage (late development disadvantage) in international competition.

However, since the reform, with opening up and active cooperation as well as importing and learning of advanced management systems from developed countries or regions, late development disadvantage has changed to late development advantage.

On one hand, since the management system is an intangible, soft technology different from technical equipment and patents, there is no price in international transfer, and is almost like a free lunch to be shared by everyone. Therefore, the import of advanced management systems and successful experience is almost free.

On the other hand, though China needs to pay the learning cost for the management system imported, there is no need to start from scratch. This saves cost, for the cost of learning, localization, and innovation is always smaller than the cost of creation. In addition, time can be saved and mistakes can be avoided.

In summary, since the opening up, it only took China 30 years to adopt the fruits of the market economy, which had been accumulated in the Western countries over hundreds of years.

7.4.2 The Early Development Effect of the Foreign Side

With long-time exploration, innovation, and accumulation, developed countries and regions lead in management and system, which is reflected in the competitive advantage (early development advantage) in international competition.

However, the early developers also face disadvantages, for example, the diminishing marginal profit of internal investment, the costly replacement of technologies, and so on. Therefore, as they export products, they always export capital and technologies as well, which brings back the early development benefit as mentioned previously. However, if the management and institution of the recipient countries are not compatible, profit will be discounted. Therefore, developed countries are willing to export management and institution for free, which saves the transaction cost for them in the international market, and ensures the high early development benefit, as well as the nonfinancial benefit in the cultural, ideological, and political dimension.

Appendix I
Collective learning of the Politburo of the 16th CCCPC

1st: December 26, 2002	Earnestly Implementing the Constitution and the Construction of a Well-off Society in an All-round Way
2nd: January 28, 2003	The World Economic Situation and the Economic Development in China
3rd: March 28, 2003	The World Trend of Employment and the Employment Policy Research of China
4th: April 28, 2003	The Modern Development Trend of Science and Technology, the Scientific Development of China, and the Adoption of Scientific Means in Combating SARS
5th: May 23, 2003	The Momentum of New World Military Development
6th: July 21, 2003	The Theoretical Thinking of the Party in the Historical Perspective
7th: August 12, 2003	The Development of the World Cultural Industry and the Development Strategy of the Cultural Industry in China
8th: September 29, 2003	The Construction of Socialist Political Civilization by Rule of Law
9th: November, 24, 2003	The Study of the Development History of Major Countries since the Fifteenth Century
10th: February 23, 2004	The World Pattern and the Security Environment of China
11th: March 29, 2004	The Current World Agricultural Development and the Agricultural Development in China
12th: April 26, 2004	The Construction of Legal System and the Perfection of Socialist Market Economy System

13th: May 28, 2004	Prospering and Developing the Philosophical Social Science in China
14th: June 29, 2004	Enhancing the Governing Capacity Building of the Party
15th: July 24, 2004	Adhering to the Coordinated Development of National Defense and Economy
16th: October 21, 2004	Several Issues Concerning the History of Relations of the Ethnic Groups of China
17th: December 1, 2004	The Historical Observation of the Exploration of Socialist Road of China
18th: December 27, 2004	The Scientific Development Strategy Facing 2020
19th: January, 24, 2005	Research on the Maintaining of the Advance Nature of the CCP Members in the New Time
20th: February 21, 2005	Striving to Build a Harmonious Socialist Society
21st: April 15, 2005	Several Issues Concerning the Social and Economic Development Strategy in China
22nd: May 31, 2005	The Economic Globalization and the New Features of Current International Trade Development
23rd: June 27, 2005	The International Energy Resource Situation and the Energy Resource Strategy in China
24th: August 26, 2005	Reflection and Thinking on the Anti-fascist War
25th: September 29, 2005	The Urbanization Model Overseas and the Path toward Urbanization with Chinese Characteristics
26th: November 25, 2005	The Research on World Marxism and the Theoretic Research and Construction Project of Marxism in China
27th: December 20, 2005	Reform on Administration Management System and Perfection of Economic Legal System
28th: January 25, 2006	About the Construction of Socialist New Countryside
29th: February 21, 2006	The Restructuring Trend of World Industry and the Strategic Decision on the Acceleration of Economic Growth Model of China
30th: March 27, 2006	The Systems and Measures for Safety Production Overseas and the Enhancement of System Building for Safety Production in China
31st: May 26, 2006	The International Protection of IPR and the Building of Law and System for the Protection of IPR in China

(continued)

32nd: June 29, 2006	Adhering to Scientific Governance, Democratic Governance and Law-abiding Governance
33rd: July 25, 2006	Review and Thinking of the Success of the Long March of the Red Army
34th: August 29, 2006	The Development Trend of World Education and Deepening of the Education System Reform in China
35th: October 23, 2006	The Medical and Health System Overseas and the Development of Medical and Health Industry in China
36th: November 30, 2006	Research on the Building of Grass-root Democracy in China
37th: December 25, 2006	About the Construction of a Resource Conservatory Society in China
38th: January 23, 2007	The Development of World Internet Technology and the Construction and Management of Internet Culture in China
39th: February 15, 2007	The Regional Development Overseas and the Promotion of Coordinated Regional Development in China
40th: March 23, 2007	Several Issues Concerning the Formulation and Implementation of Property Law
41st: April 23, 2007	The Agricultural Standardization and Food Safety in China
42nd: July 26, 2007	The Nanchang Uprise and the Building of Jinggangshan Revolutionary Base
43rd: August 28, 2007	The World Financial Situation and the Deepening of the Financial System Reform in China
44th: September 28, 2007	Expanding Opening up and Maintaining National Economic Security

Appendix II
Collective learning of the Politburo of the 17th CCCPC

1st: November 27, 2007	Implementing the Basic Strategy of Rule by Law
2nd: December 18, 2007	Implementing the Religious Policy of the Party and Improving the Work on Religions in the New Situation
3rd: January 29, 2008	Carrying out the New Request for the Construction of a Well-off Society in an All-round Manner

4th: February 23, 2008	Promoting the Construction of Service Oriented Government, Improving the Capacity to Serve People
5th: April 28, 2008	Speeding up the Work on the Transition of Economic Development Model
6th: June 27, 2008	Following the Sustainable Path and Enhancing Capacity Building to Combat Climate Change
7th: July 26, 2008	Enhancing the Preparatory Work for the Olympic Games
8th: September 28, 2008	The Theoretical System of Socialism with Chinese Characteristics

Appendix III
Chinese Officials with Overseas Educational Background

Name	Title	Overseas background
Zhou Xiaochuan	Governor of the PBOC	The US
Yi Gang	Vice Governor of the PBOC	PhD, US
Liu Mingkang	Chairman of the CBRC	Master, London City University, UK
Long Yongtu	Former Vice Minister of the MOC	LSE, UK
Yang Jiechi	Minister of the MFA	LSE, UK
Zhou Ji	Minister of Education, former Mayor of Wuhan	PhD, New York State University
Wan Gang	Minister of the MOST	PhD, Germany
Chen Zhu	Minister of the MOH	PhD, Université de Paris VII
Lu Yongxiang	Chairman of the CAS	PhD, Germany
Xu Kuangdi	Chairman of the CAE, former mayor of Shanghai	Imperial College, UK
Jin Liqun	Vice minister of the MOF	The US

CHAPTER 8

Challenges Ahead

The UK newspaper *Guardian* once commented that the UK taught the world production in the nineteenth century, the US taught the world consumption in the twentieth century, and in order to lead the world, China must be prepared to teach the world sustainable development in the twenty-first century.

The rapid economic growth over the past 30 years has brought benefit not only to China but also to all participating countries, regions, enterprises, and individuals. However, the rise of China still worries some people, and arguments like "China Threat" and "China Collapse" emerge now and then. It is true that China is facing many problems and challenges during the development process such as trade friction, energy shortages, deterioration of the eco-environment, and global financial risks. However, all these problems have solutions, and China is fully capable of taking these challenges in the future.

8.1 Challenges from the World Product Market

Since the beginning of the Reform and Opening Up process, the cheap, good, and labor-intensive products "Made in China" have flooded the whole world, bringing benefit to the world's consumers and posing great pressure upon competitors. In such context, on the macro level, some countries have attributed the trade imbalance to the competitive power of China, which has led to increasing antidumping cases, growing trade friction, and higher pressure on the RMB appreciation in recent years. On the micro level, the SMEs, labor unions, and workers abroad all blame China for the closing down of factories and loss of jobs. Trade imbalance and product quality are indeed problems, yet fair competition should not be regarded as a threat. In addition, with its low-labor-cost-based late mover advantage diminishing, China is also facing challenges and being put to the test.

8.1.1 Facing the International Economic Friction and Developing the Domestic Market

While China is still at the beginning stage of making investment overseas, the economic friction between China and other countries is largely related to trade friction on exports, which covers a wide range of areas, including the IPR, industrial policy, technical standards, and FX administration. With the gradual appreciation of the RMB and loosening of the compulsory FX settlement policy, trade friction in the coming years would be reflected in the more intangible technical barriers, IPR, safeguard measures, and so on. With the peaceful rise of the Chinese economy, the noise of the "China Threat" is always around, which, together with trade protectionism, makes trade friction unlikely to disappear in the short run. China needs to be prepared for the long-time coexistence of the noises amid economic development. To what degree the friction should be handled would be a test put to China.

Trade friction is in fact only a reflection of the more fundamental issue—the economic growth model. Therefore, in order to change its passive position, and uproot the whole problem, China needs to change its economic structure and the way of economic growth, which involves economic, educational, social security, and political reform. Economically speaking, to face the challenges of the future market, China needs to develop the hidden domestic market and reduce the reliance on the overseas market for balanced growth. With the domestic market growing larger, the magnitude of the Chinese market makes the domestic market also a world market. With a large number of foreign enterprises accessing the Chinese market, China ought to pay more attention to its domestic market, and let enterprises choose between development of the domestic market and development of the foreign market with cost yield analysis, and create demand by providing instructions on diversified supply.

8.1.2 From "Made in China" to "Created in China"

Over the years, reports on "Made in China" have given China the reputation as a "World Factory." However, a glance at the once "World Factory" countries shows that all these countries used to be leaders of the global economy at different stages with state-of-the-art technologies of the manufacturing business. Yet China is totally different. There is no reason for China to claim itself as the locomotive of the global economy. Perhaps the more precise description is the "World Processing Factory."

The wide coverage of "Made in China" comes from the late development advantage of low labor cost in the labor intensive industries of assembling, processing, OEM with little added-value, and thin profit. With the acceleration of economic globalization, the acquisition of cheap labor is not as hard as before, making competition fiercer. Currently, the "Made in China" edge is diminishing, as the late development advantage of low labor cost is diminishing. India, Vietnam, and other late movers are joining the competition, stealing away investment from South Korea, Taiwan, Hong Kong, and even from the US, Europe, and Japan.

The deeper regret of "Made in China" is the lack of product technology, excessive reliance on foreign know-how, lack of branding, and so on. Therefore, China needs to change from "Made in China" to "Created in China," which requires the move to technical and management innovation when the low cost advantage is diminishing, so that China may start to seek and establish the early development advantage.

8.2 Challenges from the World Energy and Resources Market

The high economic growth in China has created huge demand for oil and iron ore. Japan and South Korea as neighbors were the first to notice the pressure in the energy war for market and resources, and were also the first to raise the theory of "China Threat," which was echoed by the US and Europe, who extended the "China Threat" from economy to military, culture and politics, in the aim of inhibiting China. In fact, though the demand on energy and resources has created some tension in the world energy market, it has presented opportunity to suppliers and driven growth after all, not to mention China's efforts to save energy and develop a renewable economy for an economized society.

8.2.1 The "China Demand" and the Future Energy Gap

Since China is now in the process of heavy industrialization and urbanization, the demand on energy and resources increases rapidly. Prediction from the World Energy Administration shows that between 2000 and 2030, the incremental energy demand of China would account for 20% of the world total, among which coal accounts for 43%, and oil 18%. The growing economic volume naturally demands more energy supply, posing a formidable challenge in the energy market. Except for coal, the energy gap is widening and calls for solution. Table 8.1 predicts the supply-demand gap for major strategic resources (water, grain, oil, and so on).

Obviously the gap of energy and resources created simultaneously by the growing demand and limited supply is a practical issue that exists. The pressure forces China to face directly the competition and cooperation in the international energy and resources market.

Table 8.1 Prediction on supply-demand of major strategic resources in China

Resource type	Balance of supply-demand	2010	2020	2050
Oil (100 million tons)	Demand	2.8	3.5	10
	Supply	1.8	2.1	5
	Gap	1	1.4	5
Natural gas (100 million m^3)	Demand	900	2,000	3,600
	Supply	800	1,500	2,700
	Gap	100	500	900
Iron ore (100 million tons)	Demand	3.99	10	24
	Supply	3.29	5	9
	Gap	0.7	5	15
Aluminum (10,000 tons)	Demand	1,120	1,655	3,000
	Supply	805	1,456	2,000
	Gap	315	199	1,000
Copper (metal) (10,000 tons)	Demand	170	210	290
	Supply	90	115	134
	Gap	80	95	156
KcL (tons)	Demand	640	802	1,450
	Supply	100	125	160
	Gap	5,440	677	1,290
Grain (100 million tons)	Demand	5.8	6.5	12
	Supply	5.5	6	8
	Gap	0.3	0.5	4
Water/100 million m^3	Demand	5,850	7,200	7,550
	Supply	5,400	6,640	6,850
	Gap	450	560	700

Source: Bai Yongxiu, ed., *30 Years of Economic Reform in China: Resource and Environment* (Chongqing University Press, 2008).

8.2.2 The Dilemma of the International Energy and Resources Market

Case of the Iron Ore Price Negotiation. In January 2008, the International Iron and Steel Institute (IISI) headquartered in Brussels announced that in 2007 China once again ranked No. 1 for crude steel production with an output of 489 million tons, a 12-year consecutive record. However, the once proud name of the "largest producer of iron and steel" has seldom been mentioned after 2005.

In January 2005, the Chinese iron tycoon Baosteel, Hamersley of RioTinto, and CVRD agreed on the iron ore price for 2005, which was a 71.5% increase against 2004. As a result, the Chinese iron and steel enterprises paid RMB 20–30 million more for the import in 2005. As the largest importer of the world, the failure of China on the negotiation table is a lesson to learn.

With careful preparation and analysis, in the fifth International Seminar on Iron and Steel in 2006, 45 Chinese enterprises gathered in Qingdao to negotiate with the three international tycoons: BHP Billiton, Rio Tinto, CVRD. The price negotiation of 2006 was immeasurably hard, and concluded eight months later with China once again giving in to compromise. On June 20, 2006, an agreement on 19% increase was signed between China and the three producers.

Within six months after the closing of the price negotiation of 2006, a new round of talks started for 2007. The price increase for four consecutive years made it likely that the downward curve of slowed production growth of the steel makers and the upward curve of the output capacity of the mining enterprises would intersect, forming the game point of this round of talk. Ultimately Baosteel surprisingly obtained the global price setting right for the first time on December 21, 2006, and signed with CVRD on a 9.5% price increase of ore produced in the north and south of CVRD for 2007, and signed with BHP Billiton and Hamersley of Rio Tinto on a 9.5% price increase as well.

When people were still immersed in the delight of successful negotiation for the ore price of 2007, thinking that Chinese enterprises had obtained bargain power, the negotiation of 2008 came as a cold blast.

On February 18, 2008, Nippon of Japan announced that it had come to agreement with Posco and CVRD on 65% and 71% price increases for two iron ores for the fiscal year of 2008. Meanwhile the second-largest steel maker, JFE, also announced the same margin of increase with CVRD. The conclusion of the price negotiation by the Japanese and Korean steel makers cast a shadow on the Chinese steel makers, and once again the price setting right was lost. In such context, Baosteel announced on July 4, 2008 that it agreed on the benchmark price of powder ore and lump ore with BHP Billiton, with same margin of increase. According to the agreement, the price of BHP Billiton's Neumann powder ore, Yandi powder ore and Neumann lump ore would increase by 79.88%, 79.88%, and 96.5%, respectively, compared to the previous year.

The oil import by China in recent years. China is now the second-largest resource producer and the second-largest energy consumer in the world. Since 1992, China has become a net importer of product oil, and since 1996, a net importer of crude oil, with the gap between import and export ever widening (Table 8.2).

Since the world oil market and oil industry is controlled by the multinational oil companies from the US and Japan, as the third-largest oil importer, China has been distanced from the global oil market and supply system. With the strategy of going global, some Chinese oil companies walked out in the early 1990s. However, it was not until 2003 that Chinese oil companies went out for M&A in Russia, Africa, and Latin America, as boosted by the national strategy. However, the bilateral oil strategy of

Table 8.2 Import and export of oil in China (ton)

	Year	1995	1997	1999	2001	2003	2005	2006
Oil/t	Import	3,673.2	6,787	6,483.3	9,118.2	13,189.6	17,163.2	19,453
	Export	2,454.5	2,815.2	1,643.5	2,046.7	2,540.8	2,888.1	2,626.2
	Net import	1,218.7	3,971.8	4,839.8	7,071.5	10,648.8	14,275.1	16,826.8

Source: China Statistical Year Book, 1996–2007.

China remained inconsistent. In the long run, China needs to cooperate with the major oil-rich countries, during which interest conflict with the US and others would surely appear, demanding efficient policy mediation. With more development activities going on outside the Middle East, the M&A trend will likely continue, waging a war with no gunpowder.

On October 16, 2008, the "2008 Cooperation and Development Forum on International Oil Pipe" was held in the pipe city of Langfang. At the forum, it was mentioned that 2008 would be a critical year for the construction of energy networks, with many pipe projects to Central Asia, Russia, and Burma kicking off. It was also planned that by 2010, capacity would grow by 60% to satisfy the energy demand. When the Chinese oil companies are going global, attention should also be paid to the new features of the international environment, so as to take effective measures and give full play to Chinese MNCs in the international energy competition for larger breakthrough in the coopetition.

8.2.3 Promoting Energy Saving, Developing an Circular Economy, and Building a Resource-Efficient Society

While actively integrating into the global coopetition for resources and energy, China has started to give attention to energy saving and consumption reduction to build an economized society.

In recent years, energy saving and emission reduction have been key for technical development and reengineering. The efficiency index is adopted for energy saving, and the gross volume index is adopted for emission reduction, which accord the decoupling strategy separating economic growth and material consumption for higher resource productivity. There is no ready experience to refer to for higher efficiency amid fast growth of energy consumption, and China has to find its own way.

The Guidelines on the 11th Five-year Plan for the National Economic and Social Development proposed the development of renewable energy, the adoption of favorable fiscal policy, investment policy, and compulsory market share policy to encourage the production and consumption of renewable energy and its weight in the primary energy consumption.

Renewable energy is typically less competitive in the market, for it mainly serves the purpose of sustainable public interest and thus requires a whole set of laws and policies for endorsement. It also needs fiscal aid from the government, technical support from industries, and function of the market system for implementation. To be honest, China is not ready with the above-mentioned conditions so far, but the direction and goal has already been set, and the top decision-makers are prepared to introduce specific policies, such as the *Renewable Energy Law of the PRC*, national industrial policies, and the *Circular Economy Promotion Law of the PRC*, which went into effect on January 1, 2009.

One way for the building of an economized society is new industrialization. However, there lacks ready experience and a model to follow, and as a large economy, it is hard to escape from the general rules of industrialization. In the market condition, the success of an economized society lies in the actual benefit brought by the model to enterprises and people. To develop a renewable economy, it is important to let enterprises and people renew voluntarily. When enterprises are more profitable, and people benefit more from being environment-friendly, the mechanism of renewable economy would spontaneously appear. China has already started the efforts to find its way.

8.3 Challenges from Global Environmental Issues

The process of industrialization inevitably creates pollution and environmental issues. Whether to take action after pollution is done or when pollution is being done are two different strategic approaches. The early development countries mostly chose the first approach and have so far solved the environment issues quite well, though they still bear responsibility for global pollution. To avoid the repetition of the old practice, the second approach is a better choice for the late development counties. Yet, no pollution at the cost of development is too much a compromise. As a developing country now in the process of industrialization, China has experienced serious environmental pollution. The country is also blamed by Western countries for exporting pollution, which is quite untrue. But taking more responsibilities is what China is ready to accept. Though developed countries have historically contributed more to global pollution, China is willing to shoulder more responsibilities.

8.3.1 High Economic Growth and Environment Pollution in China

Like all industrialized countries, the pollution issue in China came up amid industrialization. Before the 1950s, with weak industrial foundation, pollution was not an issue. With mass industrialization after the 1950s, and in particular the fast growth of heavy industry, pollution surfaced as an issue. But the scope and degree of pollution was still manageable. By the 1980s, with fast economic development, pollution became more of an issue. The rise of township enterprises spreads pollution quickly to vast rural areas. Today the environmental issue has become a headache for the Chinese economy and society.

In 2006, the emission of waste water and industrial solid waste amounted to 1,515,410,000 tons and 53,682,870,000 tons, 16.89% and 50.90% higher than the previous year. The waste water and solid waste emission per GDP was way above the world average. Fine particles in the air (diameter smaller than 10 mm) and super-fine particles (diameter smaller than 2.5 mm) from industrial boilers and household stoves (which also emit SO_2 and nitrogen oxides) are most harmful to human health. The emission of SO_2 and nitrogen oxides per GDP is eight times higher than that of the OECD countries. In 2006, the SO_2 emissions reached 25,887,000 tons, 19.93% higher than that of 1993.

Pollution typically comes from the huge consumption of energy and resources in the industrialization process. According to the calculation of the World Bank, in the mid-1990s, two-thirds of economic growth was achieved at the cost of overconsumption of the eco-environment. The extensive economic development model was the major cause of the overexploitation and environment deterioration. In 2005, the GDP reached RMB 18.2321 trillion, or US$2.28 trillion, accounting for 5% of the world total. However, five billion tons of domestic and imported resources were consumed for that 5%, and for the major resources, the proportion consumed by China among the world total was as follows: 7.8% of oil, 39.6% of coal, 31.8% of crude steel, 24.4% of alumnium oxide, 47.7% of cement. While the water consumption of China was the same as the US, the GDP of China was merely one eighth of the US.

Most rivers in China are polluted, among which the water quality of Liao River, Hai River, Huai River, and Yellow River are worrisome. Eutrophication of the fresh water lakes has become a serious problem. The ground water in many cities is also contaminated to different degrees. In 2007, Wuxi, Jiangsu Province shocked the nation with the pollution of Taihu Lake.

In May 2007, blue algae appeared in Taihu Lake and water quality was seriously contaminated. Residents of Wuxi all rushed to buy mineral water for the lack of drinkable tap water. The causes of the blue algae were twofold: Natural and artificial, with the latter being more important. The nitrogen and phosphor content has traditionally been high in Taihu Lake. In 2006, the average nitrogen content doubled and the phosphor content grew 1.5 times compared to 1996. Since May 2007, the algae chlorophyll content in the lake has been as high as 230 per unit, providing the condition for the growth of the algae. In fact, blue algae appeared in Taihu Lake area first in the early 1980s in the Wuli Lake. Later, it became more serious and occurred more frequently. In the late 1980s, each year saw two to three algae growths, and contamination spread to Meiliang Lake. The late 1990s saw four to five growths each year, and contamination gradually spread to the central lake.

It is estimated that in 2005, RMB 10 billion was invested in the phase one project of water purification and RMB 100 billion was budgeted for the phase two project, but it may cost more to achieve an acceptable level of purification. A survey by Japanese experts indicates that to bring the water quality back to the level of the early 1980s, RMB 225.15 billion is to be invested within ten years. The drinking water crisis triggered by the blue algae disturbed the life of millions and rang the alarm bell for the whole country. Historical reasons like industrial pollution and urban waste emission, together with new causes like tourism and property development, are handicapping the comprehensive purification work. The pollution of Taihu Lake is a reflection of the backwardness of urban governance compared to the economic construction.

In addition to water pollution, desertification, acid rain, and sand storms are also found in China. Though China has started to tackle the environmental issues and has achieved some progress, more issues still remain unsolved.

8.3.2 Participating in International Environmental Cooperation

As a responsible major nation, China is an important force for international environmental cooperation. In 1972, the UN conference on human environment included the issue of the environment in the world political agenda for the first time, and with the Chinese delegation participating in this conference, it marked China's entry to the international environmental cooperation domain. Since then China has been actively participating in international environmental activities and playing a constructive role. By early 2008, China had joined 22 environmental covenants, seven protocols, and five amendments in areas of air, hazardous waste, chemicals, biological resources, ocean environment, nature protection, and nuclear security.

Judging from the economic development level of the participating countries, international environmental cooperation can be divided into the horizontal type and the vertical type, the former referring to the cooperation among countries with similar economic development, that is, within developed countries or within developing countries, and the latter referring to the cooperation among countries at different economic levels, that is, between developed countries and developing countries. In the future, with the technical progress of China, China may engage more in the vertical type of environmental cooperation, for developed countries boast sufficient capital, rich management experience, and environment technologies, which China lacks. Yet with the relatively rich natural resources and low labor cost in China, such cooperation may bring mutual benefit to both sides.

The low efficiency of resource utilization, the low recycling rate, and large emissions are related to multiple factors including the economic development level, individual awareness, and the industrial structure. It is hard for China to just skip this stage. However, with active cooperation with the international environmental agencies, the utilization of international mechanisms for capital and technologies transfer, and with the formulation and execution of supporting policies, as well as the shift from the "attend after pollution is done" model to the "attend when pollution is being done" model, at some compromise to the GDP growth, China can surely solve the environment issues in a gradual manner.

8.4 Challenges from the Global Financial Market

Reform of the financial sector has been behind other sectors in China, and the situation only changed after the accession to the WTO. The "China Collapse" prediction didn't come true. Rather, the subprime-triggered global financial crisis has had huge impact on the global economy.

In fact problems and risks in the financial sector in China exist, but collapse is yet to come. In spite of the multiple challenges ahead, China is still capable of maintaining steady growth and development.

8.4.1 Merits and Demerits of the Gradual Financial Reform in China

In the 30 years of the Reform and Opening Up process, the first part of financial reform was mainly conducted within China by bringing in foreign financial institutions and borrowing international experiences. Since the twenty-first century, and especially after the accession to the WTO, amid the "bringing in" and "going global" strategy, the financial sector has become more open to the outside, and has been exposed to financial globalization.

For the reform and opening up of the financial sector, China chose the gradual opening up strategy, which is slower in pace than the reform of the real economy. In the past ten years, this opening up strategy saved China from the impact of the Asian financial crisis at the end of the last century, and largely buffered the negative impact of the subprime crisis in 2008 and 2009. It is fair to say that the steady financial reform helped build a stable environment for the macro economy and guaranteed the reform and high growth of the real economy. However, with the further progression of the reform and accelerated globalization, the delayed financial reform started to handicap the further development of the real economy. For example, the unclear ownership of state banks leads to discrimination upon economic entities with different identity; and the underdevelopment of the capital market leads to the low efficiency in enterprise financing and resource allocation in the real economy. With the booming market economy, and limited financial tools, further financial reform, that is, further opening up and integration into the global financial system, would be the priority for the next stage.

8.4.2 Integration into the Global Financial System

Commercial banks. Talking about the Chinese state-owned commercial banks, the biggest headache is the unclear ownership and the huge amount of nonperforming loans (NPL). With nearly all the competitive industries open to the private sector, the banking industry remained tightly controlled by the government. The bad debt left by the SOEs is till today a heavy burden for all the state-owned commercial banks. In opening up the financial market and integrating into the global financial system, China does not only need the quality of the incremental financial assets, that is, liquidity and digestion of the existing bad debt, but also the mastery of new trends in the international banking industry so as to make proactive preparation. Otherwise new troubles may come before the old ones are cleared away.

Since the Great Depression of 1929, the US-led developed countries adopted the "divided operation and regulation" model, which China employs now. At a time when the financial system was not complete and the market was underdeveloped, the merits of the model were obvious in ensuring the steady development of the financial system. However, with economic development, technical progress, and market innovation, amid ever fiercer competition among the financial institutions, and even between the financial institutions and nonfinancial institutions, the traditional commercial banks are facing challenges in business development.

The unused social capital has been moved gradually from the deposit account with commercial banks to the investment account with securities firms and funds. In particular, with the government regulating the IR, the negative actual deposit IR further threatens the deposit shrinkage of the commercial banks. Although, for the time being, Chinese state-owned commercial banks have sufficient deposits, and are even restrained by the central bank in giving loans, with further opening up of the financial sector and diversification of the investment portfolio, the excessive liquidity with commercial banks will not sustain. During the stock market boom in 2007, bank deposits dropped for six consecutive months, reflecting the diversification of investment behavior.

As for the asset business, with the development of the capital market, such as the quick development of the mid-short-term investment tools like corporate bonds and commercial papers, direct financing becomes more available to enterprises, cutting the demand for commercial bank loans. Also some nonfinancial institutions have started to provide deposit and loan services to clients, such as the purchase card of chain stores, the credit service of manufacturing enterprises, the installment payment service of home electronic appliance chain stores, and so on. It is predictable that the conventional "deposit, loan, remit, acceptance" business model will be challenged, and banks would have to provide more innovative and diversified services to develop the off balance sheet business for noninterest revenue.

In the face of such challenges, M&A offers an international practice for enlarging scale, and mixed operations, and another choice for diversifying business, adopting modern electronic tools, and enhancing risks control. While referring to the foreign experience, China needs to study its own condition and walk its own way.

International capital market. Generally speaking, the international capital flow includes direct investment, securities investment, and international credit. The lessons of the financial crisis of the emerging countries indicate that for a country or a region, the larger the weight of foreign securities investment and international loan (in particular the short loan) in the international capital flow, the higher the potential financial risks. While the current account is open in China, the capital account has been rigidly controlled. In the active and prudent opening of the financial sector, China follows the strategy of loosening restriction on the long-term capital flow ahead of the short-term flow. Until now, the larger part of business is still direct investment and some international credit, with the international securities investment remaining rigidly controlled. From the perspective of development, the free flow of international capital is a long-term trend that is not to be resisted, for the multiple benefit it brings: Firstly, it promotes capital flow and lowers capital cost, which is conducive to economic growth; secondly, with the arriving of foreign capital and financial institutions comes also advanced capital operation expertise, which is conducive to capital allocation efficiency; thirdly, which is also what I believe to be the most important, it promotes the structuring of enterprise ownership and corporate governance, and forcefully pushes the financial departments to allocate resource to the most efficient sectors. However, the free flow of international capital links the finance of different countries together, and an operational error in one market or a financial crisis of one country may tumble the whole market, and even trigger a financial crisis of another country (or even many countries, as with the Asian financial crisis and the subprime crisis). If a country is to take some financial risks for the benefit of free flow of international capital, then the million dollar question is: Is there a balance between the benefit and risk of the free capital low? Or with what systematical arrangement can the risks be minimized? This might be the question to ask along financial reform for the coming several or even dozens of years.

International financial coordination and regional cooperation. In discussing the integration into the international financial system and the further opening of the Chinese financial market, research on the international financial coordination and regional cooperation seems to be rather weak. With financial globalization, financial crises spread quickly from one country to another, and the prevention of risks is no longer something that can be handled by just a few countries. More international cooperation and coordinated efforts are desired. Such work can be started on a regional level to begin with, such as the building of a regional financial coordination mechanism in Asia.

In addition to the active participation in the regional financial cooperation, China should also fully utilize its membership position of the IMF, World Bank and International Bank of Settlement. Guided by the mature market theories of Western countries and sometimes manipulated by the political and economic interest of some developed countries, in issues of principle concerning the global financial system and financial crisis, with different countries taking different positions, the crisis-handling capability of the IMF has invited criticism from developing countries and even from developed countries. However, like Frederic S. Mishkin commented, "With a large number of professionals working hard in the IMF and the World Bank, they are capable of providing highly valuable technical assistance to the developing countries and design effective systems should they adopt a more open attitude and abandon the one size fits all thinking" (Mishkin 2007). Therefore, the active participation of economists from developing countries like China is highly necessary so as to bring refreshed thinking and updated information as China develops.

8.4.3 Constructing a Financial System for China

Greenspan, the former president of the Federal Reserve, once pointed out that a combination of a weak banking system and open capital items is prone to accidents. Therefore, the urgent task for China in the coming years is to accelerate the financial system reform, build a modern enterprise system with clear ownership, improve corporate governance structure, and enhance government regulation for better transparency. While market experience can be picked up through practice, an improper system is none other than a hidden bomb, which might one day blow apart the whole system.

It is worth pointing out that the systems running well in the developed countries might not work in China, and China needs to create its own system to promote investment and development. Here we may go back to the function of finance in the overall economy, which is the provision of service and capital to the more advantageous enterprises and industries. It is in itself the forming of financial markets and financial structure that accommodates the industrial development (Lin et al. 2003). Financial development refers to the development of financial agencies and financial markets, and the transferring of capital from deposit to investment at a higher ratio with leverage tools such as interest rates and exchange rates, so to optimize the allocation and utilization of capital and promote economic growth with capital accumulation and technical advancement (Shen et al. 2004). It is obvious that the deepening and development of finance is not an ultimate goal in itself. Rather it is a systematic tool to serve for better and faster economic growth. Therefore, China should refer to the experience and lessons of the emerging markets, and combine its own conditions in tailoring a financial system with a pace and path that serves its economic development.

CHAPTER

9

Conclusion: The Theory of Development Relativity

China used to lead the world economically and technologically 500 years ago, but has lagged behind Europe, the US, and Japan for the past 200–300 years. Since the founding of the People's Republic of China in 1949, for the first 30 years, China continued to seclude itself from the outside world, and remained slow in economic development. With the adoption of the Reform and Opening Up policy, economic growth has been robust since 1978. As a super-large developing nation, China has presented the world with an unprecedented and unparalleled miracle, as well as a "riddle" that challenges modern Neo-Classical Economics.

As a quick review of the history of the world economy, the UK surpassed the Netherlands in the eighteenth century and led the world for over 100 years; the US surpassed the UK in the twentieth century and has been leading the world ever since. Though Japan failed to replace the US as the world leader after WWII, it created a catch-up miracle as well. These are not just simple issues of growth convergence, but manifestations of the development rule of "the backward striving to catch up with the advanced" and "the latecomers surpassing the old-timers."

Other than the existing neo-classical growth and endogenous growth theories, starting from the hypothesis on the advantage of backwardness by Alexander Gerschenkron, and based on the China Miracle and the successful experience on the national economic development in Europe and Asia, I developed a generalized theoretical logic of development relativity ten years ago (Lu De-ming 1999), which includes the following seven hypotheses:

1. The driving force of the early development advantage for the early development countries.
2. The driving force of the late development advantage for the late development countries.
3. Conditional increasing early development advantage by innovation.

4. Conditional diminishing late development advantage by learning.
5. The primary driving force of government for the late development countries.
6. The change of advantage and orbital transfer of development.
7. The relative advantages of international trade and international investment.

Below is a summary of the theory.

9.1 The Dual Economies Model

The concept of "developed and developing countries" and "advanced and backward countries" does not reflect the dynamic relativity of development. In accordance with the theory of development relativity, I categorize all economies (countries, regions, and enterprises) into two groups: One is the early development economies (EDEs), which are the relatively advanced early starters that enjoy a high level of development. With their driving force coming mostly from innovation, they can also be called the innovative economies (countries, regions, or enterprises). The other group is the late development economies (LDEs), which are the relatively backward, late-starting economies with a low level of development. With their driving force coming mostly from learning, they can also be called the learning economies (countries, regions, or enterprises).

The EDEs enjoy the early development advantage (EDA), including all the favorable conditions or opportunities brought by early development, such as the physical capital advantage accumulated through the early development of natural resource, the human capital advantage accumulated through the early development of human resources, the technology leadership advantage resulting from technical innovation, the institutional leadership advantage resulting from management innovation, and so on. The first two advantages concern generalized capital accumulation while the latter two advantages concern generalized technical advancement, which are mutually enhancing.

The LDEs enjoy the late development advantage, or LDA, including the special favorable conditions and opportunities brought by late development, such as the cheap resource advantage of late development of natural resources, the low wage cost advantage of late development of human resources, the advantage of capital import, the advantage of technology and knowledge import and learning, the advantage of management experience and institution learning, and so on.

9.1.1 Increase of EDA Conditional

Supposing the relative production function to be of the Cobb-Douglas type, the growth formula for the EDEs is:

$$Y = K^{\alpha} L^{1-\alpha} A e^{rt} \tag{9.1}$$

This is the aggregate production function of early development countries, which may also serve as the generalized production function of the representative early development enterprises. Y is the total output decided by the EDA.

K is the physical capital invested, and α is the output elasticity.

$$K(t) = Y(t) \cdot s - k(t) \tag{9.2}$$

$K(t)$, the capital accumulation of t year equals the total output $Y(t)$ multiplying the savings rate s, deducting the net capital outflow of t year $k(t)$. Overseas investment is one of its EDA.

L is the skilled labor (or human capital) invested, $1 - \alpha$ is the output elasticity.

$$L(t) = P(t) \cdot h + l(t) \tag{9.3}$$

$L(t)$, the skilled labor (or human capital) of t year, equals the total population of t year $P(t)$ multiplying the ratio of educated or trained labor force (or the human capital coefficient) h, and adding the net inflow of skilled external labor force (or human capital) of t year $l(t)$. The early development countries appeal to the technical immigrants and investment immigrants.

Ae^{rt} refers to the generalized technical advancement, which includes the change of technology, knowledge, management and institution and is reflected in the TFP. The technical advancement is neutral with both the enhanced (or saved) capital and labor effect.

$$A(t) = A_0 \cdot e^{rt} \tag{9.4}$$

r is the annual growth rate of technical advancement, or the annual growth rate of TFP. The technical advancement is supposed to be of the innovative R&D type with no import and learning. Since R&D and innovation is the by-product of physical capital accumulation (investment activities) and human capital accumulation (learning by doing) in the production process, technical advancement is endogenous. In other words, technical advancement and knowledge accumulation comes from the external economies (Jones 1998). Therefore Formula (9.1) features increasing returns to scale.

The derivative of Formula (9.1) is itself based on the derivative character of the exponential function with e as the base:

The first order partial derivative $\dfrac{\partial Y}{\partial t} = K^{\alpha} L^{1-\alpha} Ae^{rt} > 0$

The second order partial derivative $\dfrac{\partial^2 Y}{\partial t^2} = K^{\alpha} L^{1-\alpha} Ae^{rt} > 0$

shows when $r > 0$, the EDA increases, with the geometrical curve as follows:

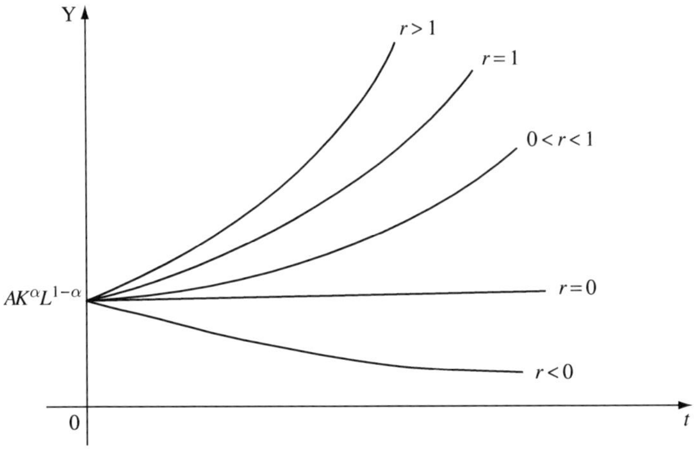

FIGURE 9.1 The output curve depicting the EDA conditional increasing

When $t = 0$, $Y = K^{\alpha} L^{1-\alpha} A$, it crosses $(0, AK^{\alpha} L^{1-\alpha})$;
When $t > 0$, $r = 0$, and $Y = K^{\alpha} L^{1-\alpha} A$, it is a horizontal line $Y = AK^{\alpha} L^{1-\alpha}$;
When $0 < r < 1$, curve $Y = K^{\alpha} L^{1-\alpha} Ae^{rt}$, monotonic increase;
When $r = 1$, curve $Y = K^{\alpha} L^{1-\alpha} Ae^{t}$, fast increase;
When $t > 1$, curve $Y = K^{\alpha} L^{1-\alpha} Ae^{rt}$, sharp increase; and
When $r < 0$, curve $Y = K^{\alpha} L^{1-\alpha} Ae^{-rt}$, monotonic decrease

The above shows the conditional increasing of EDA, with the condition being the annual growth rate of the generalized technical advancement *r* larger than 0. The larger the *r*, the faster the rate of increase. In other words, the degree that EDA increases is decided by the strength, speed, and density of the generalized technical innovation (including technical innovation, management innovation, and so on). The faster and stronger innovation happens, the quicker the EDA increases.[1]

On the contrary, there is also conditional diminishing of EDA. When the generalized technical advancement (innovation) rate *r* is smaller than 0, EDA monotonically decreases. There is no innovation, then diminishing. There are numerous examples

1. The viewpoint and proposition of revenue increasing given technical advancement conditions was mentioned in my master's thesis in 1984, and was later published in the Chinese edition of *Economic Research* in October 1986 (Lu De-ming, 1986), but with no modeling.

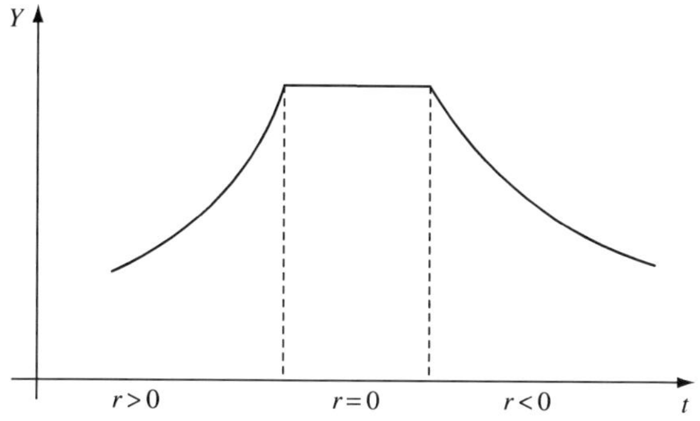

FIGURE 9.2 Three periods of EDA

of how the early development countries lost EDA and declined, and there are more examples of early development companies. See Formula (9.5) and Figure 9.2

$$Y = \begin{cases} K^{\alpha}L^{1-\alpha}Ae^{rt}, r > 0; \\ K^{\alpha}L^{1-\alpha}A, r = 0; \\ K^{\alpha}L^{1-\alpha}Ae^{-rt}, r < 0. \end{cases} \tag{9.5}$$

9.1.2 Diminishing of LDA Conditional

Assuming the relative production function of the LDEs that have already started development to be of the Cobb-Douglas type too, the growth formula for the LDEs is

$$Y = K^{\alpha} L^{1-\alpha} Ae^{rt\frac{1}{2}ct^2} \ (r>0, c>0) \tag{9.6}$$

This is the aggregate production function of late development countries, which may also serve as the generalized production function of the representative late development enterprises. Y is the total output decided by LDA.

$$K(t) = Y(t) \cdot s + k(t) \tag{9.7}$$

$k(t)$ is the net capital inflow that reflects LDA.

$$L(t) = P(t) \cdot \mathrm{h} \mp l(t) \tag{9.8}$$

Here the supposition of simple labor input is abandoned, for even for an illiterate laborer in a developing country, once he or she takes a job, there is the experience-type human capital accumulation effect of "learning by doing," and he or she will naturally become experienced. As for the international flow of skilled laborers (or human capital), it features net outflow in the beginning stage for the drain of talents, with the $l(t)$ being negative, and features net inflow later as the talents return, with the $l(t)$ becoming positive, which reflects the transition of the late development disadvantage into late development advantage in the late development countries.

$Ae^{rt\frac{1}{2}ct^2}$ refers to the generalized learning-type technical advancement of LDEs, with the formula being

$$A(t) = A_0 e^{rt\frac{1}{2}ct^2}, (r > 0, c > 0). \tag{9.9}$$

Here, c is defined as the acceleration of catching-up of the LDEs, referring to the acceleration of the narrowing of the economic and technical gap between the LDEs and EDEs after LDEs begin to learn.

If there is no innovation with the LDEs, technical advancement is categorized as the import and learning type. The learning-type technical advancement is decided by the growth rate r of the innovative-type technical advancement of EDEs, and the acceleration c of catching up (or narrowing of the gap) for the LDEs. The faster the r, the larger the gap and the LDA, and the more technologies available for import. The larger the c, the faster it catches up, and the fewer technologies there are available for import.

$$Ae^{rt-\frac{1}{2}ct^2} = \frac{Ae^{rt}}{Ae^{\frac{1}{2}ct^2}}, (r>0, c>0) \tag{9.10}$$

There is a positive linear ratio between the learning-type technical advancement $Ae^{rt-\frac{1}{2}ct^2}Ae^{rt\frac{1}{2}ct^2}$ and the technologies available for import and learning Ae^{rt}, and a negative linear ratio between $Ae^{rt-\frac{1}{2}ct^2}$ and the technologies already imported and adopted $Ae^{\frac{1}{2}ct^2}$. In the utilization process, the learning-type LDA diminishes with the narrowing of the gap, and once the gap becomes 0, the acceleration c would also become 0, and the LDEs would converge to the EDEs category.

The learning-type technical advancement is also endogenous though it comes from outside. This is because the generalized technical import and learning is the by-product of the generalized capital import and accumulation, which comes from the external economy of human capital investment and learning process. The import, learning, and advancement of technologies is the outcome of the opening policy of a nation, and each and every piece of technology is bought from outside by the government or enterprises of the LDEs. Therefore Formula (9.6) also shows the increasing returns to scale.

Find the derivative for Formula (9.6):

The first order partial derivative $\frac{\partial Y}{\partial t} = K^{\alpha} L^{1-\alpha} Ae^{rt-\frac{1}{2}ct^2} \cdot (r - ct)$

$\because K^{\alpha} L^{1-\alpha} Ae^{rt-\frac{1}{2}ct^2} > 0$

$\therefore$ only when $(r - ct) = 0$, then $\frac{\partial Y}{\partial t} = 0$

i.e., only if $t = \frac{r}{c}$, then $\frac{\partial Y}{\partial t} = 0$

If $(r - ct) > 0$ or $t < \frac{r}{c}$, then $\frac{\partial Y}{\partial t} > 0$

If $(r - ct) < 0$ or $t > \frac{r}{c}$, then $\frac{\partial Y}{\partial t} < 0$

The economic meaning of which is: The function of total output monotonic increases before reaching the point $t = \frac{r}{c}$, namely LDA, leading to economic growth; Y monotonically decreases after reaching the point $t = \frac{r}{c}$, namely LDA diminishing, leading to the cessation of economic growth.

The second order partial derivative,

$$\begin{aligned}\frac{\partial^2 Y}{\partial t^2} &= K^{\alpha}L^{1-\alpha} Ae^{rt-\frac{1}{2}ct^2} \cdot (r - ct)^2 + K^{\alpha}L^{1-\alpha} Ae^{rt-\frac{1}{2}ct^2} \cdot 2(r - ct) \cdot (0 - c) \\ &= K^{\alpha}L^{1-\alpha} Ae^{rt-\frac{1}{2}ct^2} \cdot [(r - ct)^2 - 2c(r - ct)] \\ &= K^{\alpha}L^{1-\alpha} Ae^{rt-\frac{1}{2}ct^2} \cdot \{(r - ct) \cdot [(r - ct) - 2c]\}\end{aligned}$$

The above first order partial derivative shows that discussion should only be focused on the $t < \frac{r}{c}$ (or $r > ct$) zone. Since in this zone, $K^{\alpha} L^{1-\alpha} Ae^{rt-\frac{1}{2}ct^2} > 0$, $r - ct > 0$, $\frac{\partial^2 Y}{\partial t^2}$ is only subject to the plus-minus of $(r - ct - 2c)$:

$$\text{If } (r - ct - 2c) = 0,\ t = \frac{r - 2c}{c} = \frac{r}{c} - 2, \text{ then } \frac{\partial^2 Y}{\partial t^2} = 0$$

$$\text{If } (r - ct - 2c) < 0,\ t > \frac{r}{c} - 2, \text{ then } \frac{\partial^2 Y}{\partial t^2} < 0$$

$$\text{If } (r - ct - 2c) > 0,\ t < \frac{r}{c} - 2, \text{ then } \frac{\partial^2 Y}{\partial t^2} > 0$$

The economic meaning of which is: The marginal output of the function increasing before reaching the point $t = \frac{r}{c} - 2$, and after reaching the point $t = \frac{r}{c} - 2$, the diminishing of LDA leads to the diminishing of marginal output.

The corresponding curve of Formula (9.6) is as follows:

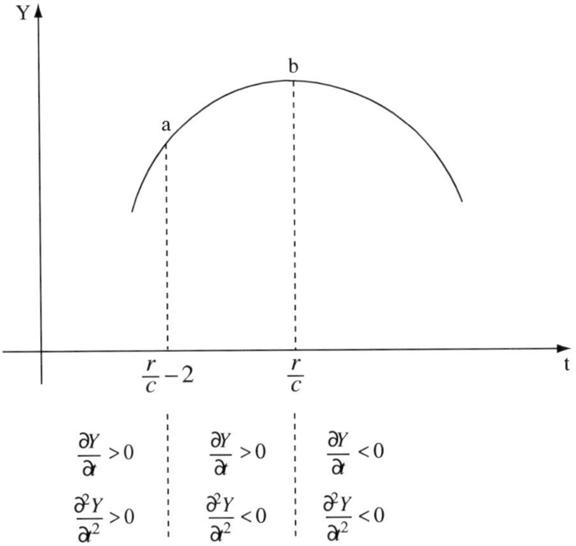

FIGURE 9.3 The output curve of conditional diminishing of LDA

In period one, ($t < \frac{r}{c} - 2$) before point a, the first order derivative is larger than 0, and the second order derivative is larger than 0, indicating the output increasing due to LDA. This is because when the gap is wide in the beginning, growth goes fast with technology imports and management learning, with both the total output and marginal output increasing.

In period two, ($\frac{r}{c} - 2 < t < \frac{r}{c}$) between *a* and *b*, the first order derivative is larger than 0, and the second order derivative is smaller than 0, indicating the further increase of total output while the marginal output diminishes due to LDA. This is because the technologies imported in period one are outdated by then, and re-importation was desired. Each time technologies are imported, the gap becomes smaller and LDA decreases. Later importation becomes increasingly difficult, since LDA gets smaller and the cost of importation and learning gets ever higher.

In period three, ($t > \frac{r}{c}$) behind point *b*, the first order derivative is smaller than 0, and the second order derivative is smaller than 0, indicating the diminishing of marginal output and total output, and no growth. This is because LDA disappears, the gap disappears, and the acceleration becomes 0, with no technology available for import, forcing the seeking of a new driver for development.

The above shows the conditional diminishing of LDA, with the condition of the acceleration of catching up *c* of the LDEs being larger than 0. The scenario of $c \leq 0$ is not discussed here, since without import and learning, LDA does not play its role, and hence the discussion on increase or decrease does not have practical meaning.

9.2 The Two Stages Model

Assuming an economy (country or enterprise) development from a relatively backward status, then there are generally two development stages: The learning-type growth stage driven by LDA, and the innovative development stage driven by EDA, with the model as follows:

$$Y = \begin{cases} K^{\alpha}L^{1-\alpha}\, Ae^{rt-\frac{1}{2}ct^2}, r>0, c>0; \\ K^{\alpha}L^{1-\alpha}\, Ae^{rt}, r>0, c=0. \end{cases} \tag{9.11}$$

This is a two-segment function and curve (Figure 9.4). The first segment is driven by LDA with c larger than 0, and the second segment is driven by EDA with c equaling 0, indicating the completion of catching up and the disappearance of gap, when the LDA runs out and the development driver becomes competing innovation. The complete path of development is indicated by the real line part of LDA-P-EDA in Figure 9.4.

Let us first make a comparison of the two types of growth. To begin with, the early stage of LDA increases on a greater tangent than EDA. Shapewise, the front part of LDA is steeper while EDA looks flatter. Namely,

$$\frac{\Delta LDA}{\Delta t} > \frac{\Delta EDA}{\Delta t}$$

This indicates that the learning-type growth in the early stage is generally faster than the innovative-type growth later on. In reality the learning-type growth of a developing country is typically faster than the innovative-type growth of a developed country.

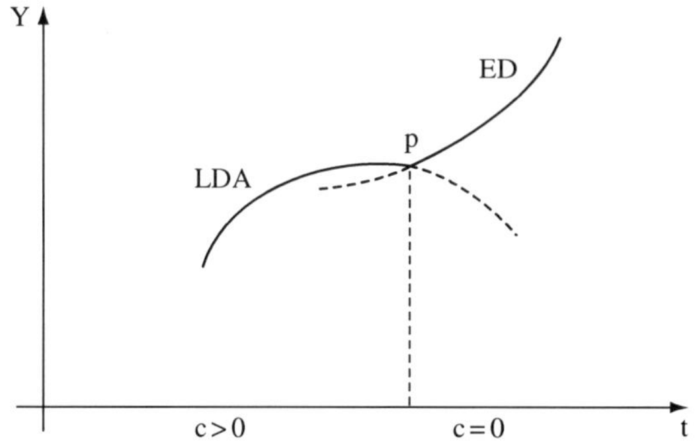

FIGURE 9.4 The development path and orbital transfer of development

Secondly, suppose country (enterprise) A differs from country (enterprise) B for 50 years in terms of development level. Theoretically speaking, the EDA of 50 years in advance for A and the LDA of 50 years behind for B is the same in quantity and opposite in direction, namely,

$$\Sigma EDA = \Sigma LDA$$

However, to acquire the EDA of 50 years in advance, A has to pay a high innovation cost (IC), which includes direct cost (R&D input) and opportunity cost (R&D time consumption). With the LDA of 50 years, B also needs to pay some learning cost (LC), which includes direct cost (import and purchase) and opportunity cost (learning time consumption). Comparing A and B, we find

$$\Sigma IC > \Sigma LC$$

because the innovative R&D input is generally higher than the tuition fee paid for import and purchase, and the bigger variance lies in the opportunity cost. While R&D and innovation takes a pretty long period of time with incredibly high risk of success, import and learning can usually be completed within a short period with less or no detour and thus much smaller risk and opportunity cost. Therefore, $\frac{\Sigma LDA}{\Sigma LC} > \frac{\Sigma EDA}{\Sigma IC}$, indicating the LDA-driven growth to be higher than the EDA-driven growth. If only the time consumption cost is studied, then the effect of "compressive growth" as driven by LDA can be seen. It only takes a few dozen years to cover the development path that once took others hundreds of years to complete.

Thirdly, let us look at the growth trend. Should LDA play its role, it definitely gives rise to high growth in the early stages, and then gradually diminishes and disappears in the end. Therefore, the LDA-driven high growth cannot be sustained in the long run, and the EDA-driven growth momentum is decided by innovation. When innovation is rapid, the EDA line rises upward to the left in Figure 9.4, and when innovation slows, the EDA line drops downward to the right.

9.2.1 Development Starting Point: The Primary Driving Force of Government

The start of the economic growth engine of the late development countries depends on the government as the primary driving force.

Though there is LDA for late development, the conditions for development are usually poor in the starting stage, such as the narrow internal market, insufficient capital, backward technology and management, and so on. When development is underway, it is typically the late development disadvantages and barriers that are mostly confronted.

When faced with the disadvantages and barriers, there are two options: Passively wait for the slow emergence and formation of conditions, or actively seek for substitution, that is, the government plays the primary driving force for industrialization and economic growth, when conditions are not ready. On one hand, the government may partially replace the market function and private enterprise through industrial policy and planning, so as to make up for the insufficient market mechanism and civil force. On the other hand, the government can help to open doors to the outside world, strike a balance between the Opening Up and Protection policy, import foreign capital and technologies in an organized manner, and roll out the export-oriented and globalized development strategy in a gradual manner from import substitution to export substitution, and so on.

After WWII, the successful East Asian economies, such as Japan, South Korea, Singapore, China, and Taiwan, all pursued fast growth as driven by government in the early stages of development. Meanwhile, in most developing countries in Africa, Asia, and Latin America, government either did nothing and missed favorable opportunities, or was caught in political chaos and set wrong policies, or even buried the country in its closed-door tradition.

In fact, if government takes action, the disadvantages and barriers of late development can be overcome thanks to the market, resource, experience, and lessons available in the outside world. For all late development countries, the potential of LDA exists, although the extent to which it does depends on previous policies.

9.2.2 The Turning Point: The Change of Driving Force and the Transformation of Development

The asymmetrical double-winged output curve in Figure 9.3 indicates the change of development track, with point p being the turning point or flex point.

Before reaching point p, the driving force of LDA comes from import and learning. Yet if import and learning continues, when LDA diminishes in utilization, an economy can be caught in the "late development trap" of "import-imitation-import again-imitation again." In this case, only by adopting innovative learning, namely "import-digestion and absorption-improvement and innovation" can one get out of the trap. The innovative learning or learning-type innovation can create EDA while utilizing LDA, and realize the change of driving force and the transformation of development. Therefore the condition for reaching the turning point or the condition of orbital transfer of development is: The technical advancement changes from import and learning to R&D innovation, and the majority of capital investment changes from foreign capital to domestic capital. In short, the growth engine must shift from LDA to EDA.

Through import and learning, the gap can be narrowed but will not disappear. In consideration of maintaining competitive leadership, the EDEs would not usually diffuse the latest and most advanced technologies. Those transferred are typically the rather new or sub-new technologies, namely the second- and-third-class technologies that still have market while the upgraded version has already been developed. For this reason, the LDEs may catch up quickly through learning and import, but there is always a constant distance that is hard to cover toward the end of the journey, which may take three to five years or even as long as eight to ten years. I define this constant distance as the "last minimum gap (LMG)." To cover this LMG, the transition from import and learning to innovation must be adopted, and the jump from LDA-driven catching up to EDA-driven surpassing must be done.

The turning point is a time point in theory but a time period in reality, which may be a year, several years or even longer. This is a special transitional period to update driving force and change strategy, which usually starts from the critical point of the LMG, but sometimes earlier in a period when the LDA is diminishing prior to the occurrence of the LMG. This is the time to adopt both learning and innovation to ensure a smooth and fast transition.

9.2.3 The Growth Convergence: There is no Perfect Tense for Development

According to the logic of existing Growth Economics, once a developing country succeeds in catching up, there is a convergence (or convergence club) of the developing and developed countries, and the mission of development is fulfilled. Convergence is one of the themes of empirical research on the growth theory. No matter what the result of the empirical research is, convergence is not the finality or end of development. There is no end to development. As with the development on the enterprise level, there is no perfect tense for development on the national level as well.

Currently, the most widely and frequently used categorization of countries is the "developed countries" and "developing countries." Developed countries refer to those that have already completed industrialization. The problem with this categorization is that it assigns absolute values to the issue of development. According to the theory of development relativity and the generalized thinking, I believe development is the common task of all nations in the world, and the eternal theme of mankind. There is no perfect tense for development, and even developed countries need to further develop. The US today, as I think, is also a developing country, which is developing fast.

First of all, the assumption of "development=industrialization" should to be abandoned. For if development equals industrialization, then once industrialization is done, development is done. In reality, the task of development is not just limited to industrialization, but also covers service provision, a knowledge-based economy, and so on. It also includes the evolution of institution, which will never finish and have perfect tense.

Secondly, assuming there to be a relative variance of development, with high and low level of development, an early and late stage of development, and advanced and backward stage of development, if we take a look at the cross-section of development, except for the first and the last one which are absolutely the early developer and the late developer, the remaining N-2 economies are all relative early developers and late developers. For example: For country A, B, and C, B is a late developer compared to A, and an early developer compared to C. The early developer of yesterday might be late developer today, and the late developer today might be early developer tomorrow. If we look into the structural difference of development, department I of country A is in a leadership position compared to country B, but department J of country A might be in backward position compared to country B.

It is for this reason that I categorize all economies (countries and enterprises) into the EDEs and the LDEs in the book according to the dynamic displacement thinking. Once the LDEs pass point P, the development task of stage one is done, but the task of stage two only just begins. The development task for EDEs today is knowledge-based economy upon industrialization, with the driving force of development shifting from LDA to EDA. The form of development also changes from import and learning to R&D and innovation, which is infinite and boundless.

9.3 Historical Facts and Cases

Theories ought to stand test and interpret reality, so let us review the world history of development.

In the middle ages, China and India in the Eastern world used to be the developed countries, the European countries used to be developing countries, and the US was simply not there. After the industrial revolution of the eighteenth century, the Europeans overtook, and the late US surpassed.

9.3.1 China

For many years before the fourteenth century, China led the world in economy, science, and technology. Gun powder, the compass, paper making, movable type printing, the clock, shipbuilding, the spinning wheel, and iron casting were just a few original Chinese innovations. In medical science, chemistry, textile, machinery, metallurgy, and many other industries, China was ahead of the Western world (Elvin 1973). Historical data shows that China was the most open nation, the most technically advanced and economically powerful nationality then, due to the fact that scientific innovation before modern times was mostly experience-based innovation (Lin 1994). Due to its ancient agricultural civilization base, together with its huge population and skilled workforce, China obtained the EDA in science, technology, and economy.

However the scientific revolution and industrial revolution of modern times didn't take place in China. After the fifteenth century, China adopted a closed-door policy. Its feudal bureaucracy handicapped innovation. When the model of scientific advancement shifted from the experience type to the scientific experiment type in modern times, China was still dependent on experience. Constrained by the royal court examination system as the dominant talent selection mechanism, innovation stagnated, and the EDA diminished. By the sixteenth century, most technical invention was left unimproved, and some failed to pass down. In the end, the conservative nation of China failed to innovate and maintain its leadership, and was surpassed by the Western world.

9.3.2 Portugal, Spain, and the Netherlands

Between 1500 and 1800, the Eastern world (Asia), with China and India as the center, was still the developed region in the world while the Western world (Europe) was the backward marginal region. However, the once separated Eastern world and Western world started to approach each other.

In the fifteenth and sixteenth century, with innovative thinking (adventure) and innovative technology (sailing), Portugal, and Spain obtained early development opportunities and established the leading position in Europe, which led to the geographic discovery of America, discovery of wealth (gold and silver) and the discovery of the sailing route between the East and the West. Portugal and Spain obtained the EDA and benefited from the exploration of America and Asia markets.

Later Europe and Asia started trading through the shipping industry. Europe obtained gold and silver from America, which it later used to buy products from China and India (ceramics, textiles, tea, and spices). Asia was the production center then, with competitive products and technologies in the market, and Europe was the trade center. As a transshipment harbor, the Netherlands controlled world trade and led the world economy with innovative advantages in its shipbuilding technologies, shipping expertise, and foreign trade policy and systems.

It is fair to say that before the eighteenth century, Europe acquired money capital by stepping on the back of America, and commercial capital by climbing on the shoulder of Asia, and accumulated advantages through the "learning by doing" effect in international trade. Yet, Portugal, Spain, and the Netherlands failed to extend their technical innovation in shipping and sailing or the EDA in trade to the industrial sector. For the lack of investment and production, consumption and trade alone failed to form the advantage in productivity. The leading position was later surpassed by the UK which first industrialized the nation on the basis of scientific revolution and industrial revolution.

9.3.3 The United Kingdom

The United Kingdom is a remote island country with scare resources, and the earliest industrial center as driven by the EDA in the modern world. The industrial revolution of the late eighteenth century took place in the UK because it was the first to establish a modern democracy as well as the values, system, and social structure that were conducive to the nurturing of capitalism. The door to scientific innovation was opened. The industrial revolution has a two-fold meaning: The abundant technical innovation and its application in production, such as the invention of the steam engine by Watt which pushed forward machinery industry, the innovation of Jean spinning machine which pushed forward the textile industry, the emergence of ships and trains which pushed forward the transportation revolution, and the institution innovation that interacts with technical innovation, such as the factory system for enterprise organization, the congress system for national politics, and the financial and legal systems that favored free market competition. The above technical innovation and institution innovation helped the UK to establish its EDA in the world. Between 1846 and 1860, all tariff barriers and trade restrictions were lifted, and free trade was adopted. After that, the UK took great efforts to expand colonies and make itself the "world factory" and the "Empire on which the sun never sets." Over 70% of its savings were invested overseas, reaping the EDA worldwide and diffusing the new technologies and systems to the outside world.

Nevertheless, after dominating the world for over 100 years, the UK failed to maintain its leading position and was surpassed by the US and Germany in the twentieth century. The reasons for the relative decline of the UK are as follows:

1. Decadence of the innovative and enterprising spirit. The noble social culture of the UK is innovative and conservative at the same time. After nurturing the modern systematic civilization and industrial civilization, the inert and conservative nature surfaced amid the sense of superiority. With the success of its pioneering work, its entrepreneurship diminished step by step.
2. The innovative advantage of industrialization was gradually lost. Being the forerunner and leader of the first industrial revolution, the UK failed to grasp the opportunity of the second industrial revolution and enhance its EDA.
3. The outdated industrial structure was not updated in a timely manner. The leading advantage in the early stage was mainly reflected in the pillar industries such as textile, coal mining, iron and steel, and shipbuilding, which suffered from backward and timeworn equipment after years of operation. The UK failed to upgrade and

replace the equipment, and failed to obtain the substitutive advantage in R&D with the emerging industries.

9.3.4 France and Germany

Compare to the UK, France, and Germany were both late development countries then, and only developed in the process of catching up with the UK.

As a second industrialized nation, France benefited from the Enlightenment and the French Revolution. Yet before the French Revolution, the Watt steam engine and the spinning mule had already entered France. In 1825, the UK deregulated the export of machinery and technology, and France increased its efforts in importing technology from the UK. At that time, almost all the key technologies and equipment of all major industrial sectors, and even the technicians and experts were imported from the UK. As verified by J. H. Clapham the economic historian: "the progress of France can mostly be attributed to the imitation of the UK and the arriving of the British experts and British capital" (Clapham 1965). France is the first successful example of a case driven by the learning-type LDA.

The industrialization of Germany was under the dual impact of the British industrial revolution and the French Revolution. However, Germany did not simply copy everything from the UK. Rather it is a typical example of learning-type innovation. It grasped the opportunity of the second industrial revolution, protected the infant industry moderately and greatly developed the then new industries like electric power, chemical engineering, petrol, electric equipment, and automobile. Soon it surpassed the UK and France, and led Europe.

9.3.5 The United States of America

Compared to Western Europe, the US is a late development country. As a British colony in the early days, it started its developmental journey on top of the capital of immigrants (physical capital and human capital), immigrant technology, and immigrant culture. The Westward Movement expanded the domestic market, yet the key for the success in surpassing the old timers was innovation. Since the end of the eighteenth century, a great amount of industrial technologies from the first industrial revolution of the UK were adopted by the US. At the beginning of the nineteenth century, the US government set up the State Patent Bureau and drafted the patent law to give incentive and protection to invention and innovation. Since then innovation has mushroomed, especially during the second industrial revolution, when US technical innovation and invention attracted worldwide attention with a series of electric and technical inventions such as the electromotor, light bulb, telephone, and telegraph, which gave rise to the development of the electric and electronics industries. Many of the then emerging industrial enterprises were founded by the inventors themselves, such as Bell, Westinghouse, and Edison. The invention of the automobile and airplane triggered the transportation revolution. By the beginning of the twentieth century, the US had replaced the UK as the world leader.

The US secured its leading position with not only the technical innovation advantage but also the institution innovation advantage. Though it inherited most of the culture, philosophies, notions, ideologies, and systems from Europe, with Americanized reform, a unique innovative vitality later came into existence. The national political system, market competition system, legal system, and modern enterprise system all serve as examples for the rest of the world. The US not only promotes trade liberalization but also financial liberalization, and with the current subprime crisis and financial crisis happening, there would be further innovation on the financial system later. In fact the institution innovation advantage that made the US the leader of the latest technical revolution is the IT industrial revolution, which left Japan chasing behind. Today the US has stored energy for the next industrial technical revolution. With the ever-increasing EDA, no one else is in a position to challenge the US position as the world leader.

9.3.6 Japan and South Korea

Compared to the US and Germany, Japan is a late development country and, like the UK, an island country with no resource advantage. The development of the Japanese economy followed a typical road of importation and learning with learning-type innovation. In history, ancient Japan copied its culture, technology, and system from China. Following the seventeenth century, Japan was feudal and conservative with a closed-door policy. The arrival of the "black ship" from the US in 1853 pushed the door open, and Japan was forced to open up in 1859. In 1868, Meiji Reform started and set the beginning of the learning of the Western civilization. In 1871, a delegation of envoys was sent to 12 countries in Europe and America to conduct investigations and learning for 22 months. It only took Japan 40 years to complete the main part of the industrial revolution through importation and learning, while it had taken the US and the UK 60 and 70 years, respectively, to do the same thing. After WWII, through various channels, in various forms and by various means, Japan managed to absorb the latest technical achievements from the US and Europe in a quick and vast manner and, as a result, acquired considerable late development benefit. On a heap of ruins after WWII, Japan went all out and developed its economy within a mere 20-odd years. Nevertheless, after Japan succeeded in catching up, the LDA diminished and finally disappeared. Japan failed to find a new driving force to maintain the development momentum, in the absence of originality. Compared to Germany, Japan owns the manufacturing advantage but lacks the knowledge production advantage. Therefore it is always one step behind the US, and the "LMG" is hard to cover.

As one of the NIEs of Asia, South Korea developed after Japan, and copied many of its enterprise systems, market structures, and industrial policies from Japan. Yet the US has the same degree of impact on South Korea, if not more. South Korea deserved the name as an excellent importer and learner of technologies in the following two ways: The first being the "apprentice" type, by sending people outside to study and train in order to transfer technologies. Once the apprentices finish learning, they immediately replace the foreign masters. The second was the "copycat" type, where they repaired the imported machinery equipment to start with and then copied the repaired ones later. Innovation and improvements are achieved each time with increasingly advanced machinery imported. The industrialization of South Korea is materialized in importation and learning, and the LDA enabled the country to catch up quickly. Currently some of its industrial technologies such as micro-electronics are already world-class.

9.3.7 Back to China

Because China had secluded itself from the outside world, it gradually became backward in economy and technology. In the Opium War in 1840, the British forced open the door of the inventor of gunpowder in 1900 the eight powers of the UK, France, Germany, Austria, Italy, Japan, Russia, and the US occupied Beijing, and in the 1930s Japan invaded China. The backward old China suffered and was reduced to a semi-colony. Efforts like the "Westernization Movement" and the reform of Sun Yet San all ended in failure. The industrial foundation was only established after 1949 when the New China was founded. Yet with sanction from outside and the system of planned economy adopted inside, the path to modernization was still beyond China on the whole.

In 1978, China adopted the Reform and Opening Up policy and started to embark on the journey of learning-type growth as driven by the LDA. Within 30 years, China achieved the surpassing miracle that amazed the world. Yet although the gap between China and the outside world has narrowed, compared to the US, Japan, and the developed European countries, there is still a gap of at least 30–50 years. China still has the LDA, though it has started to diminish. At the beginning of the twenty-first century, China raised the concept of building an "innovative country," and is preparing for the change of driving force and the transformation of development ahead of schedule.

9.4 Development Strategies

Economic development is just like a marathon race. All economies in the world (grouped as countries and enterprises) are runners. Those running in tier one are the developed countries, mostly the members of Organization for Economic Cooperation and Development (OECD), with the US being the pacemaker, followed by Japan and Europe. In tier two are the Newly Industrializing Economics (NIEs), and in tier three are the vast numbers of developing countries, including most of the late development countries in Asia, Africa, and Latin America.

This is a historical global competition, with the ranking often changing in the middle. With all runners going all out to catch up, the late comers surpass the old timers now and then. Those who led yesterday might fall behind today, and those who are behind today might set the pace tomorrow, which is even more typical with the enterprise group. The once-leading enterprises in each sector may fall behind all of a sudden, and those behind may overtake by grasping a single opportunity, and enterprise runners can be squeezed out of the track at any time. The ranking and listing of the Global 500 is a perfect example of this.

Economies in different tiers and on different development levels have their own special opportunities and relative advantages: EDA or LDA. Each economy can make its strategic selection or correction at any time, to change its relative position. There are mainly three types of strategies to choose: EDA Strategy, LDA Strategy and the Leapover Development Strategy.

9.4.1 EDA Strategy

The EDA strategy takes the form of leadership, and reflects in both technical and institutional innovation. Innovation enhances EDA, and the absence of innovation implies lockstep and diminishing of EDA. For instance, the US strategy features leadership and innovation, by leading the world in economy and dominating the world in military and political affairs, which is based on its leadership in science and education. For other countries that want to lead, they also have to innovate, and be original as well, so as to find opportunities for early development, create EDA and embark on the journey to leadership.

In the business world, there are usually one or two leaders in each sector, who determine the industrial standard and game rules, and lead the market price. It is also their strategy to innovate, and in an original way, for if they stop innovating, they would have to give their place to others. Those enterprises competing for leadership also need to innovate, and can only succeed through innovation.

9.4.2 LDA Strategy

The LDA Strategy takes the form of catching up, and reflects both technical and institution learning. LDA can be acquired through learning for faster economic growth.

Without learning, one will unavoidably make mistakes and waste time and money. France of the nineteenth century, Japan of the twentieth century, and China today are examples of the LDA-driven, learning-type growth. Learning may accelerate growth and narrow the gap with the leaders.

In commercial competition, the late development enterprises generally adopt the imitation strategy, which is a shortcut to fast growth, although imitation often invites legal disputes. Learning does not equal simple imitation, but even simple imitation is better than not learning. Some late development countries are still fast asleep with doors closed, not ready for competition. Others have not found the way to LDA, and only follow passively, which always leaves them further behind the leaders in the ever dynamic and fiercer competition. In this case, the government should be blamed, since it is the responsibility of the government to exercise the "primary driving force" with acceleration. The late development countries might borrow a management tool—benchmark learning—from enterprises, which has helped many late development enterprises succeed in catching up.

9.4.3 Leapover Development Strategy

The leapover strategy takes the form of leapfrogging, and is in essence the learning-type innovation strategy that combines both advantages. It also manages the conversion of advantages. With learning and catching up, the LDEs narrow the gap and get developed, but with the LDA diminishing, the "LMG" appears, and the only option left is to surpass. But in what way? Surpassing is not possible in normal development, and can only happen in the following two scenarios.

First is the import and learning in large scale, which is to import the most advanced technologies and follow up with innovation by utilizing the lock-in effect of EDEs, and surpass the old timers by leapfrogging. For example, the Maglev technology has long been developed, but for the high cost of replacing the old technologies in Germany, it was locked in the old technologies. China later imported the first Maglev train unit and followed up with innovation. Yet this is only for one single technology, which applies to enterprises but not countries.

Second is breakthrough innovation, which is especially true for the original or primal innovation that enables leapfrogging and advancement at one stroke. This applies more to enterprises than countries, for innovation on the country level can only happen with accumulation: Only when innovation reaches a certain degree in quantity, strength and speed, can a country surpass others. For example, the US succeeded in surpassing the UK at the beginning of the twentieth century, but Japan failed to surpass the US at the end of the same century.

Leapfrogging is highly impossible in scenarios other than the above two. Even if efforts are made, most end up in failure simply because it is not feasible to skip a certain stage of development without importation and learning on a large scale, or breakthrough innovation. For example, the Great Leap Forward movement in China in the 1950s—which was meant to catch up with the US and overtake the UK—and the former USSR-type strategy with priority on heavy industry, both serve as lessons of failure.

Bibliography

Amin, Samir. *Unequal Development: An Essay on the Social Formations of Peripheral Capitalism*, translated by Gao Xian. Beijing: The Commercial Press, 2000.

Andre Gunder Frank. *Reorient: Global Economy in the Asian Age.* Berkeley: University of California Press, 1998.

Bai, Yongxiu, ed. *Zhongguo Jingji Gaige Sanshi Nian: Huanjing Ziyuan Juan (30 Years of Economic Reform in China: Resource and Environment)*, Chongqing: Chongqing Chubanshe (Chongqing Publishing House), 2008.

Barro, Robert J. and Xavier Sala-l-Martin. New York: *Economic Growth.* McGraw-Hill, Inc, 1995.

Bi, Jieqi et al. *Gaige Kaifang Duben (The Book on Reform and Opening Up).* Beijing: Zhonguo Shuili Shuidian Chubanshe (China Water Conservancy and Electricity Press), 1996.

Bongiorni, Sara. *A Year without Made in China.* Beijing: Jixie Gongye Chubanshe (China Machine Press), 2008.

Bryan, Lowell, and Diana Farrell. *Market Unbound: Unleashing Global Capitalism.* New York: John Wiley & Sons, 1996.

Bryan, L. and D. Farrell. *Market Unbound*, translated by Wang Zhong. Taiwan: Taiwan Shibao Wenhua Chuban Gongsi (China Times Cultural Press), 1997.

Cai, Fang. Zhongguo Liudong Renkou Wenti (The Issue on Floating Population in China). Henan: Henan Renmin Chubanshe (Henan People's Press), 2000.

Cai, Fang, Du Yang, and Chen Fan. "Zhongguo Jingji Zengzhang: Laodongli, Renli Ziben Yu Jiuye Jiegou" (The Economic Growth in China: Labor, Human Capital and Employment Structure). *Zhongguo Nongcun Guancha (China Rural Observation)*, no. 1 (2002).

Cai, Fang, and Wang Dewen. "Zhongguo Jingji Zengzhang De Kechixuxing Yu Laodong Gongxian" (The Labor Contribution and the Sustainability of the Economic Growth in China). *Jingji Yanjiu (Economic Research)*, no. 10 (1999).

Cao, Jianhai. "Jingji Quanqiuhua Yu Zhongguo Qiche Gongye Fazhan" (Economic Globalization and Development of the Chinese Auto Industry). *Guanli Shijie (The Management World)*, no. 4 (2003).

Cardoso, Fernando Henrique, and Enzo Faletto. *The Dependence and Development in Latin America.* Chinese translation. Beijing: World Knowledge Press, 2002.

Chen, Baosen. "Yuanzi Shidai De Kaolü—Zhongmei Qidong Zhanlue Jingji Duihua Jizhi" (Considerations Originated from Generation: the Sino-US SED Mechanism). *Shijie Zhishi (The World Knowledge)*, no. 21 (2006).

Chen, Huai. *Riben Chanye Zhengce Yanjiu (Research on the Japanese Industrial Policy).* Beijing: Zhongguo Renmin Daxue Chubanshe (China Renmin University Press), 1991.

Chen, Ping, and Li Guangzhong. "Zhongguo De Jiegou Zhuanxing Yu Jingji Zengzhang" (The Structural Transformation and Economic Growth in China). *Shijie Jingji (The World Economy)*, no. 3 (2001).

Chen, Wei. "Di Shibaci Shanghaishi Shizhang Guoji Qiyejia Zixun Huiyi: Jujiao Guojia Fazhan Zhanlue Tisheng Chengshi Chuangxin Nengli" (The 18th Mayor Consultation Conference with International Entrepreneur: the Boosting of Innovation Capability through National Development Strategy). *Wenhui Bao, (Wenhui Daily)*, November 3, 2006.

Chen, Xiangdong. *Guoji Jishu Zhuanyi De Lilun Yu Shijian (The Theory and Practice of International Technology Transfer)*. Beijing: Beijing Hangkong Hangtian Daxue Chubanshe (Beijing Aviation and Spaceflight College Press), 2008.

Chen,Yushan, and Chen Shaojing. *1984: Yuangeng Yu Shekou (1984:Yuan Geng and Shekou)*, Economic Observation: Opening up China: 30 Years' Memory of the Reform, ed. Beijing: Zhongxin Chubanshe (CITIC Press), 2008.

Cheung, Steven N.S. "The Economic System of China." *(Discussion Paper)*, 2008.

China Intellectual Property Right Society, ed. *Ge Hangye Zhuanli Jishu Xianzhuang Ji Fazhan Qushi Baogao 2007–2008 (Report on the Current Condition and Development Trend of Industries 2007–2008)*, Beijing: Kexue Chubanshe (Science Press), 2008.

Chiu, Henry W. "Income Inequality, Human Capital Accumulation and Economic Performance." *The Economic Journal* 106 (1998): 458–470.

Clapham, John H., *The Economic Development of France & Germany from 1815 to 1914*. Beijing: The Commercial Press, 1965

Cui, Dawei, Chen Changgui, and Stanley Rosen. *Quanqiuhua He Kuaguo Renli Ziben—Zhongguo De Haigui Xuezhe (Globalization and The Cross Nation Human Capital-the Returned Scholars). Guoji Zhengzhi Jingjixue Yu Zhongguo De Quanqiuhua (The International Political Economy and the Globalization of China)*, Chen Zhiming and Cui Dawei. ed. Shanghai: Shanghai Sanlian Chubanshe (Shanghai Sanlian Press), 2006.

Dahlman, Carl J., and Jean-Eric Aubert. "China and the Knowledge Economy." *The World Bank*, 2001.

Deng, Xiaoping. *Deng Xiaoping Wenxuan Dierjuan (The Selected Works of Deng Xiaoping, Volume 2)*. Beijing: Renmin Chubanshe (The People's Press), 1994.

———. *Deng Xiaoping Wenxuan Disanjuan (The Selected Works of Deng Xiaoping, Volume 3)*. Beijing: Renmin Chubanshe (The People's Press), 1993.

———. *Deng Xiaoping Wenxuan Diyijuan (The Selected Works of Deng Xiaoping, Volume 1)*. Beijing: Renmin Chubanshe (The People's Press), 1994.

Department of Book Publication and Administration, General Administration of Press and Publication. Zhongguo Tushu Chuban Chanye Baogao (Industrial Report on Book Publishing in China 2005–2006). Beijing: Renmin Daxue Chubanshe (China Renmin University Press), 2008.

Du, Xin. *Guanlian Jingji (The Connected Economy)*. Beijing: Xinhua Press, 2007.

Elvin, Mark. *The Pattern of the Chinese Past*. Stanford: Methuen Publishing Ltd, 1973.

Fang, Yu. "1979: Coca Cola, Kaifang De Biaoqian" (1979: Coca Cola, the Label